GRAPHIC DESIGN AND PRINT PRODUCTION

GRAPHIC DESIGN AND PRINT PRODUCTION

– Author –

Pavalan Buddhavarapu

Nagulan Bhogaraju

Wordpen Academics

Publishing Science That Matter

ISBN: 9789389183917 (Hardback)

Published by : **WORDPEN ACADEMICS**
4736/23, Ansari Road, Darya Ganj,
New Delhi – 110 002
Phone: +91-011-35004336
E-mail: info@wordpenacademics.com

Printed at **:** **Replika Press Pvt. Ltd.**

Exclusive Distributor: ***Bio-Green Books, New Delhi***

Preface

Graphic design is a craft where professionals create visual content to communicate messages. By applying visual hierarchy and page layout techniques, designers use typography and pictures to meet users' specific needs and focus on the logic of displaying elements in interactive designs, to optimize the user experience. Graphic design is an ancient craft, dating back past Egyptian hieroglyphs to at least 17,000-year-old cave paintings. It's a term that originated in the 1920s' print industry. It continues to cover a range of activities including logo creation. Graphic design in this sense concerns aesthetic appeal and marketing. Graphic designers attract viewers using images, color and typography. However, graphic designers working in user experience (UX) design must justify stylistic choices regarding, say, image locations and font with a human-centered approach. That means you need to focus on—and seek to empathize the most with—your specific users while you create good-looking designs that maximize usability. Aesthetics must serve a purpose—in UX design we don't create art for art's sake. So, graphic designers must branch into visual design.

Print production in advertising is the process of turning a creative idea into printed material including magazine or newspaper ads, billboards, brochures, flyers, and direct mail. A designer who's well-versed in print requirements communicates well with the printing company both before and during the life of the print job. And I want you to be able to ask the right questions when talking to a printer, especially at the beginning of a project. And I hope I can give you more realistic expectations of the print manufacturing process as you come to understand how everything works. In fact, these are the two recurring themes in this video course, the value of communication and the realities of the printing process. But here's some good news. Printers appreciate a designer who has a curiosity about the print process, who wants to make sure that they give the printer healthy files. And the printer's really going to value their working relationship with that kind of designer as a result. Graphic design and print production are two closely related fields that play a vital role in the creation of marketing materials, advertisements, and other visual content. The process of graphic design involves creating visual concepts and ideas to communicate a message or promote a product, service, or brand. Print production, on the other hand, involves the physical production of printed materials, such as brochures, posters, business cards, and other marketing collateral.

This book provides an overview of the history of graphic design, including key movements, styles, and designers that have influenced the field. It covers the design process, including research, ideation, conceptualization, and execution and describes the fundamental elements of design, such as line, shape, form, texture, and space. It also discusses the principles of design, such as balance, contrast, harmony, and hierarchy, and how these elements and principles can be used to create effective compositions. Describes the principles of color theory, color models, color management systems, and color calibration and also discusses the importance of consistent color reproduction across various output devices. It covers the pre-press process, including file preparation, proofing, imposition, and trapping and discusses the importance of understanding printing processes and finishing techniques. It focuses on the importance of resolution, files formats, and color spaces in image reproduction and also describes the basics of web-to-print technology, including online ordering, variable data printing, and automated workflows. The book is an excellent resource for students studying graphic design, printing technology, or related fields and is also suitable for anyone interested in learning more about graphic design and print production, from beginners to experts in the field.

We are grateful to all those persons as well as various books, manuals, periodicals, magazines, journals etc. that helped in the preparation of this book. In spite of the best efforts, it is possible that some errors may have occurred into the compilation and editing of the book. Further queries, constructive suggestions and criticisms for the improvement of the book are always welcomed and shall be thankfully acknowledged.

Pavalan Buddhavarapu
Nagulan Bhogaraju

Contents

Introduction

Figure I.1 Car graphics are an example of modern day print design

On any given day, you can look around your surroundings and come in contact with print design. Information comes to you in many forms: the graphics on the front of a cereal box, or on the packaging in your cupboards; the information on the billboards and bus shelter posters you pass on your way to work; the graphics on the outside of the cup that holds your double latte; and the printed numbers on the dial of the speedometer in your car. Information is communicated by the numbers on the buttons in an elevator; on the signage hanging in stores; or on the amusing graphics on the front of your friend's T-shirt. So many items in your life hold an image that is created to convey information. And all of these things are designed by someone.

Figure I.2 Times Square has many examples of print design

Traditionally referred to as graphic design, communication design is the process by which messages and images are used to convey information to a targeted audience. It is within this spectrum that this textbook will address the many steps of creating and then producing physical, printed, or other imaged products that people interact with on a daily basis. Design itself is only the first step. It is important when conceiving of a new design that the entire workflow through to production is taken into consideration. And while most modern graphic design is created on computers, using design software such as the Adobe suite of products, the ideas and concepts don't stay on the computer. To create in-store signage, for instance, the ideas need to be completed in the computer software, then progress to an imaging (traditionally referred to as printing) process. This is a very wide-reaching and varied group of disciplines. By inviting a group of select experts to author the chapters of this textbook, our goal is to specifically focus on different aspects of the design process, from creation to production.

Each chapter begins with a list of Learning Objectives, and concludes with Exercises and a list of Suggested Readings on the Summary page. Throughout, key terms are noted in bold and listed again in a Glossary at the end of the book.

In Chapter 1, we start with some history. By examining the history of design, we are able to be inspired by, and learn from, those who have worked before us. Graphic design has a very rich and interesting heritage, with inspirations drawn from schools and movements such as the Werkbund, Bauhaus, Dada, International Typographic Style (ITS), as well as other influences still seen in the designs of today.

Figure I.3 Johannes Itten was a designer associated with the Bauhaus school

We now work in an age where the computer has had an influence on the era of Post Modernism. Is this a new age? Are we ushering in an era unseen before? Or are modern-day designs simply a retelling of the same tropes we have seen for hundreds of years?

Chapter 2 follows with a discussion about the design process. Contrary to what we tend to see in popular television shows and movies where advertising executives are struck with instant, usable, and bold ideas, design strategies are seldom insights gained through such a sudden outburst of inspiration. The design process is a deliberate, constructive, and prescriptive process that is guided by specific strategies. For example, before any piece of designed communication can be started, some very detailed research needs to be performed. This happens well before any graphic design or layout software is opened on a computer. Designing is a form of problem solving, where a system is created to communicate a specific and targeted message. The design process is the way that a designer breaks the problem into discrete creative activities. First is an exploration of what is trying to be achieved. Facts are gathered about the problem, and the problem itself is often defined very specifically. The idea phase is where brainstorming and ideation occurs, often without judgment, as a way to gather as many different ideas and directions as possible. From this, solutions are evaluated, both for their perceived impact on the target audience and for their perceived effectiveness in portraying the desired message. Finally, all of this information is distilled into an accepted solution. Designers do not sit around waiting for ideas to just happen; they follow a process in order to make it happen.

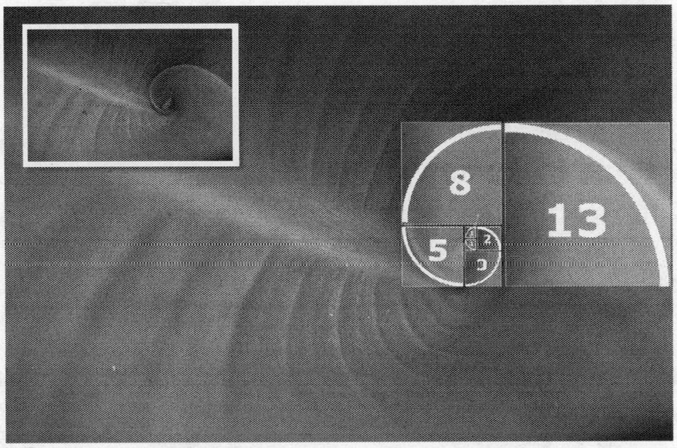

Figure I.4 The golden ratio is a constant that appears in nature

Chapter 3 presents the most important and necessary design elements required for effective graphic layout and design. When designing a layout, the designer cannot just 'throw' all of the information onto the page. Design is a thoughtful process that makes use of many different skills to create a design that is both appealing and legible. We discuss the grid in its many forms, including different types of grid such as the ITS grid, the golden ratio, and even strategies for using no grid at all. Space is an important design element, with different items on the page requiring more or less area to be effective. We also talk about the density, or 'colour' of type on the page, along with a number of different typographical conventions for making the most of the collection of words on the layout.

In Chapter 4, we begin to move along in the production process and discuss some of the more physical attributes of design. And one of the most important topics in creating printed products is that of colour. It is a complex part of the design process, affecting how an image is transmitted to the eye, how the colours are perceived, and what makes one thing look different from another, even if it is the same colour. Have you ever printed something on your home printer only to be disappointed that it doesn't look like it did on your computer screen? Highly detailed systems of colour management are put in place to mitigate these differences.

As we proceed toward creating printed output, Chapter 5 is where it all starts to come together. In the print process, this stage is called prepress. Prepress is where all the design work is translated from a file on the computer in front of you into a form that can be 'printed' onto a given surface. Imagine the requirements for creating not just one copy of a design, but thousands! This is a very important step, and if mistakes or production hurdles are not discovered and overcome at this step, then the project can end up being very costly for all parties involved, from the designer, to the printer, to the client. This chapter deals with topics such as preflight, imposition, separations, platemaking, and considerations for other print and finishing processes.

Chapter 6 is a comprehensive look at how all of this design work will result in a finished product. The many ways that a design can be printed are varied and complex, but having some knowledge about how the print process works will help to create a more successful project. Is it going to be printed on a box, or on a billboard? How many copies are needed: one or one million? These and many more decisions influence how a product will be produced. This chapter outlines some of the more popular printing technologies, along with industry standard procedures for working with them. Suggestions for choosing the right paper (or other types of **substrates**) are also made along with best practices for working with colour on the printed page.

Chapter 7 rounds out this textbook with a look at online technologies and how they affect, and are affected by, the printed word. We examine online web-to-print solutions and their contribution to bridging the process from graphic design to printed work. We also highlight other considerations such as branding and digital file resolution strategies. As the world has moved into an Internet-connected, always-on compendium of information, print remains a vital, relevant, and important part of the media mix. Effective communication campaigns make the most of *all* opportunities that media design and, in particular, print design can offer.

The goal of this text is to bridge the disciplines of communication design and print production to form a concise, accessible compendium outlining the design process in this modern, computer-driven age. While it is common, or perhaps easy, to surmise that graphic design is solely a computer-driven pursuit, when we take a step back, and look at the entire process, we see that computer-aided design is only one part of a larger picture. And by including this larger domain in our studies, we can truly gain an appreciation for the influences and strategies needed to be successful in this field.

Media Attributions

Chapter 1. Design History

1.1 Introduction

Learning Objectives

- Identify the unique attributes of major modern graphic design styles, beginning with William Morris. The design styles discussed will be those that have a presence or an influence in our current visual culture:
    - Morris
    - Werkbund
    - Bauhaus
    - Dada
    - International Typographic Style (ITS)
    - Late Modern
    - Post Modern
- Evaluate the influence of past design styles on one another
- Explain the influence of culture on major modern graphic design styles
- Identify the cross-cultural influences of visual culture that impacted graphic design style
- Identify the technological influences that affected and advanced graphic design

Industrial Revolution Overview

The Craftsman

Before the Industrial Revolution (1760-1840 in Britain) most aspects of design and all aspects of production were commonly united in the person of the craftsman. The tailor, mason, cobbler, potter, brewer, and any other kind of craftsman integrated their personal design aesthetic into each stage of product development. In print, this meant that the printer designed the fonts, the page size, and the layout of the book or broadsheet; the printer chose (even at times made) the paper and ran the press and bindery. Unity of design was implicit.

Typography in this pre-industrial era was predominantly used for books and broadsheets. The visual flavour of the fonts was based on the historic styles of western cultural tradition — roman, black letter, italic, and grotesque fonts were the mainstay of the industry. Typography was naturally small scale

— needed only for sheets and pages — and was only large when it was chiseled into buildings and monuments.

Technological Shift

The Industrial Revolution radically changed the structure of society, socially and economically, by moving vast numbers of the population from agrarian-based subsistence living to cities where manufacturing anchored and dominated employment and wealth. Agrarian-based society was tied to an aristocracy overseeing the land and controlling and directing production through the use of human labour. In contrast, urban production, though still very much in need of human labour (female and child labour in particular was in huge demand), was dominated by the mechanized production of goods, directed and controlled by industrialists instead of the aristocracy. The factories were powered initially by steam, and eventually by gasoline and electricity. These new manufacturing models were dominated by an engineering mentality that valued optimization of mechanical processes for high yields and introduced a compartmentalized approach to production.

Design and Production Separate

The design process was separated from the production-based process for a number of reasons. Primary was the efficiency-oriented mindset of the manufacturers who were focused on creating products with low unit costs and high yield outcomes, rather than on pleasing aesthetics or high-quality materials. Design process is time consuming and was considered unnecessary for each production stage of manufactured goods.

Manufactured products were intended for the working and middle classes, and high-quality output was not a goal. These products were never intended to vie for the attention of the upper classes — enticing them away from the services and bespoke products of the craftsman (a contemporary example is Tip Top Tailors attracting Savile Row customers). Rather, they supplied common people with goods they had not been able to afford before. This efficient line of thinking created the still existing equation of minimal design plus low material integrity equalling low-cost products.

Design, rather than being a part of each step of production (implicit in the craftsman's approach), was added for form development and when a product needed more appeal for the masses — usually during the later stages of production through decorative additions. Design was now directed by the parameters and constraints of the manufacturing process and its needs.

Advertising Emerges

Despite low product standards, the high quantities and low costs of manufactured goods "stimulated a mass market and even greater demand" (Meggs & Purvis, 2011, p. 127). The historic role of graphic design for broadsheets and books expanded at this point to include advertising. Each company and product needed exposure to sell these manufactured products to the mass market — no earlier method of promotion could communicate to this number of people.

The design aesthetic of these times was relatively untouched by stylistic cohesion or design philosophy. Industrialists used a pastiche of historic styles that aspired to make their products look more upscale, but did not go as far as to create a new visual language. This was a strategy that made sense and has since been repeated (consider early computer design aesthetics). Usually, when a new medium or communication strategy is developed (advertising in print and the posters of the Industrial Revolution), it uses visual and language styles that people are already familiar with, and introduces a new way to deliver the message. Too much change alienates, but novelty of delivery works by adding a twist on the shoulders of an already familiar form.

Font Explosion

In addition to its new role in promoting products to the mass market, graphic design moved forward with an explosion of new font designs as well as new production methods. The design of fonts had earlier been linked to the pragmatic and cultural objectives of producing books and broadsheets. With large format posters and numerous other print components, text needed to do much more than represent a phonetic symbol. Innovations in production affected — perhaps infected — printers with the pioneer spirit of the times, and all products and their potential were examined and re-evaluated. This attitude naturally included the function and design of fonts and the methods used to reproduce them. Text was often the only material used to promote its subject and became integral to a visual communication. Jobbing printers who used either letterpress or lithographic presses pushed the boundaries of both, competing with each other by introducing innovations and, in turn, pushing artists and type foundries to create more products they could use. An entirely new font category, slab serif — sometimes called Egyptian — was created. Thousands of new fonts emerged to meet the demand of the marketplace.

Photography

In addition to font development, the Industrial Age also contributed the photograph and ultimately its use in books and advertising. Photography (for print design) was originally used as a research tool in developing engravings, but this was costly and time consuming. Numerous inventors searched for ways to integrate photography into the press process since the early years of its development in the 1830s. Photo engraving eventually arrived in 1871 using negatives and plates. From that time forward, photography has been used to conceptually and contextually support the communication of graphic design in its many forms.

1.2 William Morris and the Arts & Crafts Movement

Conditions and Products of the Industrial Age

The Arts & Crafts movement emerged in the second half of the 19th century in reaction to the social, moral, and aesthetic chaos created by the Industrial Revolution. William Morris was its founder and leader. He abhorred the cheap and cheerful products of manufacturing, the terrible working and living conditions of the poor, and the lack of guiding moral principles of the times. Morris "called for a fitness of purpose, truth to the nature of the materials and methods of production, and individual expression by both artist and worker" (Meggs & Purvis, 2011, p. 160). These philosophical points are still pivotal to the expression of design style and practice to this day. Design styles from the Arts & Crafts movement and on have emphasized, in varying degrees, either fitness of purpose and material integrity, or individual expression and the need for visual subjectivity. Morris based his philosophy on the writings of John Ruskin, a critic of the Industrial Age, and a man who felt that society should work toward promoting the happiness and well-being of every one of its members, by creating a union of art and labour in the service of society. Ruskin admired the medieval Gothic style for these qualities, as well as the Italian aesthetic of medieval art because of its direct and uncomplicated depiction of nature.

Many artists, architects, and designers were attracted to Ruskin's philosophy and began to integrate components of them into their work. Morris, influenced by his upbringing in an agrarian countryside, was profoundly moved by Ruskin's stance on fusing work and creativity, and became determined to find a way to make it a reality for society. This path became his life's work.

Pre-Raphealite Brotherhood

Morris met Edward Burne-Jones at Exeter College when both were studying there. They both read extensively the medieval history, chronicles, and poetry available to them and wrote every day. Morris published his first volume of poetry when he was 24, and continued to write and publish for the rest of his life. After graduation, Morris and Burne-Jones tried a few occupations, and eventually decided to become artists. Both became followers of Dante Gabriel Rossetti who founded the Pre-Raphealite brotherhood that was based on many of Ruskin's principles. Morris did not last long as a painter, eventually finding his design vocation while creating a home for himself and his new wife (Rosetti's muse and model).

Discovering the lack of design integrity in Victorian home furnishings and various additional deficiencies in other aspects of home products, he chose to not only design his home, but all its furniture, tapestries, and stained glass.

Morris & Co.

In 1860, Morris established an interior design firm with friends based on the knowledge and experiences he had in crafting and building his home. He began transforming not only the look of home interiors but also the design studio. He brought together craftsmen of all kinds under the umbrella of his studio and began to implement Ruskin's philosophy of combining art and craft. In Morris's case, this was focused on making beautiful objects for the home. The craftsmen were encouraged to study principles of art and design, not just production, so they could reintegrate design principles into the production of their products. The objects they created were made and designed with an integrity a craftsman could feel proud of and find joy in creating, while the eventual owner would consider these products on par with works of art (an existing example is the Morris chair). The look of the work coming out of the Morris studio was based specifically on an English medieval aesthetic that the British public could connect to. The English look and its integrity of production made Morris's work very successful and sought after. His organizational innovations and principled approach gained attention with craftsmen and artisans, and became a model for a number of craft guilds and art societies, which eventually changed the British design landscape.

William Morris and the Kelmscott Press

Morris's interest in writing never waned and made him acutely aware of how the book publishing industry had been negatively affected by industrialization. One of his many pursuits included the revitalization of the book form and its design components through the establishment of the Kelmscott Press. The press was created in 1888 after Morris, inspired by a lecture about medieval manuscripts and incunabula publications, began the design of his first font, Golden, which was based on the Venetian roman face created originally by Nicolas Jenson.

In his reinterpretation of this earlier font, Morris strove to optimize readability while retaining aesthetic integrity — in the process reviving interest in font design of earlier periods. Morris used this font in his first book, *The Story of Glittering Plain*, which he illustrated, printed, and bound at his press. The design approach of this publication and all others Kelmscott produced in its eight years was based on recreating the integrated approach and beauty of the incunabula books and manuscripts of the medieval period. All aspects of the publication were considered and carefully determined to create a cohesive whole. The press itself used hand-operated machinery, the paper was handmade, and the illustrations, fonts, and page design were all created and unified by the same person to make the book a cohesive, beautiful object of design. Morris did not wholly reject mechanization, however, as he recognized the advantages of mechanical process. He considered, redesigned, and improved all aspects of design and production to increase physical and aesthetic quality.

Kelmscott Press produced over 18,000 volumes in the eight years of its existence and inspired a revival of book design on two continents. In addition, Morris inspired a reinterpretation of design and design practice with his steadfast commitment to Ruskin's principles. Future generations of designers held to Morris's goals of material integrity — striving for beautiful utilitarian object design and carefully considered functionality.

1.3 Deutscher Werkbund

In the early years of the 20th century, the German Hermann Muthesius returned to Germany from England with Morris's Arts & Crafts concepts. Muthesius published the *The English House* in 1905, a book wholly devoted to the positive outcomes of the English Arts & Crafts movement. Muthesius was a sometime cultural ambassador, possibly an industrial spy, for Germany in England. His interest in the Arts & Crafts movement was not based on returning German culture to the romantic values of an earlier pre-manufacturing era. He was focused on infusing the machine-made products of Germany with high-quality design and material integrity. Muthesius believed manufacturing was here to stay. He was one of the original members of the state-sponsored Deutscher Werkbund — an association that promoted the union of art and technology. The Werkbund integrated traditional crafts and industrial mass-production techniques, and put Germany on a competitive footing with England and the United States. Its motto "Vom Sofakissen zum Städtebau" (from sofa cushions to city-building) reveals its range.

Design Embraces the Manufacturing Process

Peter Behrens and Henry van de Velde were also part of the original leadership, and with Muthesius developed the philosophy of *Gesamtkultur* — a cohesive cultural vision where design was the driving force of a wholly fresh, man-made environment. Every aspect of the culture and its products was examined and redefined for maximum use of mechanization in its production. The new visual language of *Gesamtkultur* was a style stripped of ornament in favour of simplicity and function. All areas of cultural production were affected by this new philosophy — graphic design, architecture, industrial design, textiles, and so forth — and all were reconfigured and optimized. Sans serif fonts dominated the reductive graphic design style as did standardization of sizes and forms in architecture and industrial design. Optimization of materials and mechanical processes affected every area. Germany embraced this new philosophy and visual style for its simplicity and exactness. In 1919, Walter Gropius, a modernist architect whose work was inspired by Werkbund ideals, was finally successful in opening a school he called the Bauhaus (in Weimar where artists, industrialists, and technicians would develop their products in collaboration). These products would then build a new future for German exports by virtue of their high level of functional utility and beauty.

1.4 Bauhaus

The Bauhaus philosophy has become famous for its integrated approach to design education; "it precipitated a revolution in art education whose influence is still felt today" (Whitford, 1995, p. 10). Most art colleges and universities still base much of their foundational curriculum on its fundamental ideas.

The Bauhaus school was founded with the idea of creating a 'total' work of art in which all arts, including architecture, would eventually be brought together. The first iteration of the school brought together instructors from all over Europe working within the latest art and design styles, manufacturing ideologies, and technologies. An example of this new teaching style can be found in its first-year curriculum. This foundation year exposed all students to the basic elements and principles of design and colour theory, and experimented with a range of materials and processes. This allowed every student the scope to create projects within any discipline rather than focus solely on a specialty. This approach to design education became a common feature of architectural and design schools in many countries.

In addition to its influence on art and design education, the Bauhaus style was to become a profound influence upon subsequent developments and practices in art, architecture, graphic design, interior design, industrial design, and typography.

The school itself had three iterations in its 14-year run. With each iteration, the core concepts and romantic ideals were modified and watered down to work within the realities of the difficult Nazi culture. When the school was finally closed by its own leadership under pressure from the Nazi-led government, most of the faculty left the country to teach in less difficult circumstances and continued to spread Bauhaus precepts all over the world. Many of its artists and intellectuals fled to the United States. Because the Bauhaus approach was so innovative and invigorating, the institutions that were exposed to the Bauhaus methodology embraced its principles. This is why the Bauhaus had a major impact on art and architecture trends in Western Europe, the United States, and Canada.

Later evaluation of the Bauhaus design philosophy was critical of its bias against the organic markings of a human element, an acknowledgment of "… the dated, unattractive aspects of the Bauhaus as a projection of utopia marked by mechanistic views of human nature" (Schjeldahl, 2009, para. 6). And as Ernst Kállai proposed in the magazine *Die Weltbühne* in 1930, "Home hygiene without home atmosphere" (as cited in Bergdoll & Dickerman, 2009, p. 41).

The very machine-oriented and unadorned aesthetic of the Bauhaus refined and evolved, eventually informing the clean, idealistic, and rigorous design approach of the International Typographic Style.

1.5 Dada

> Dada does not mean anything. We read in the papers that the Negroes of the Kroo race call the tail of the sacred cow: dada. A cube, and a mother, in certain regions of Italy, are called: Dada. The word for a hobby-horse, a children's nurse, a double affirmative in Russian and Rumanian, is also: Dada. (Tzara, 1992)
> – Tristan Tzara, *Dada Manifesto*

Dada was an artistic and literary movement that began in 1916 in Zurich, Switzerland. It arose as a reaction to World War I, and the nationalism and rationalism, which many thought had brought war about. Influenced by ideas and innovations from several early avant-gardes — Cubism, Futurism, Constructivism, and Expressionism — its influence in the arts was incredibly diverse, ranging from performance art to poetry, sculpture, and painting, to photography and photographic and painterly collage.

Dada's aesthetic, marked by its mockery of materialistic and nationalistic attitudes, became a powerful inspiration for artists and designers in many cities, including Berlin, Paris, and New York, all of which generated their own groups. The movement radically changed typographic ideals and created fresh approaches to text. Unburdened of its rules and conventions, type was allowed to become expressive and subjective. The poetic output of the group was fresh and different, and needed its typography to be as expressive and innovative as its content. Dada, in combination with aspects of Constructivist and Suprematist typography, balanced the cultural discipline created and applied to typography by other streams of contemporary design like the Bauhaus. This movement in particular advanced typography as a medium of its own. It promoted the use of typography as an art material that could be manipulated by artists and designers expressively and without preordained rules and structural principles.

> Words emerge, shoulders of words, legs, arms, hands of words. Au, oi, uh. One shouldn't let too many words out. A line of poetry is a chance to get rid of all the filth that clings to this accursed language, as if put there by stockbrokers' hands, hands worn smooth by coins. I want the word where it ends and begins. Dada is the heart of words. (Ball, 1996)
> – *Hugo Ball's manifesto*, read at Zunfthaus zur Waag on July 14, 1916

1.6 International Typographic Style

International Typographic Style (ITS), also known as the Swiss Style, emerged in Switzerland and Germany in the 1950s. ITS became known for design that emphasized objective clarity through the use of compositional grids and sans serif typography as the primary design material (or element).

Guiding Principles

ITS was built on the shoulders of the 'less is more' ideal of the German Werkbund and the Bauhaus school. But its pioneers pursued ideologies that had much more depth and subtlety. Ernst Keller, whose work in design spanned over four decades, brought an approach to problem solving that was unique. His contribution to design was in defining the problem. For Keller, the solution to a design problem rested in its content. Content-driven design is now a standard practice. Max Bill, another pioneer, brought a purist approach to design that he had been developing since the 1930s. He was instrumental in forming Germany's Ulm School of Design, famous for its ITS approach. The school introduced Greek rhetorical devices to amplify concept generation and produce greater conceptual work, while the study of semiotics (creating and understanding symbols and the study of sending and receiving visual messages) allowed its design students to understand the parameters of communication in a more scientific and studied way. At this time, there was also a greater interest in visual complexity. Max Huber, a designer known for his excellent manipulation of presses and inks, layered intense colours and composed chaotic compositions while maintaining harmony through the use of complex grids that structured and unified the elements. He was one of many designers who began using grids in strategic ways. ITS design is now known for its use of anchored elements within a mathematical grid. A grid is the "most legible and harmonious means for structuring information" (Meggs & Purvis, 2011, p. 355). Visual composition changed in many ways due to the grid. Design was already moving toward asymmetrical compositions, but now even the design of text blocks changed — from justified text to aligned flush left, ragged right. Fonts chosen for the text changed from serif fonts to sans serif, a type style believed to "express the spirit of a more progressive age" by early designers in the movement. Sans-serif typefaces like Helvetica, Univers, and Akzidenz Grotesk were favoured because they reflected the ideals of a progressive culture more than traditional serif fonts like Times or Garamond. ITS balanced the stabilizing visual qualities of cleanliness, readability, and objectivity with the dynamic use of negative space, asymmetrical composition, and full background photography.

Photography

ITS did not use illustrations and drawings because of their inherent subjectivity. Photography was preferred because of its objective qualities, and was heavily used to balance and organically complement the typography and its structured organizational grid. Often the photograph sat in the background with the type designed to sit within it; the two composed to strengthen each other to create a cohesive whole. ITS refined the presentation of information to allow the content to be understood clearly and cleanly, without persuading influences of any kind. A strong focus on order and clarity was desirable as design was seen to be a "socially useful and important activity … the designers define their roles not as artists but as objective conduits for spreading important information between components of society" (Meggs & Purvis, 2011, p. 355).

Josef Müller-Brockmann, another one of its pioneers, "sought an absolute and universal form of graphic expression through objective and impersonal presentation, communicating to the audience without the interference of the designer's subjective feelings or propagandistic techniques of persuasion" (Schneider, 2011). Müller-Brockmann's posters and design works feature large photographs as objective symbols meant to convey his ideas in particularly clear and powerful ways.

After World War II, international trade began to increase and relations between countries grew steadily stronger. Typography and design were crucial to helping these relationships progress — multiple languages had to be factored into a design. While clarity, objectivity, region-less glyphs, and symbols were essential to communication between international partners, ITS found its niche in this communicative climate and expanded beyond Switzerland, to America.

ITS is still very popular and commonly used for its clarity and functionality. However, there is a fine line between clean and simple, and simply boring. As the style became universal, its visual language became less innovative and was perceived to be too restrictive. Designers wanted the freedom to be expressive, and the culture itself was moving from cultural idealism to celebratory consumerism. ITS can be a very successful design strategy to adopt if there is a strong concept binding all of the design components together, or when there is a vast amount of complexity in the content and a visual hierarchy is needed to calm the design to make it accessible.

1.7 Late Modern | New York Style

Late Modernism encompasses the period from the end of World War II to the early 21st century. Late Modernism describes a movement that arose from and reacted to trends in ITS and Modernism. The Late Modern period was dominated by American innovations spurred on by America's new-found wealth. The need for more advertising, marketing, and packaging was matched by a new mood in the culture — a mood that was exuberant and playful, not rigid and rule-oriented.

Late Modern was inspired by European avant-garde immigrants. These immigrants found work in design and quickly introduced Americans to early modern principles of an idealistic and theoretical nature. American design at this point had been pragmatic, intuitive, and organic in composition. The fusion of these two methodologies in a highly competitive and creative climate produced design work that was original in concept, witty, and provocative and, as personal expression was highly prized, full of a variety of visual styles. Paul Rand is one of the great innovators of this style. Rand was adept at using ITS when its rules and principles were called for, but he was also very influenced by European art movements of the times. In his work, he fused the two and made works that were accessible, simple, engaging, and witty. His work was inspirational, but his writing and teaching were as important, if not more, to redefining the practice of design. He restructured the design department at Yale and published books on design practice informed by ITS principles, softened by wit, and espoused the value of the organic look of handmade marks. As a result, artists and designers began to merge organic shapes with simple geometry.

The look of graphic design also changed through advancements in photography, typesetting, and printing techniques. Designers felt confident in exploring and experimenting with the new technologies as they were well supported by the expertise of the print industry. Designers began to cut up type and images and compose directly on mechanical boards, which were then photographed and manipulated on the press for colour experimentation. As well, illustration was once again prized. Conceptual typography also became a popular form of expression.

Push Pin Studios

An excellent example of this expansive style can be found in the design output of New York's Push Pin Studios. Formed by Milton Glaser and Seymour Chwast, Push Pin was a studio that created innovative typographic solutions — I♥NY— brand identities, political posters, books, and albums (such Bob Dylan's album *Dylan*). It was adept at using and mixing illustration, photography, collage, and typography for unexpected and innovative visual results that were always fresh and interesting as well as for its excellent conceptual solutions. The influence of Push Pin and Late Modern is still alive and has recently experienced a resurgence. Many young designers have adopted this style because of its fresh colours, fine wit, and spontaneous compositions.

1.8 Post Modern

By the early 1970s, the idealistic principles of Modernism were fading and felt flat and lifeless. Pluralism was again emerging as people craved variety as a reaction to the reductivist qualities that modernism espoused.

Punk

In the late 1970s in Britain, Australia, and parts of the United States, a youthful rebellious culture of anger and distain arose against the establishment. In many ways, the design language of Punk echoed the Dadaist style, though Punk was anchored with a pointed, political message against the tyranny of society and the disenfranchisement of youth. A use of aggressive collages, colours, and experimental photography were its hallmarks. These free-form, spontaneous design works incorporated pithy tag lines and seethed with anger in a way that Dada work never attempted to achieve. Punk actively moved away from the conformities of design, and was anti-patriotic and anti-establishment. Punk established the do-it-yourself (DIY) ethos and stylized it with the angry anti-establishment mood of the mid 1970s, a time of political and social turbulence. DIY style was considered shocking and uncontrolled. However, the influence on design has been far reaching and subsequently widely emulated.

Jamie Reid, a pioneer of the Punk style, developed the visual signature look for the Sex Pistols and many other punk bands. His personal signature style was known for a collaged 'ransom note' typography that became a typographic style of its own. Reid cut letters out of newspapers and magazines, and collaged them together to be photographed. By doing this, he could see what he was creating as he went along, trying out different font styles and sizes and seeing the results instantly. Treating type as if it were a photograph also freed him from the restrictions of typesetting within a structured grid and allowed him to develop his ideas and concepts as he created. This unguided, process-free approach to design became a part of the Post Modern experimentation that was to come.

When Punk first exploded in the 1970s, it was deemed a youthful rebellion. In actuality, it was one of the many forms of visual expression that manifested as part of the Postmodernist movement that began as a reaction to the rigid restrictions of Modernism.

Early Post Modernism

Early Swiss Post Modern design was driven by the experimentations and teachings of Wolfgang Weingart who taught at the Basel School of design in Basel, Switzerland. Weingart was taught ITS by the masters of the style, Emil Ruder and Armin Hofmann at the Basel School. But once he became an instructor there, he questioned the "value of the absolute cleanliness and order" (Meggs & Purvis, 2011, p. 465) of the style. He experimented vigorously with breaking all typographic and organizational rules to see what the effect on the audience would be. He invigorated typography with energy and in turn changed the viewer's response to the visual information. Instead of a simple fast reading, the reader now faced dynamic complexity free of any rules or hierarchies. The viewer was now compelled to spend more time with a design piece to understand its message and parse the meaning of its symbolism.

One of his American students, April Greiman, brought this new design language back to California with her and heavily influenced the youth culture there. David Carson, a self-taught designer working in the surf magazine world, took the ideas of the style and adopted them to his own typographic experiments in the surfing magazines he designed. For Carson, Post Modern design reflected the free spirit of the surf community.

Post Modernism is actually an umbrella term for many visual styles that came about after the 1980s. They are unified by their reaction to Modernism's guiding principles — particularly that of objectivity. A key feature of Post Modern design is the subjective bias and individual style of the designers that practise it. Additional defining stylistic characteristics can be summarized in the idea of 'de-construction.' The style often incorporates many different typefaces breaking every traditional rule of hierarchy and composition. Visual organization becomes more varied and complicated with the use of layers and overlapping. The use of image appropriation and culture jamming is a key feature. Dramatic layouts that do not conform to traditional compositions are another common characteristic. A traditional grid is not used to organize the layout of the elements, making composition look 'free-style.' Other organizational systems for the elements developed — axial, dilatational, modular, and transitional systems created a fresh way to organize the information. The combination of multiple geometric shapes layered with photographs created depth that worked well on the computer monitor — now a component of contemporary society.

Post Modernism is still in use today, though selectively. The chaos created by our technological advancements needs to be balanced with the ease of accessing information. The Apple brand is a good example of a contemporary design approach that feels fresh and current, while delivering massive amounts of information in a clean and simple way. The Post Modern methods of built-in visual difficulty are less welcome in our data-saturated culture.

1.9 Summary

The technological revolution of the 1990s brought the mobile phone and computer to every home and office and changed the structure of our current society much as manufacturing in the 1800s changed Britain and the Western world. As with the Industrial Revolution, the change in technology over the last 20 years has affected us environmentally, socially, and economically. Manufacturing has slowly been moved offshore and replaced with technology-based companies. Data has replaced material as the substance we must understand and use effectively and efficiently. The technological development sectors have also begun to dominate employment and wealth sectors and overtake manufacturing's dominance. These changes are ongoing and fast-paced. The design community has responded in many novel ways, but usually its response is anchored by a look and strategy that reduce ornament and overt style while focusing on clean lines and concise messaging. The role of design today is often as a way-finder to help people keep abreast of changes, and to provide instruction. Designers are once again relying on established, historic styles and methods like ITS to connect to audiences because the message is being delivered in a complex visual system. Once the technological shifts we are experiencing settle down, and design is no longer adapting to new forms of delivery, it will begin to develop original and unique design approaches that complement and speak to the new urban landscape.

Questions to consider after completing this chapter:

1. What design principles do Dada and Punk have in common?
2. What influence does ITS have on Post Modern design?
3. What influence does ITS have on current design practice?
4. How did World War II influence design education?
5. How did Morris and the Arts & Crafts movement help to create the Bauhaus design philosophy?
6. How did technology influence early German design?
7. How does technology influence contemporary design practice?

References

Ball, H. (1996). Dada Manifesto. *Flight out of time: A Dada diary*. Retrieved from https://theanarchistlibrary.org/library/hugo-ball-dada-manifesto.a4.pdf

Bergdoll, B., & Dickerman, L. (2009). *Bauhaus 1919-1933: Workshops for modernity*. New York City, NY: The Museum of Modern Art.

Meggs, P. B., & Purvis, A. W. (2011). *Meggs' history of graphic design* (5th ed.). Hoboken, NJ: Wiley.

Schjeldahl, P. (2009, November 16). Bauhaus rules. *New Yorker.* Retrieved from http://www.newyorker.com/magazine/2009/11/16/bauhaus-rules

Schneider, S. (2011, September 20). Josef Müller-Brockmann: Principal of The Swiss School. Retrieved from http://www.noupe.com/design/josef-muller-brockmann-principal-of-the-swiss-school.html

Tzara, T. (1992). Dada Manifesto 1918. In Motherwell, R., Schwitters, K., et al. (Eds). *The Dada Painters and Poets* (81). Boston, MA: GK Hall & Co.

Whitford, F. (1995). *Bauhaus*. London, England: Thames and Hudson.

Suggested Reading

Meggs, P. B. (1998). *A history of graphic design* (3rd ed). New York City, NY: John Wiley & Sons.

Chapter 2. Design Process

2.1 Introduction

Learning Objectives

- Explain the role of communication design in print and media
- Describe how the creative process relates to strategic problem solving
- Contrast how the creative process relates to the design process
- Define critical phases of the design process
- Discover how project research helps to define a communication problem
- Give examples of brainstorming techniques that generate multiple concepts based on a common message
- Learn about metaphors and other rhetorical devices to generate concepts
- Explore how concepts translate into messages within a visual form

Communication Design and The Design Process

The practice of graphic or communication design is founded on crafting visual communications between clients and their audience. The communication must carry a specific message to a specific audience on behalf of the client, and do so effectively — usually within the container of a concept that creates context and builds interest for the project in the viewer.

See an illustrated model of the design process here: A Model of the Creative Process

Overview of the Design Process

The process of developing effective design is complex. It begins with research and the definition of project goals. Defining goals allows you to home in on precisely what to communicate and who the audience is. You can then appropriately craft the message you are trying to communicate to them. Additional information regarding how to deliver your message and why it's necessary are also clarified in the research stage. Often the preferred medium becomes clear (i.e., web, social media, print, or advertising) as does the action you want your audience to take. Asking a millennial to donate to a cause is a good example. Research reveals that transparency of donation use, donor recognition, and ease of making the donation are vital to successfully engaging a millennial audience (Grossnickle, Feldmann, White, & Parkevich, 2010). Research also reveals that millennials resist negative advertising, so the message must be crafted in positive terms that are anchored to a realistic environment (Tanyel, Stuart, & Griffin, 2013). Knowing this information before the concept development begins is vital to crafting a message that will generate the response your client needs. Critiquing and analysis allow you to evaluate the effectiveness of the design approach as it develops through the stages of an iterative process.

In order to design visual materials that communicate effectively, designers must understand and work with the syntax of visual language. Meaning is expressed not only through content but through form as well, and will include both intellectual and emotional messages in varying degrees.

Developing Concepts into Design Solutions

Designers are responsible for the development of the creative concepts that express the message. A **concept** is an idea that supports and reinforces communication of key messages by presenting them in interesting, unique, and memorable ways on both intellectual and emotional levels. A good concept provides a framework for design decisions at every stage of development and for every design piece in a brand or ad campaign. An early example of this is the witty and playful 'think small' Volkswagen Beetle (VW) advertising campaign of the 1960s. By amplifying the smallness of its car in a 'big' car culture, VW was able to create a unique niche in the car market and a strong bond between the VW bug and its audience (see Figure 2.1).

Figure 2.1 Volkswagen Beetle

When you implement solutions, you put concepts into a form that communicates effectively and appropriately. In communication design, form should follow and support function. This means that what you are saying determines how you say it and in turn how it is delivered to your audience. Design is an **iterative** process that builds the content and its details through critiquing the work as it develops. Critiquing regularly keeps the project on point creatively and compositionally. Critiquing and analysis allow you to evaluate the effectiveness of the whole design in relation to the concept and problem. The number of iterations depends on the skill of the designer in developing the content and composition as well as properly evaluating its components in critique. In addition, all of this must occur in the context of understanding the technologies of design and production.

As you begin to build and realize your concepts by developing the content, the elements, and the layouts, you must apply compositional and organizational principles that make sense for the content and support the core concept. Compositional principles are based on psychological principles that describe how human beings process visual information. Designers apply these principles in order to transmit meaning effectively. For example, research has shown that some kinds of visual elements attract our attention more than others; a designer can apply this knowledge to emphasize certain parts of a layout and give a certain element or message importance. These principles apply to all forms of visual materials, digital media, and print.

When dealing with text, issues of legibility and readability are critical. Designers organize information through the use of formal structures and typographic conventions to make it easier for the viewer to absorb and understand content. The viewer may not consciously see the underlying structures, but will respond positively to the calm clarity good organization brings to the text.

Media Attributions

- Volkswagen Beetle © IFCAR is licensed under a Public Domain license

2.2 Design Research and Concept Generation

Defining Design Problem Parameters

Many designers define communication design as a problem-solving process. (The problem/opportunity is how to deliver information effectively to the desired audience.) The process that takes the designer from the initial stages of identifying a communication problem to the final stage of solving it covers a lot of ground, and different models can be used to describe it. Some are very complicated, and some are simple. The following sections break the design problem-solving process into four steps: (1) define, (2) research, (3) develop concepts, and (4) implement solutions.

2.3 Define

Step 1: Define the Communication Problem

The inventor Charles Kettering is famously quoted as saying "a problem well-stated is half-solved." Clearly the first step in any design activity is to define the communication problem properly. To do this, you will need to meet with clients to establish initial goals and objectives.

Here are some of the questions you should ask:

- What is the business of the client; what products or services does the client offer?
- What are the client's long-term business goals? (What does the client want its business to have accomplished in 5 or 10 years?)
- What is the purpose of the project? What does the client hope to achieve with it? (The goals of a specific project are usually narrower than overall long-term business goals, but should fit within the larger picture.)
- What are the performance criteria that will be used to evaluate whether project goals are met?
- Who is the target audience?
- What is the client's message to this audience?
- How does this project fit in with existing corporate materials?
- Does this piece require more than one format or medium?
- What corporate guidelines (if any) must be adhered to?
- Are illustration, photography, or any other special services required?
- Are there any special or unusual considerations around this project?
- What quantity is needed (for print)?
- What distribution method will be used (for print)?
- What is the budget?
- Who will approve the project? Will that person be available for sign-off when required?

Good planning at the beginning can make a project run smoothly and without surprises. Don't assume anything; both the designer and the client should listen closely to each other and ask plenty of questions. Keep in regular communication, document discussions, and ensure that you have written confirmation of decisions.

2.4 Research

Step 2: Conduct Research

Gather and analyze information What else do you need to know? The information you collected in the first stage is just a starting point — now you need to do more research in order to fine-tune your goals and process. Check every assumption, ask more questions, and add detail.

Research practices may involve:

- Competitor analysis: analyzing the competition to see what they do and determine their strengths and weaknesses
- **Ethnographic** research: observing user behaviour and culture
- Site research: observing and understanding the strengths and weaknesses of a space to optimize the effectiveness of the design experience you will be creating; site research is necessary to any design project that is situated in a built environment
- Marketing research: analyzing behaviour in terms of consumer practices, including demographic profiling (grouping people based on variables such as age/income/ethnicity/location to create profiles generally describing their thinking/behaviour)
- User testing: measuring the ability of the product or service to satisfy users' needs
- Co-creation: inviting end-users to **brainstorm** solutions with the design team before the concept phase of design begins

Incorporating Research into the Design Process

Research should be a part of all design process, but what kind of research is done, and who does it, will be determined by the scope and budget of the project. Some information may be publicly available, for example, through corporate publications or previously published marketing studies or market data, but a design company may need to partner with a research firm in order to do targeted in-depth research.

At the very least, design research should include:

- A literature review (gathering and reviewing all existing material that is relevant to your subject)
- Collected details (existing materials, corporate guidelines) of your client's business and the services the client offers
- Information on the **target audience** (What do they want? need? expect?)
- Analysis of competitors (Who are they? how are they different? how are they the same? how

do they advertise or make information available?)

- Estimates and technical advice from subcontractors (e.g., printers)

Some things to consider:

- Is a full design audit required? Much like a SWOT analysis, which assesses strengths, weaknesses, opportunities, and threats, a design audit applies the same stringent methodology to analyzing your competitors' visual presence in the marketplace.

> A graphic design audit is a fantastic and relatively easy way to get a clear picture of how your competitors are perceived, what key messages they are communicating and how you look when placed alongside them. It's also a valuable exercise that informs you about the type of communication your customers are receiving on a regular basis from your key competitors. (Clare, 2006)

- What are the implications of the audience profile in relationship to the project goals?
- What is the most appropriate means to communicate with this audience (i.e., what media and marketing tools should you use)?
- How do the goals of this project fit into your client's long-term goals?
- Is your client's message what actually needs to be communicated in order to further the client's business goals?

Research takes time and can cost money, but in the larger picture will save time and money by helping to focus the direction of the design process. It also helps you provide justification for your proposed communication solutions to your client. Remember that all research must be carefully documented and raw sources saved and made available for future reference.

Now that you have gathered all the information, it's time to craft the design problem into a well-defined, succinct statement.

A Problem Well-stated is Half-solved

The writer Mark Levy, in his article A Problem Well-stated is Half-solved, developed six steps you can take to state a design problem so its solutions become clearer:

> 1. State the problem in a sentence. A single sentence forces you to extract the main problem from a potentially complex situation. An example of a problem statement: "We need to increase revenue by 25%."
> 2. Make the problem statement into a question. Turning the problem statement into a question opens the mind to possibilities: "How do we increase revenue by 25%?"
> 3. Restate the question in five ways. If you spin the question from a variety of perspectives, you'll construct new questions that may provide intriguing answers.
> For instance, try asking: "How could we increase revenue by 25% in a month?" "How could we increase it by 25% in an hour?" "How could we increase it by 25% in a minute?" "What could we stop doing that might cause a 25% revenue increase?" "What ways can we use our existing customer base to affect the increase?"
> 4. Give yourself thinking quotas. An arbitrary production quota gives you a better shot at coming up

with something usable, because it keeps you thinking longer and with greater concentration.
When I asked you to "Restate the question five ways," that was an example of an arbitrary quota. There's nothing magical about five restatements. In fact, five is low. Ten, or even a hundred, would be far better.

5. Knock your questions. Whatever questions you've asked, assume they're wrong-headed, or that you haven't taken them far enough.
You might ask, "Why do we need an 25% increase at all? Why not a 5% increase? A 500% increase? A 5,000% increase? What other things in the business might need to change that would be as important as revenue?"
6. Decide upon your new problem-solving question. Based on the thinking you've already done, this step may not even be necessary. Often, when you look at your situation from enough angles, solutions pop up without much more effort.

However, if you still need to pick a single question that summarizes your problem, and none seems perfect, force yourself to choose one that's at least serviceable. Going forward is better than standing still.

Now you can start brainstorming.

Concept Mapping

A good way to begin the process of research and problem definition is to write down everything that you already know about your subject. This brainstorming can be done in a linear way by developing lists, or in a non-linear way, popular with designers, called *concept mapping*. Concept mapping is a non-linear approach that allows a designer to see what is known and what still needs to be researched. Concept mapping is also used to generate concepts and to create associations and themes.

W5 + 1

The first step is to take a sheet of paper and write a central title or topic in the centre. Then surround this central idea with information gathered by answering the following questions, based on the 5 Ws (who, what, where, why, and when), plus one more, how:

- What are you trying to communicate? (the problem)
- Why must communication occur? (what is its purpose?)
- Who is the target audience?
- Where will communication take place? (in what medium and location?)
- When will communication take place?
- How will you implement the concept?
- What if? (what would be ideal?)

Once you've added all the information you have at hand, you will see any assumptions and gaps in that information, and you can begin specific directed research to create a larger, more objective picture.

Here is an example of a concept map (See Figure 2.2). To see a concept map that details the scope of visual communication.

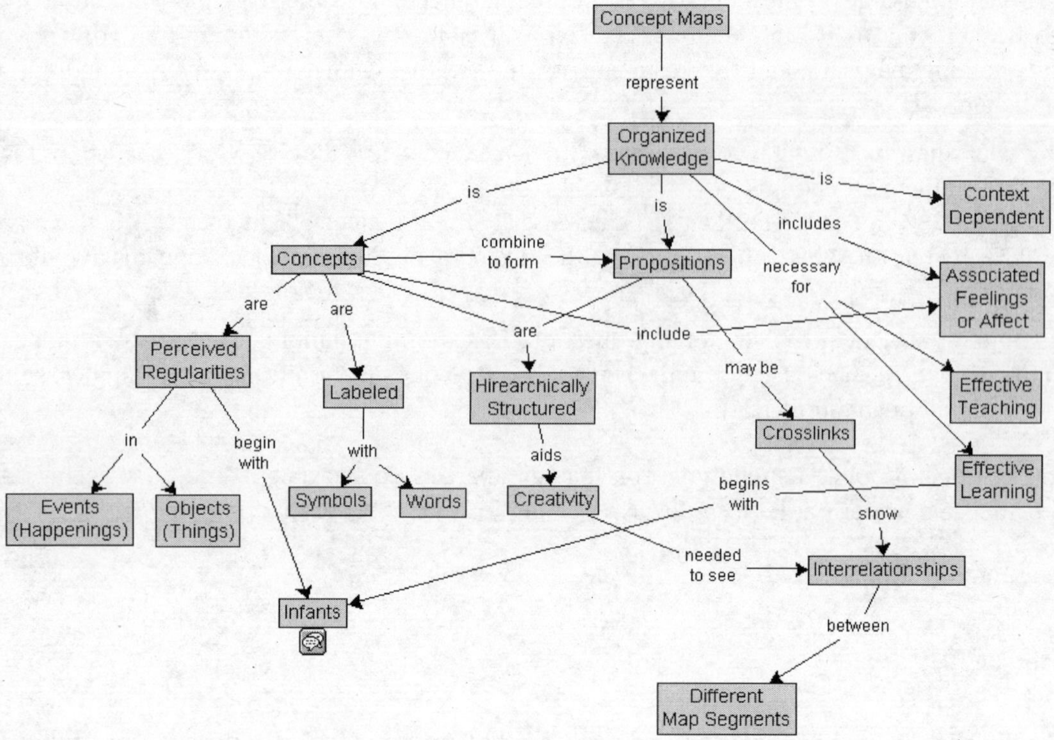

Figure 2.2 Example of a concept map

You can use the information in a concept map to generate other themes and concepts for your project. For example, in the concept map above, you could develop another theme by highlighting in yellow all information from the 1970s. This would reveal the parameters of design practice in the 70s and would additionally reveal what has been added and changed in design practice since.

Text Attributions

2.5 Develop Concepts

Step 3: Developing Concepts

Concept development is a process of developing ideas to solve specified design problems. The concepts are developed in phases, from formless idea to precise message in an appropriate form with supportive visuals and content. Once you have done your research and understand exactly what you want to achieve and why, you are ready to start working on the actual design. Ideally, you are trying to develop a concept that provides solutions for the design problem, communicates effectively on multiple levels, is unique (different and exciting), and stands out from the materials produced by your client's competitors.

Generate, test, and refine ideas

A good design process is a long process. Designers spend a great deal of time coming up with ideas; editing, revising, and refining them; and then evaluating their results every time they try something. Good design means assessing every concept for effectiveness.

The design process looks roughly like this:

- Generating a concept
- Refining ideas through visual exploration
- Preparing rough layouts detailing design direction(s)
- Setting preliminary specifications for typography and graphic elements such as photography, illustration, charts or graphs, icons, or symbols
- Presenting design brief and rough layouts for client consideration
- Refining design and comprehensive layouts, if required
- Getting client approval of layouts and text before the next phase

Developing Effective Concepts

A concept is not a message. A concept is an idea that contextualizes a message in interesting, unique, and memorable ways through both form and design content.

A good concept reinforces strategy and brand positioning. It helps to communicate the benefits of the offer and helps with differentiation from the competition. It must be appropriate for the audience, facilitating communication and motivating that audience to take action.

A good concept provides a foundation for making visual design decisions. For example, Nike's basic message, expressed by its tagline, is “Just Do It.” The creative concept Nike has used since 1988 has been adapted visually in many ways, but always stays true to the core message by using images of individuals choosing to take action.

> “It was a simple thing,” Wieden recalls in a 2009 Adweek video interview in which he discusses the effort’s genesis. Simplicity is really the secret of all “big ideas,” and by extension, great slogans. They must be concisely memorable, yet also suggest something more than their literal meanings. Rather than just putting product notions in people’s minds, they must be malleable and open to interpretation, allowing people of all kinds to adapt them as they see fit, and by doing so, establish a personal connection to the brand (Gianatasio, 2013).

A good concept is creative, but it also must be appropriate. The creativity that helps develop effective, appropriate concepts is what differentiates a designer from a production artist. Very few concepts are up to that standard — but that’s what you should always be aiming for.

In 1898, Elias St. Elmo Lewis came up with acronym AIDA for the stages you need to get consumers through in order for them to make a purchase. Modern marketing theory is now more sophisticated, but the acronym also works well to describe what a design needs to do in order to communicate and get people to act.

In order to communicate effectively and motivate your audience, you need to:

A — attract their attention. Your design must attract the attention of your audience. If it doesn’t, your message is not connecting and fulfilling its communication intent. Both the concept and the form must stand out.

I — hold their interest. Your design must hold the audience’s interest long enough so they can completely absorb the whole communication.

D — create a desire. Your design must make the audience want the product, service, or information.

A — motivate them to take action. Your design must compel the audience to do something related to the product, service, or information.

Your concept works if it makes your audience respond in the above ways.

Generating Ideas and Concepts from Concept Mapping

You can use the information in a concept map to generate additional concepts for your project by reorganizing it. The concept tree method below comes from the mind-mapping software blog (Frey, 2008)

1. Position your design problem as the central idea of your mind map.
2. Place circles containing your initial concepts for solving the problem around the central topic.
3. Brainstorm related but non-specific concepts, and add them as subtopics for these ideas. All related concepts are relevant. At this stage, every possible concept is valuable and should not be judged.

4. Generate related ideas for each concept you brainstormed in step 3 and add them as subtopics.
5. Repeat steps 3 and 4 until you run out of ideas.

Applying Rhetorical Devices to Concept Mapping

After you have placed all your ideas in the concept map, you can add additional layering to help you refine and explore them further. For example, you can use rhetorical devices to add context to the concepts and make them come alive. **Rhetoric** is the study of effective communication through the use and art of persuasion. Design uses many forms of rhetoric — particularly metaphor. If you applied a metaphor-based approach to each idea in your concept map, you would find many new ways to express your message.

Rhetorical Devices Appropriate for Communication Design

Allusion is an informal and brief reference to a well known person or cultural reference. In the magazine cover linked below, an allusion is used to underline the restrictive nature of the burqa, a full body cloak worn by some Muslim women, by applying it to Sarah Jessica Parker, an actor whose roles are primarily feminist in nature. (Harris, 2013)

Follow the link to see an example: Marie Claire Cover

Amplification involves the repetition of a concept through words or images, while adding detail to it. This is to emphasize what may not be obvious at first glance. Amplification allows you to expand on an idea to make sure the target audience realizes its importance. (Harris, 2013)

Follow the link to see an example: Life's too short for the wrong job Marketing Campaign

Analogy compares two similar things in order to explain an otherwise difficult or unfamiliar idea. Analogy draws connections between a new object or idea and an already familiar one. Although related to simile, which tends to employ a more artistic effect, analogy is more practical; explaining a thought process, a line of reasoning, or the abstract in concrete terms. Because of this, analogy may be more insightful. (Harris, 2013)

Follow the link to see an example: WWF Lungs Before It's Too Late

Hyperbole is counter to understatement. It is a deliberate exaggeration that is presented for emphasis. When used for visual communication, one must be careful to ensure that hyperbole is a clear exaggeration. If hyperbole is limited in its use, and only used occasionally for dramatic effect, then it can be quite attention grabbing.

Follow the link to see an example: Final Major Project by Mark Studio

A written example would be: *There are a thousand reasons why more research is needed on solar energy.*

Or it can make a single point very enthusiastically: *I said "rare," not "raw." I've seen cows hurt worse than this get up and walk.*

Hyperbole can be used to exaggerate one thing to show how it differs from something to which it is being compared: *This stuff is used motor oil compared to the coffee you make, my love.*

Hyperbole is the most overused rhetorical device in the world (and that is no hyperbole); we are a society of excess and exaggeration. Handle it like dynamite, and do not blow up everything you can find (Harris, 2013).

Metaphor compares two different things by relating to one in the same terms commonly used for the other. Unlike a simile or analogy, metaphor proposes that one thing is another thing, not just that they are similar (Harris, 2013).

Follow the link to see an example: Ikea Bigger Storage Idea

Metonymy is related to metaphor, where the thing chosen for the metaphorical image is closely related to (but not part of) that with which it is being compared. There is little to distinguish metonymy from synecdoche (as below). Some rhetoricians do not distinguish between the two (Harris, 2013).

Follow the link to see an example: London Logo

Oxymoron is a paradox presented in two words, in the form of an adjective and noun ("eloquent silence"), or adverb-adjective ("inertly strong"), and is used to impart emphasis, complexity, or wit (Harris, 2013). See Figure 2.3 for another example.

Figure 2.3 Example of an oxymoron

Personification attributes to an animal or inanimate object human characteristics such as form, character, feelings, behaviour, and so on. Ideas and abstractions can also be personified. For example, in the poster series linked below, homeless dogs are placed in environments typical of human homelessness (Harris, 2013).

Follow the link to see an example: Manchester Dogs' Home Street Life

Simile is a comparison of one thing to another, with the two being similar in at least one way. In formal prose, a simile compares an unfamiliar thing to a familiar thing (an object, event, process, etc.) known to the reader. (Harris, 2013)

Follow the link to see an example: Strong Handle Billboard

Synecdoche is a type of metaphor in which part of something stands for the whole, or the whole stands for a part. It can encompass many forms such that any portion or quality of a thing is represented by the thing itself, or vice versa (Harris, 2013).

Follow the link to see an example: A Global Warming Poster

Understatement deliberately expresses a concept or idea with less importance as would be expected. This could be to effect irony, or simply to convey politeness or tact. If the audience is familiar with the facts already, understatement may be employed in order to encourage the readers to draw their own conclusions (Harris, 2013).
For example: *instead of endeavouring to describe in a few words the horrors and destruction of the 1906 earthquake in San Francisco, a writer might state: The 1906 San Francisco earthquake interrupted business somewhat in the downtown area.*

Follow the link to see an example: Nike's Just Do It

An excellent online resource for exploring different rhetorical devices is "A Handbook of Rhetorical Devices" (Harris, 2013). The definitions above have been paraphrased from this site.

Developmental Stages of Design

No design work should ever be done without going through an iterative development process in which you try out different ideas and visual approaches, compare and evaluate them, and select the best options to proceed with. This applies to both form and content.

The development of the concept starts with brainstorming as wide a range of ideas as possible, and refining them through a number of development stages until you are left with those that solve the communication problem most effectively.

The development of graphic forms starts with exploring a wide range of styles, colours, textures, imagery, and other graphic devices and refining them through development stages until you are left with those that best reinforce the concept and message.

The development process starts with **thumbnails** and works through rough layouts and comprehensives to the final solution. Thumbnails are small, simple hand-drawn sketches, with minimal information. These are intended for the designer's use and, like concept maps, are visuals created for comparison. These are not meant to be shown to clients.

Their uses include:

- Concept development and visualization of ideas
- Preliminary evaluation of content (they allow you to sift and sort ideas quickly and effectively)

- Preliminary evaluation of form (value studies, compositional studies, potential placement of elements)
- Note-taking (a tool to record verbal or visual information quickly and accurately)

Quantity is very important in thumbnails! The idea is to get as many ideas and options down as possible. Designers typically take one of two approaches when they do thumbnails: they either brainstorm a wide range of ideas without exploring any of them in depth, or they come up with one idea and create many variations of it. If you use only one of these approaches, force yourself to do both. Brainstorm as many ideas as possible, using a mix of words and images. The point here is the quantity of ideas — the more the better. Work fast and don't judge your work yet.

Once you have a lot of ideas, take one you think is good and start exploring it. Try expressing the same idea with different visuals, from different points of view, with different taglines and emotional tones. Make the image the focal point of one variation and the headline the focal point of another. The purpose here is to try as many variations of an idea as possible. The first way of expressing an idea is not necessarily the best way, much like the first pancake is not usually the best.

After you've fully explored one idea, choose another from your brainstorming session and explore it in the same way. Repeat this with every good idea.

Roughs are exactly that — rough renderings of thumbnails that explore the potential of forms, type, composition, and elements of your best concepts. Often a concept is explored through the development of three to five roughs. These are used to determine exactly how all of the elements will fit together, to provide enough information to make preliminary evaluation possible, and to suggest new directions and approaches.

The rough:

- Uses simple, clean lines and basic colour palettes.
- Accurately renders without much detail (the focus is on design elements, composition, and message)
- Includes all of the visual elements in proper relationship to each other and the page

Comps are created for presenting the final project to the client for evaluation and approval. The comp must provide enough information to make evaluation of your concept possible and to allow final evaluation and proofing of all content.

The comp:

- Is as close as possible to the final form and is usually digital
- May use final materials or preliminary/placeholder content if photographs or illustrations are not yet available

Hand-drawn or Digital?

Comps might be hand-drawn when you are showing a concept for something that doesn't yet exist, such as a product that hasn't been fabricated, a structure that hasn't been built, or to show a photographer how you want material to be laid out in a photograph that has not yet been taken. Although you could create these comps digitally, it's often more cost effective to create a sketch.

Designers sometimes create hand-drawn comps in order to avoid presenting conceptual work that looks too finished to a client, so they will not be locked into a particular approach by the client's expectations.

Even in this digital age, you should draw all thumbnails by hand (using pen, pencil, or tablet) for the following reasons:

- You don't have to make time-wasting decisions that you shouldn't be making at this early stage (e.g., what typeface should I use? what colour should this be?)
- It's much faster than doing it digitally.
- Work done on a computer tends to look finished and professional, and this can trick you into thinking an idea is better than it is.
- The technology of a tool tends to define the way it is used. If you are using a computer, you will tend to come up with solutions that can be executed only on a computer, and that limits your creative options. For example, would you think of creating an illustration from coloured paper if you were using the computer?
- Hand-drawn sketches provide a paper trail that shows your concept development process and can be presented in case studies to reveal your entire design process in a more personal and engaging way.

Media Attributions

- nothing-is-written-in-stone-527756_1920 © SBM is licensed under a Public Domain license

2.6 Implement Solutions

Step 4: Solution Implementation

In this step, we are ready to select the final concept options and carry their application through to completion in producing the final design(s). This part of the process requires that you know how to work with photographers and illustrators, as well as with people in production technologies — primarily, programmers and printers. You may also require project management skills. You should also put a process in place so your final solutions can be evaluated for their effectiveness. Did they work? Did they achieve their goals?

There are many components that require attention during the production phase:

Production and Implementation

- Copy placement and preparation of layouts from approved text
- Liaison with suppliers and subcontractors
- Completion of photography, illustration, charts/graphs, icons/symbols
- Ongoing client liaison for proofreading and corrections
- Scanning and electronic preparation of images (black and white, duotones/tritones, colour); may include colour correction and/or digital manipulation
- Preparation of electronic files in line with press/prepress/web requirements
- Supervision of all prepress materials (final files and proofs)
- Organization, maintenance, and archiving of all digital materials related to the job

Production Supervision

- Discuss production options with client, solicit quotes, and select printer/programmer
- When contract is awarded, liaise with production services to discuss and refine project details
- Prepare or review production specifications
- Liaise with client and production to check proofs
- Oversee production to ensure quality control
- Follow up after production work is complete

Evaluation

Every step of a project should be evaluated in terms of the goals you have defined. Two fundamental questions about every design decision you make are:

- What does this accomplish?
- How does what is accomplished help to meet the project goals?

After the original design challenge has been defined, evaluate every stage of the process in that context. It's surprisingly easy to stray off track when you're designing. If you find yourself designing something brilliant, but it doesn't communicate what it should to the right audience, then all that brilliance is wasted.

Communication

Whether they are in print or multimedia, all design works are intended to communicate to a specific audience, and the design must support that function. All concepts must be evaluated with that end in mind. For example:

- Does the work communicate the key message(s) and support the client's goals?
- Does the work effectively integrate images, design, and text (form and content) to support that communication; create an overall 'look'; make the piece work as a unified whole with no distractions?
- Is the piece physically easy to read and/or understand?
- Do the design choices amplify material (subject matter, mood) in the text?
- Is the piece appropriate to the audience? (children, youth, adults, seniors have particular interests and needs)

Economic Efficiency

- What is possible and most effective within the budget?
- Will this method attract the desired audience/buyer?

Design and Materials

- Are the design choices compatible with technological requirements for production?
- For print materials, is there efficient and economical use of paper?
- Will the materials chosen support the intended use and method of distribution?

2.7 Summary

Communication design can be described as a problem-solving process that can be broken into four steps: (1) define, (2) research, (3) develop concepts, and (4) implement solutions. Research should be a part of all design process determined by the scope and budget of the project. Concept mapping is a non-linear approach that outlines what is known, what is needs, creates associations and themes, and helps generate ideas. Good design takes time that involves generating and assessing concepts. Time is also spent editing, revising, refining , and evaluating ideas.

In conclusion, defining the design process is complicated as it has many stages and involves many steps at each stage. Complicating it further is the reality that every project is unique in its parameters, goals, time period, and participants. This chapter is meant to facilitate the beginning of how you define your individual design process by basing it on general guidelines. If you are still developing an understanding of your personal design strengths and weaknesses, allow extra time for each stage and track your time for each stage. You'll soon discover if you fall into the category of a brainstorming, conceptual, or project development type. Conceptual designers find it easy to develop multiple concepts, but less easy to take the steps to develop them to their full potential. Project development types are the opposite — finding concepts hard to create, but developing projects quite easy. Allow extra time to discover which category you fall into and also to develop strengths in your weaker area. As you gain experience developing design projects, you will start to personalize your design process and be able to estimate how long it takes with a fair degree of accuracy. This will help you to estimate project design costs more accurately and gauge the steps needed to bring a project to a successful conclusion.

Questions to consider after completing this chapter:

1. How does communication design work within the constraints of print and media?
2. How does the creative process relate to strategic problem solving?
3. How is the creative process related to the design process?
4. What are the critical phases of the design process?
5. How does project research help to define a communication problem?
6. What are some examples of brainstorming techniques that generate multiple concepts based on a common message?
7. How does using a metaphoric device generate concepts?
8. How do concepts translate into messages within a visual form?

References

Clare, R. (2006). Competitor analysis – A graphic design perspective. *Ezine Articles*. Retrieved from http://ezinearticles.com/?Competitor-Analysis—A-Graphic-Design-Perspective&id=306043

Frey, C. (2008). *How to generate breakthrough ideas using a concept tree*. Retrieved from http://mindmappingsoftwareblog.com/concept-tree/

Gianatasio, D. (2013, July 2). Happy 25th birthday to Nike's 'Just Do It,' the last great advertising slogan. *Adweek*. Retrieved from http://www.adweek.com/adfreak/happy-25th-birthday-nikes-just-do-it-last-great-advertising-slogan-150947

Grossnickle, T., Feldmann, D., White, A., & Parkevich, N. (2010). *Millennial donors: A study of millennial giving and engagement habits.* Achieve and Johnson Grossnickle Associates. Retrieved from http://cdn.trustedpartner.com/docs/library/AchieveMCON2013/MD10%20Full%20Report.pdf

Harris, R. A. (2013). A handbook of rhetorical devices. *VirtualSalt*. Retrieved from http://www.virtualsalt.com/rhetoric.htm

Tanyel, F., Stuart, E. W., & Griffin, J. (2013). Have "Millennials" embraced digital advertising as they have embraced digital media? *Journal of Promotion Management*, *19*(5), 652–673. http://doi.org/10.1080/10496491.2013.829161

Suggested Reading

Dubberly Design Office. (2009, March 20). *A model of the creative process*. Retrieved from http://www.dubberly.com/concept-maps/creative-process.html

Chapter 3. Design Elements, Design Principles, and Compositional Organization

3.1 Introduction

Learning Objectives

- Utilize basic design principles relating to visual composition
- Define design terminology pertaining to form
- Describe organizational systems and core principles for layout grids
- Differentiate between typographic categories
- Establish a visual hierarchy within a layout
- Express ideas using the principles of composition and form

Communication design is essentially the crafting of a message meant for a specific section of the public. This written message is infused with meaningful and relevant visual components. The composition of these components should amplify, clarify, and enhance the message for the viewer. To assist in making sound design choices, a designer applies principles of composition and principles of organization to the design elements selected for a project.

Understanding how to utilize the fundamentals of design elements, principles, and composition is necessary to be able to confidently move through the stages of the design development process and build a project from the initial design brief to the final published design work.

Definitions from various design sources about what comprises a design element are consistent for the most part, but defining design principles is not as consistent and varies from one text to the next. Marvin Bartel's (2012) definitions of these categories are both simple and on point. He defines a visual element as any "basic thing that can be seen," and a design principle as a method for "arranging things better." Also included in this chapter are organizational systems that can focus and direct the overall direction a composition will take.

3.2 Visual Elements — Basic Things That Can be Seen

> Point, line, and plane are the building blocks of design. From these elements, designers create images, icons, textures, patterns, diagrams, animations, and typographic systems. (Lupton & Phillips, 2014, p. 13)

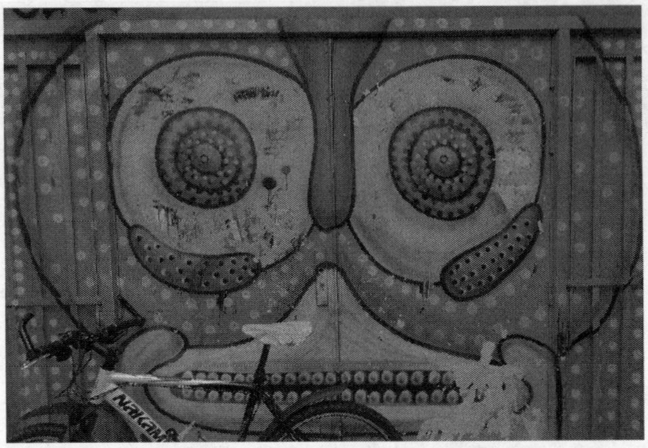

Figure 3.1 Design using points, lines, planes

Point

A point is a precise position or location on a surface. In purely mathematical terms, a point marks a set of coordinates — it has no mass at all. In this objective definition, a point is essentially a place. Visually, a point is a dot and therefore the basic building block of every variation of line, texture, and plane.

Subjectively, the term *point* has a lot of power. *Point* can direct attention, be the focus of attention, create emphasis, and cut through veiled information. The compositional term *focal point* brings the objective and subjective together by being the first place the eye is drawn to in a composition and usually contains the most important piece of visual communication.

Line

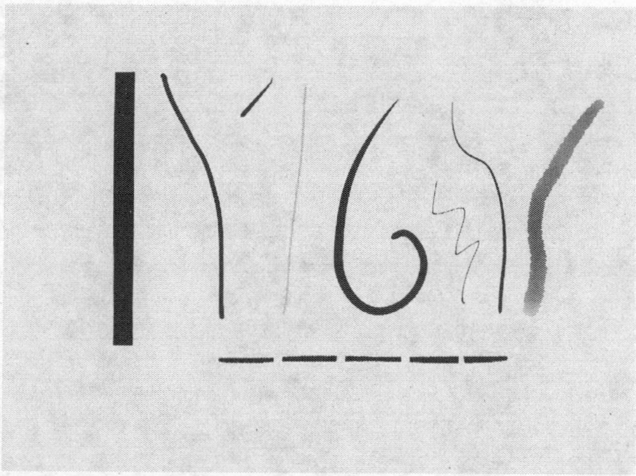

Figure 3.2 Lines (by Ken Jeffery)

A line is the second most basic element of design — a line is a collection of points arranged in a linear manner (see Figure 3.2). A line connects two points, or traces the path of a movement. A line can be actual or implied — for instance, as a composition of two or more objects in a row. Lines in nature act as defining planes — examples are a horizon or the silhouette of a forest against the sky. Long straight lines do not often occur in nature, and therefore when they are present, they tend to dominate the landscape visually. Natural settings are usually parsed by the eye into shorter sequences of curved or straight lines and organic shapes.

When made by the hand, a line is created by the stroke of a pencil, pen, brush, or any mark-making tool. These lines can be thin or wide, and are expressive and distinct, reflecting the texture of the tool used to make them. Lines can create a plane (a shape) by being clustered together or by defining a shape. If the line is thickened, it changes and becomes a plane. When lines are made digitally, they can acquire many of the same qualities possessed by hand-drawn lines through the application of effects.

Plane

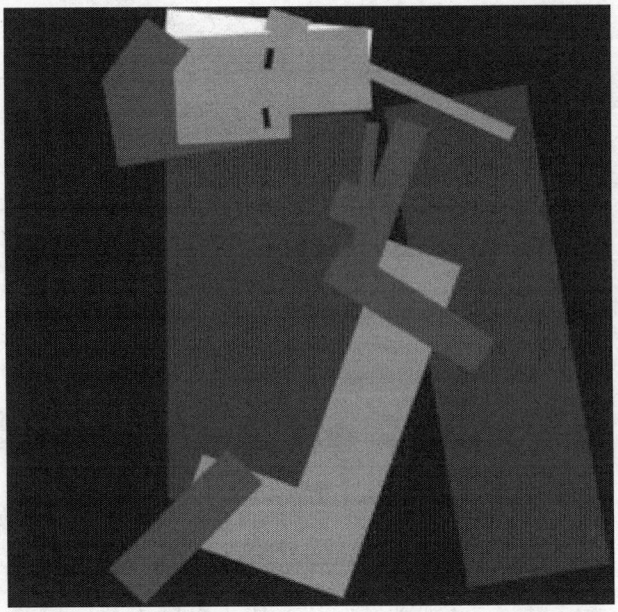

Figure 3.3 Planes

Like lines, planes (shapes) can be organically made or they can be geometric, as in the example shown in Figure 3.3. A plane is a flat surface that has defined borders. "A line closes to become a shape, a bounded plane" (Lupton & Phillips, 2014, p. 38). Planes are excellent compositional tools for clustering visual elements into visual fields. A plane can also act as a separating device and allow the viewer to see that one section of information is not linked to another.

In design software, a vector graphic is a shape created by defining its parameters with a line, and then filling it with a solid or textured fill. Grids help to create and define typographic planes that float or interact with solid planes of image, texture, or colour. In the physical world, everything is composed of shapes that are either two- or three-dimensional. How you choose to organize and arrange the planes in your photograph, your illustration, or your design will structure the composition and determine not only how the elements intersect with one another but also how the viewer interacts with the composition.

Colour

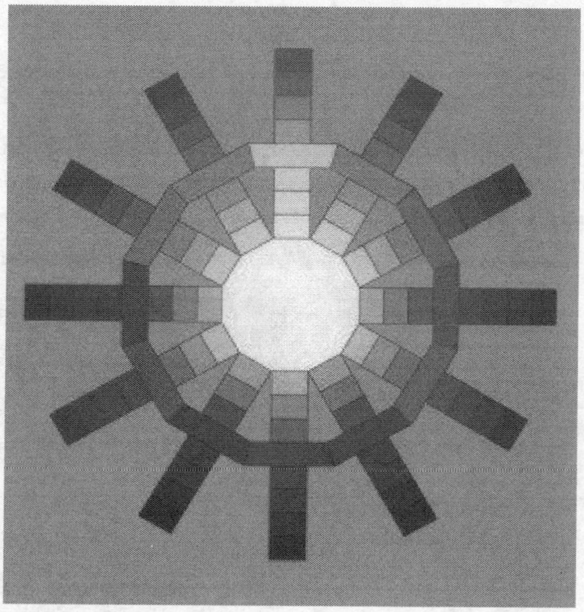

Figure 3.4 Colours

Graphic design has evolved over the last two centuries from a craft that designed text and images primarily in black and white for books and broadsheets, to a craft that works with full colour in analog and digital media and on every kind of substrate. Controlling and effectively using colour to support communication is now more important than it has ever been. Both media and advertising have become very sophisticated over the last few decades and are adept at creating exciting, sensuous, and energetic environments that are crafted with the skillful use of colour and texture. The public, in turn, has absorbed these unprecedented levels of image saturation with a variety of outcomes. One is an expectation that the visual palette match and enhance the message. A second outcome is a high expectation for strong and authentic visuals of places or objects. A third outcome is a cultural nostalgia for earlier looks created by various devices. Examples like 8-bit graphics or 1950s Kodachrome both possess unique colour and texture palettes and have properties the public can discern. When one of these nostalgic colour palettes is applied to an image, it adds another layer of meaning to the work, and that meaning has to make sense for the viewer.

The explosion of tools for making and sharing digital photography and graphics also reveals how good the general public has become at crafting visuals with relevant atmosphere and texture. The bar has been raised very high with colour use in contemporary times, and understanding colour basics is an absolute necessity.

RBG and CMYK Colour Spaces

Given that design and colour are united in every project, it is important to realize that there are two colour systems, and often a project needs to work in both. Digital media works in the additive colour system, and its primary colours are red, green, and blue (RGB). In this system, the absence of colour equals black, while combining all colours results in white. RGB is the colour system of visible light (see

Figure 3.5). This light system is called *additive* because the three primaries together create all the hues in the spectrum.

Subtractive colour is the system needed for print media, and its primary colours are cyan, magenta, yellow, and black (CMYK), as shown in Figure 3.5. In CMYK, the absence of colour equals white, while combining all colours creates black. Both of these systems have many overlapping colours but their colour spheres are not exactly the same. Understanding where the overlaps e xist and where they don't correspond is vital to the success of a project. If your print materials cannot be replicated on screen, you will have a major design problem that will have to be corrected. Always choose colours that will work in both systems.

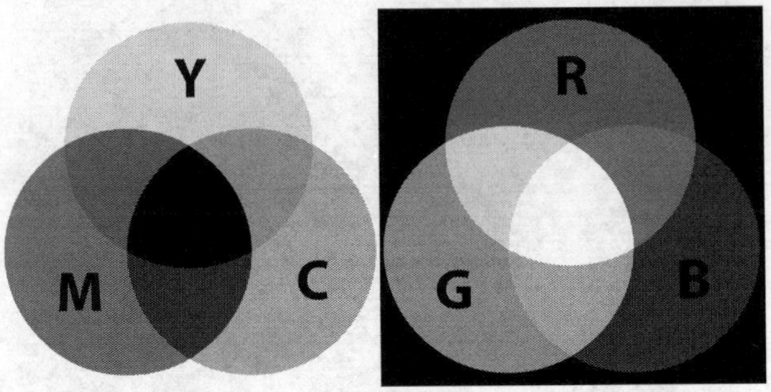

Figure 3.5 Primary colours for the additive and subtractive colour schemes

Environment is another aspect of colour choice that is very important. Both the natural world and the world within the screen vary from moment to moment and screen to screen. Colours are affected and influenced by the amount of atmospheric light available to them as well as by the colours in contact with the object they are viewing. Texture also changes our perception of a colour as does the brightness or darkness around it.

However much a designer hopes to define the parameters of a colour palette, there will always be unknown factors influencing the palette on the viewers' end. Create a palette that is focused enough to create the right atmosphere and energy level for your project, but one that doesn't rely too heavily on a specific colour. Careful, considered colour use will help define a message and create a mood that supports the composition and concept of a design work. Always create a palette that will work with both colour systems and also be robust enough to work in less than optimal environmental circumstances.

Negative Space

Negative space, which is also called *white space,* is the visually quiet area that surrounds the active area of a composition (see Figure 3.6). It is also referred to as figure/ground, and has a very important role in composition as it shapes the visual perception of the subject. Without negative space, there is no positive space — the effect is similar to seeing a polar bear in a snowstorm. Negative space is often thought of as as passive and unimportant, but the active elements or 'figure' are always perceived in relation to their surroundings by the mind of the viewer. The composition of the negative space frames and presents the active elements in a flat or dynamic way. If the surrounding area is busy with many other elements, the focal point loses its power because the elements all have a similar visual value. The works of Gustav Klimt exhibit this quality.

Figure 3.6 Example of negative or white space

If, on the other hand, the work is balanced and the negative space is active, it brings energy to the form and its space. The focal point or figure increases its visual power because there is contrast for the eye. Another way to look at this is to see that the range or gamut of visual activity is increased and therefore the experience is more satisfying to the eye.

When designers play with reducing or confusing positive and negative space, they create ambiguity. Ambiguity creates tension, which increases the interest of a composition to the viewer and also increases the visual energy of a design. There are three types of figure/ground relationships.

Stable figure/ground is the most common type. The positive element is clearly separate and defined against its negative space. A good example of this is text blocks in magazines or books.

Reversible figure/ground is the second type and is found in most of the work of M.C. Escher. Both the positive and negative space delivers 'active' information that feels equal to the eye and therefore creates a toggling effect in the viewer. One shape is comprehended while the other acts as its negative space, then the opposite happens and the negative space becomes meaningful and its opposite becomes the neutral 'holding' space.

Ambiguous figure/ground creates a confusing lack of focal point. The eye searches for a dominant visual 'starting point' in the composition but can't find one. Often this creates energy, and if the effect is compelling, it invites the viewer to stay with the work for a long period of time, absorbing all of the visual information.

Figure 3.7 FedEx express truck

Designers often utilize figure/ground in the crafting of symbols, wordmarks, and logos because of its capacity to create meaning with the space surrounding a mark. An excellent example of figure/ground is the FedEx wordmark (see Figure 3.7). The negative space needed to define the letterforms also augments their meaning by creating a forward pointing arrow. In print design, negative space can also allude to what is outside the frame and makes the field of the page or poster larger that it physically is. On a static or moving screen, negative space has the ability to change the flow of time, to introduce a break, or to create space around an important point.

Composing strong figure/ground tension is an excellent skill to acquire for designers of any media. Crafting white space eventually becomes as important to a designer as selecting the words and the elements of a project. Composing the negative spaces of a composition will allow you to vary visual emphasis of the elements, and control and increase the visual energy overall.

Texture

Figure 3.8 Example of texture

Texture is a visual and a tactile quality that designers work with (see Figure 3.8). Texture is used both in composition and also on the printed substrate or media space. Designers create textures for their projects with anything at hand. A texture can be made with typography, generated in raster or vector software like Photoshop or Adobe Illustrator, or by using a camera and capturing elements in the material world.

Using texture thoughtfully will enhance a visual experience and amplify the context for the content. Often adding texture adds visual complexity and a bit of visceral depth to a two-dimensional design project. It can also tie one piece of design to another, or become a defining element of a brand or a series of communications.

The tactile aspect of a design work comes into play with the choices we make for the substrate we print on. The surface can be smooth or rough, glossy or matte, thick or thin, translucent or opaque, paper, plastic, concrete, metal, wood, or cloth. Paper can even have two or more of these qualities if we augment the original look of the paper with layers of varnish that reverse the tactile effect of the substrate. Often the choice of substrate is most effective if it is sympathetic to or contrasts with the concept and content of the piece. The choice of substrate texture affects how the viewer perceives the content — both physically and optically. Glossy substrates often feel sophisticated, hard, and cold. They are imbued with a sense of precision because the ink sits on top of the surface of the paper and retains almost all of its original integrity. A textured matte paper feels organic, accessible, and warm because the ink is partially absorbed by the paper, and is therefore influenced by and fused to its softer characteristics.

Pattern is part of the element of texture, but because of its special ability to hold content that is meaningful, and its long and significant cultural history, it deserves a special mention. All patterns can be reduced to dot and line and are organized by a grid system of some kind. Their 'flavour' is a reflection of the culture and time they come from and of the materials that created them. Patterns can be a subtle addition to the content of any design work. A pattern can be created using a relevant graphic (like a logo) or repeated multiple times, or it can support the organizational principles developed by the designer in a decorative way; for example, if a grid is based on the square and the texture of the pattern is also based on the square.

When the pattern is seen as a whole, its individual components melt away and lose their identity to the larger field of the pattern. This ability to focus on a pattern in multiple ways creates a second purpose for the graphic element (such as a circle, a square, a logo, or symbol) the designer has used. In modern design practice, pattern is an opportunity to augment the clean and simple material surfaces we work with and ornament a page or a website with a relevant texture.

Typography

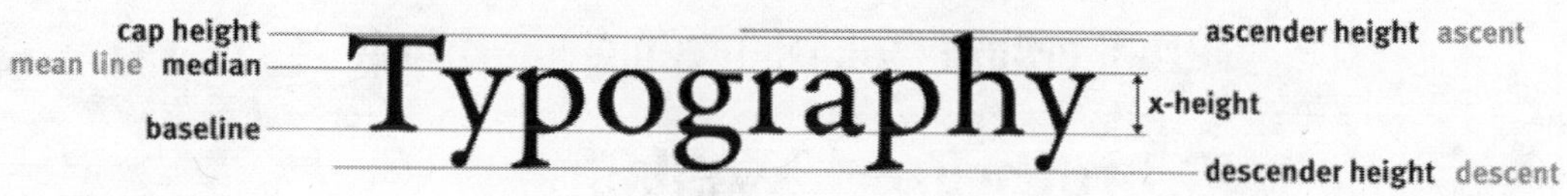

Figure 3.9 Typography

Typography is the medium of designers and the most important element we work with (see Figure 3.9).

Typography not only carries a message but also imbues a message with visual meaning based on the character of a font, its style, and its composition. Words are meaningful in and of themselves, but the style and composition of words tells a reader you are serious, playful, exciting, or calm. Typography is the tonal equivalent of a voice and can be as personal or as general in flavour.

Typography traditionally has two functions in most design projects. One function is to call attention to or to 'display' the intent of a communication. This function is called titling or display typography and it is meant to call attention to itself. The second function is to present the in-depth details of a communication within a text block. This function requires a different typographic approach — one that is quiet and does not call attention to itself. Instead, it is intended to make the content accessible and easy to read.

Font Categories

There are many ways to categorize and subcategorize type. This overview discusses the seven major historical categories that build on one another. Serif fonts comprise four of these categories: humanist, old style, transitional, and modern. Italics, first designed in the 1500s, have evolved to become part of a font 'family' and were at one time a separate category. They were initially designed as independent fonts to be used in small pocket books where space was limited. They were not embraced as text fonts, but were considered valuable for adding emphasis within a roman text and so became part of the set of options and extensions a font possessed. The trajectory of use is the opposite for the sans serif category. Sans serif fonts have historically been used for display only, but in the 20th century, they became associated with the modern aesthetic of clean and simple presentation and have now become very popular for text-block design. Egyptian or slab serif fonts can be used as either display or text depending on the characteristic of the font design.

Blackletter

Figure 3.10 Example of Blackletter type

Blackletter was the medieval model for the first movable types (see Figure 3.10). It is also know as

Block, Gothic, Fraktur, or Old English. The look of this font category is heavy and dark. The letterforms are often condensed and put together tightly in a text block creating a dark colour (tone) for a page — between 70% and 80% grey. To put the tone in context, the usual tone of a modern text page is between 55% and 70% grey. The look of the letterforms makes it hard to read the page, because legibility was not their first function as it is today. The beauty of the font and the form of the book was the primary goal for early publications. Books were considered to be objects of wealth and beauty, not solely as a means to convey information.

Humanist

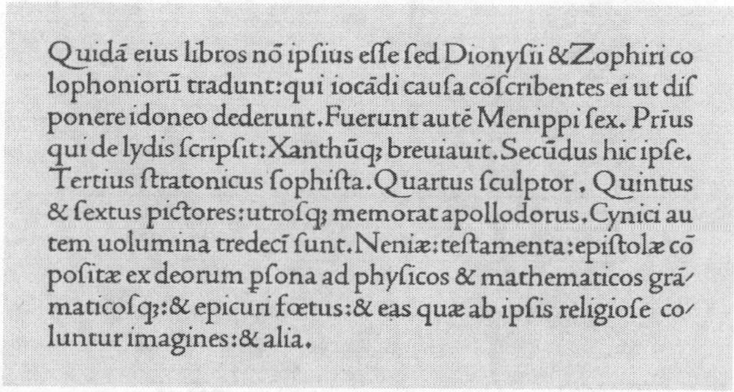

Quidā eius libros nō ipſius eſſe ſed Dionyſii &Zophiri co
lophoniorū tradunt:qui iocādi cauſa cōſcribentes ei ut diſ
ponere idoneo dederunt.Fuerunt autē Menippi ſex. Prīus
qui de lydis ſcripſit:Xanthūq; breuiauit.Secūdus hic ipſe.
Tertius ſtratonicus ſophiſta.Quartus ſculptor. Quintus
& ſextus pictores:utroſq; memorat apollodorus.Cynici au
tem uolumina tredecī ſunt.Neniæ:teſtamenta:epiſtolæ cō
poſitæ ex deorum pſona ad phyſicos & mathematicos grā
maticoſq;:& epicuri fœtus:& eas quæ ab ipſis religioſe co
luntur imagines:& alia.

Figure 3.11 Example of Humanist type

Humanist fonts are also referred to as Venetian, because they were developed in and around Venice in the mid-15th century (see Figure 3.11). Their design was modelled on the lighter, open serif letterforms and calligraphy of the Italian humanist writers. The designers strove to replicate many of the characteristics found in this writing style, including multiple variations of a glyph (letterform) that a written document possessed. For instance, a font could have up to 10 different lowercase a's to set a page with. Humanist types were the first roman types. Though they were much easier to read and lighter on the page than blackletter, they still created a visually dark and heavy text block in contrast to the fonts we have become accustomed to. Humanist fonts have little contrast between the thick and thin strokes — the strokes are usually heavy overall. The x-height of a humanist font is small compared to contemporary fonts, and this impedes quick comprehension and legibility. Humanist fonts are not often used for these reasons, though they are well respected because they are the original model so many other fonts are based on. It is important to remember that these fonts were a perfect match to the earliest printing technologies and that those presses could not have printed our light and delicate fonts. Fonts have evolved alongside the technological advancements of the printing industry.

Examples of humanist fonts include Jenson, Centaur, Verona, Lutetia, Jersey, and Lynton.

Old Style

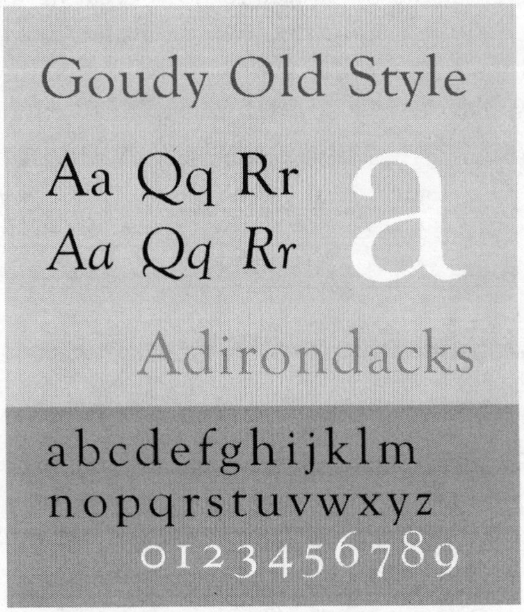

Figure 3.12 Example of Old Style type

Old style fonts, also known as Garalde fonts, are the next leap in font design, and their stylistic developments were driven by the technological advancement of presses and the improved skills of punchcutters (see Figure 3.12). Font designers began to explore the possibilities of their medium — both the metal of the punches and the abilities of the presses and their papers. The letterforms became more precise, their serifs more distinct. The contrast of the stroke weights was also increased, and the presses held true to the design and didn't distort them. The aim of these new fonts ceased to be about replicating the look of handwriting and more about refining the letterforms to create a lighter overall tone.

Examples of old style fonts include Goudy Old Style, Granjon, Janson, Palatino, Perpetua, Plantin, and Sabon.

Transitional

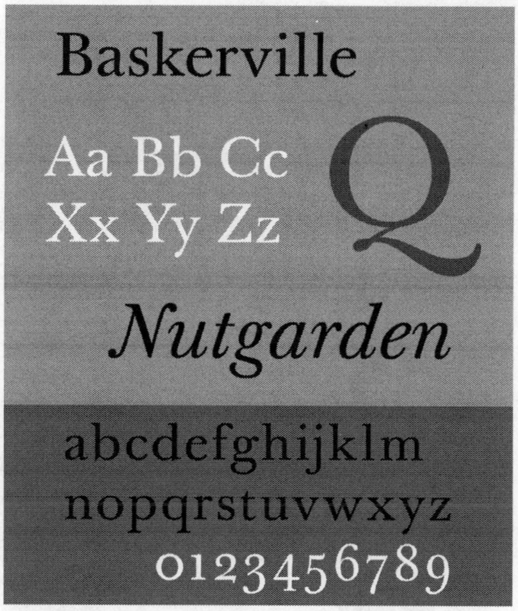

Figure 3.13 Example of Transitional type

A few centuries later, font design was again refined, and this time the impetus came from France and the Enlightenment movement. Fonts were created along the rationalist principles of the times. The strokes were contrasted further with very thick main strokes and very thin sub-strokes, and the serif, which capped the stroke, did not use bracketing (the rounding underneath the intersection of the two strokes). The letterforms took on a look that implied they were constructed mathematically and anchored within a grid. These new fonts broke with humanist and old style tradition and ceased to reference calligraphy.

Examples of transitional fonts include Baskerville, Bookman, Fournier, and Joanna (see Figure 3.13).

Modern

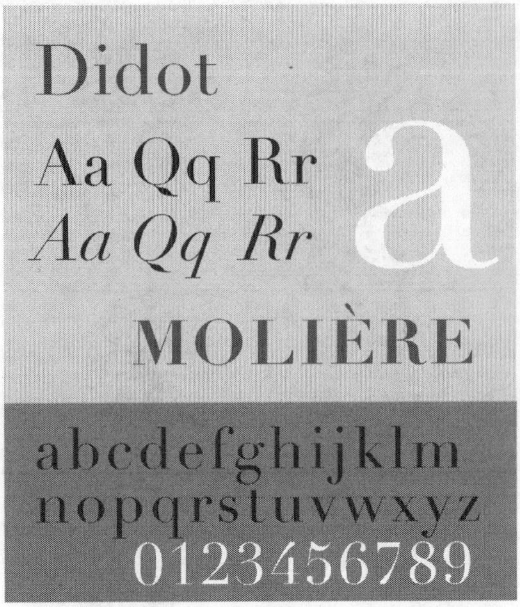

Figure 3.14 Example of Modern type

Modern fonts are also known as Didones and take the contrast started by the transitional fonts much, much further (see Figure 3.14). Bodoni is an excellent example font as nearly everyone can bring to mind the extreme contrast of its thick and thin strokes. The Frenchman Didot and the Italian Bodoni were the first to bring this design style to the public. Its major attributes align with the Romantic period's aesthetics.

> Romantic letters can be extraordinarily beautiful, but they lack the flowing and steady rhythm of the Renaissance forms. It is that rhythm which invites the reader to enter the text and read. The statuesque forms of Romantic letters invite the reader to stand outside and look at the letters instead. (Bringhurst, 2004, p. 130)

The major characteristics of modern fonts are extreme contrast between thick and thin strokes, clean, unbracketed, hairline serifs, and a completely vertical axis. These fonts have an almost mechanical look because of their precise, sharp, and clean appearance. They also possess an elegance that complrments the time period they emerged in. Modern fonts are often used as display fonts and can sometimes be used for text, though very carefully.

Examples of modern fonts include Fenice, Zapf Book, New Caledonia, Bodoni, and Didot.

Egyptian

Figure 3.15 Example of Egyptian type

Egyptian is also known as slab serif, square serif, or mechanical (see Figure 3.15). This category of font was created in England in the 1880s — a design expression of the industrial revolution. The category was named Egyptian because of the popularity of all things Egyptian after Napoleon's return from a three-year Egyptian expedition. The name of the style has nothing to do with any element of Egyptian culture. The style was created initially for display copy, but over the centuries, fonts like Clarendon have become popular for setting text blocks because they contain the quality of objectivity and yet still feel traditional.

Examples of Egyptian fonts include Officina Sans and Officina Serif, Clarendon, and every typewriter font.

Sans Serif

Figure 3.16 Example of Sans Serif

Sans serif fonts have existed since ancient times, but it was only in the late 19th century that font designers began to consider removing serifs and letting the letterforms stand on their own (see Figure 3.16). These fonts were initially considered appropriate only for titling and display purposes, and only became text fonts in the hands of the 20th-century modernists. The first sans serif forms were created on the early humanist and old style calligraphic forms, but eventually the forms were influenced by objective modernist principles and geometry.

Examples of sans serif fonts include Univers, Helvetica, and Akzidenz-Grotesk.

Media Attributions

- Point Grafitti © Steve Collins is licensed under a CC BY (Attribution) license
- Line © Ken Jeffrey
- Plane is licensed under a CC BY-SA (Attribution ShareAlike) license
- Color_AddSub © SharkD is licensed under a Public Domain license
- Coles_Phillips2_Life © Coles Phillips is licensed under a Public Domain license
- FedEx_Express_truck © Coolcaesar is licensed under a CC BY-SA (Attribution ShareAlike) license
- An_example_of_texture © Tomas Castelazo is licensed under a CC BY-SA (Attribution ShareAlike) license
- Typography_line_terms_alternate.svg © Damian Adrian is licensed under a CC BY-SA (Attribution ShareAlike) license
- Rudolf_Koch_gebrochene_Schriften © BK is licensed under a Public Domain license

3.3 Compositional Principles — Strategies for Arranging Things Better

> We have many words for the frustration we feel when an interface isn't directing us to what we need to know. Loud, messy, cluttered, busy. These words. . . express our feeling of being overwhelmed visually by content on a screen or page. We need them to express how unpleasant a user experience it is to not know where to direct our attention next. (Porter, 2010, para 1)
>
> If everything is equal, nothing stands out. (Bradley, 2011)

The proper composition of visual elements generates not only visual stability, it enhances mood through composition and generates order that prevents visual chaos. Designers use compositional rules in their work to make the reader enter their work and experience a design environment that is calm yet exciting, quiet yet interesting. A magazine designer, for example, creates a grid and applies an order to the typographic elements creating a comprehensible hierarchy. This design system is interpreted in different ways, in pages and spreads, issue after issue. If the organizational system is versatile and planned with thought and depth, it can be used to produce unique and exciting layouts that remain true to the rules determined for the overall system initially designed. Organizational principles create a framework for design without determining the end results.

Compositional rules can be used to generate content as well as organize it. The Bauhaus artist and designer Laszlo Moholy-Nagy created a series of paintings by calling in a set of instructions to a sign painter using the telephone. Here is his account of the experience, written in 1944:

> In 1922 I ordered by telephone from a sign factory five paintings in porcelain enamel. I had the factory's color chart before me and I sketched my paintings on graph paper. At the other end of the telephone, the factory supervisor had the same kind of paper divided in to squares. He took down the dictated shapes in the correct position. (It was like playing chess by correspondence). (Moholy-Nagy, 1947, p. 79)

Designing visual elements into a strong composition is a complex endeavour on its own, but increasingly designers are being asked to create vast compositional systems that other people will implement. Much like Laszlo Moholy-Nagy, designers need to be able to make strong compositional systems and also convey how their systems work, how to apply their rules, and how to apply them so they retain a relevant freshness.

Alignment

Figure 3.17 Alignment

Alignment refers to lining up the top, bottom, sides, or middle of a text, composition, or grouping of graphic elements on a page. Often a design composition includes a grid where the alignment of text blocks is dictated by the design of the columns of the grid (see Figure 3.17).

Typographically, horizontal alignment includes flush left (also called left justified or ragged right), flush right (also called right justified or ragged left), centred, and fully justified. Vertical alignment in typography is usually linked to baseline alignment. A baseline grid exists in digital software that is meant for layout of type and is the invisible line where font characters sit.

Contrast

Contrast is a visual device that increases the special character of both elements that have been paired. Contrast assists composition by creating focal points, and adds energy and visual range to a composition. Using contrast enables us to distinguish the qualities of one object by comparing differences with another. Some ways of creating contrast among elements in the design include the use of contrasting colours, sizes, and shapes. Johannes Itten, a design instructor and artist at the Bauhaus focused his research on the concept of contrast in both composition and colour. Itten's list of contrasts can be applied to both the composition and the atmosphere of a design work. His list includes these pairings: large/small, hard/soft, thick/thin, light/heavy, straight/curved, continuous/intermittent, much/little, sweet/sour, pointed/blunt, light/dark, loud/soft, black/white, strong/weak, diagonal/circular. No design makes use of only one kind of contrast, but usually one dominates the others.

Colour Contrast

Johannes Itten also worked with contrast in his seminal theory of colour and determined that there are seven kinds of contrast.

1. *Contrast of hue* occurs when a hue or colour is separated by being outlined in black or white lines. White lines weaken the 'strength' and appearance of the colour and the colours around the white lines seem darker. In contrast, a black line around a colour strengthens the appearance of the colour, while the colours around the black lines appear to be lighter.
2. *Light-dark contrast* is the contrast between light values and dark values.
3. *Cold-warm contrast* refers to the contrast between cool and warm colours. Warm colours are the red, orange, and yellow colours of the colour wheel, while cool colours are blue, green, and purple.
4. *Complementary contrast* is the contrast between colours directly opposite each other on the colour wheel.
5. *Simultaneous contrast* occurs between two colours that are almost complementary. One colour is one section to the left or right of the complementary colour of the other.
6. *Contrast of saturation* refers to the contrast between intense colours and tertiary or muted colors. Muted colours appear duller when placed next to intense colours, and intense colours appear more vivid when next to a muted colour.

7. *Contrast of extension* refers to the contrast between the area of one colour and another. Different areas of one colour are needed to balance another.

For text, contrast is achieved by using varied colours, serif and sans serif, type styles that are not often paired, or type in place of an image. As contrast in elements diminishes, the elements begin to feel similar, and the level of visual interest decreases.

Emphasis

A focal point in a composition draws the eye to it before the eye engages with the rest of the visual information. This is called *emphasis* and is achieved by making a specific element gain the attention of the eye. Emphasis is created in graphic design by making only one focal point and clearly emphasizing it by placing the elements on the page in positions where the eye is naturally drawn to the proper entry into the work. Designers rely on additional compositional principles to support the hierarchy of a composition such as contrast, repetition, or movement.

Designers use emphasis to assist viewers in identifying the relative importance of each element in a composition. Emphasis is strongly linked to visual hierarchy. Both emphasis and visual hierarchy create order for the viewer, allowing the eye to see the first element of importance, then the second, then the third, and so on. Graphic elements gain or lose emphasis by changing in size, visual intensity, colour, complexity, uniqueness, placement on the page, and relationship to other elements.

Movement

Figure 3.18 Example of movement

Movement is made by creating visual instability — like motion in a photograph that blurs the image, as shown in the example in Figure 3.18. Creating the illusion of movement photographically or artistically is not difficult because a blur translates into movement in the mind of the viewer. However, it is not the only option for a designer. A composition can also achieve movement if the graphic elements are arranged in a way that directs the eye to move in a specific direction — usually by creating a diagonal that takes the eye up to the right corner (forward motion) or down to the left corner (backward motion). Movement can also be created using overlapping planes that imply depth and distance by becoming progressively smaller and lighter in tone (mimicking depth). Using typography as a visual medium is also an option. Overlapping the text blocks and/or sentences effectively creates both depth and movement (though it destroys legibility). David Carson is a designer who often uses this technique to create movement in his work.

Scale

Varying scale (size) is one of the major tools in the designer's toolbox. Changing scale is important on two levels. The first is purely compositional — a composition needs variety in the size of its elements to be dynamic and effective. If all the elements have the same visual weight, the composition will be flat. Another aspect to varied scale is conceptual. If a design visually distorts the size relation of one element to another, the viewer is instantly engaged in discovering why. This is a great method to engage the viewer and add a twist to the message embedded in the design. A great example of this is the 'think small' ad campaign of the 1960s for Volkswagen Beetle.

The series is witty and engaging and plays on how we perceive size. This distortion is witty and playful, and presents smallness as desirable. Subtle scale differences do not make much visual impact, but large ones are very dramatic. The concept and context of a project should determine the relationship of scale differences for a composition. Large differences in scale are suited to dramatic and energetic design content, while smaller differences in scale are appropriate for professional and institutional content.

Proximity and the Gestalt Theory of Visual Relationships

Proximity of elements is part of Gestalt theory, which is a framework of spatial relationships developed in the 1920s by the German psychologists Max Wertheimer, Wolfgang Kohler, and Kurt Koffka. The term Gestalt means *unified whole,* and points to the underlying conceptual structure of this framework. Gestalt works because the mind seeks to organize visual information. A composition created using Gestalt principles predetermines how each of the elements within it interacts with the others spatially. In this system of relationships, close proximity of objects, regardless of shape, size, or content, indicates a connection. There are six basic Gestalt principles: (1) similarity, (2) continuation, (3) closure, (4) proximity, (5) figure/ground, and (6) symmetry and order.

Similarity

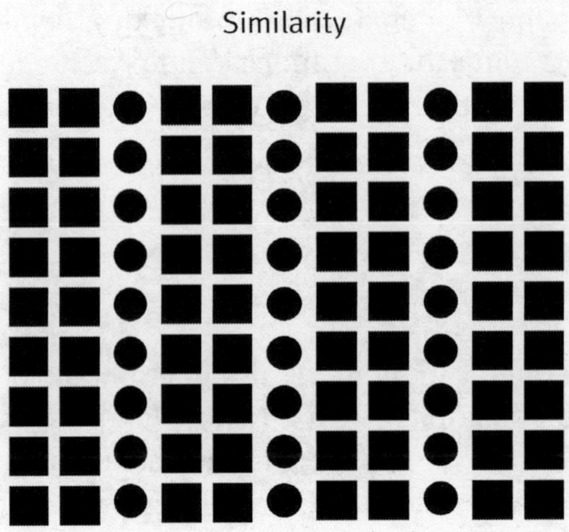

Figure 3.19 Similarity

When visual elements have a similar shape or look as one another, a viewer will often connect the discrete components and see a pattern or grouping (see Figure 3.19). This effect can be used to create a single illustration, image, or message from a series of separate elements. Similarity of medium, shape, size, colour, or texture will trigger a sense of similarity. The sense of grouping will be strengthened or weakened by increasing or decreasing the commonality of the individual elements.

Continuation

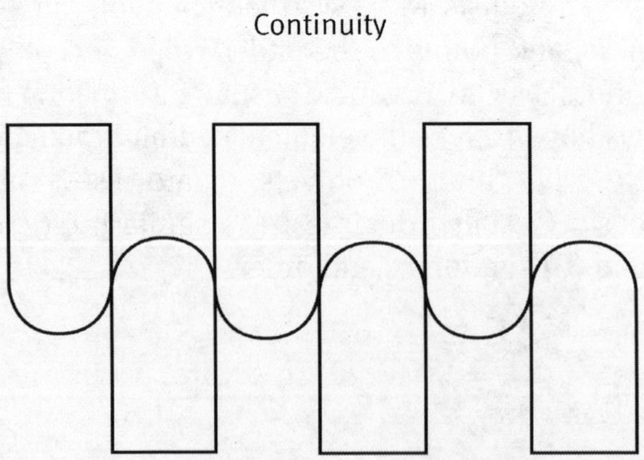

Figure 3.20 Continuity

Continuation is the tendency of the mind to see a single continuous line of connection rather than discrete components (see Figure 3.20). The eye is drawn along a path, line, or curve, as long as there is enough proximity between objects to do so. This tendency can be used to point toward another element in the composition, or to draw the eye around a composition. The eye will continue along the path or direction suggested by the composition even when the composition ends, continuing beyond the page dimensions.

Closure

Figure 3.21 Closure

Closure is a design technique that uses the mind's tendency to complete incomplete shapes (see Figure 3.21). The principle works if the viewer is given enough visual information to perceive a complete shape in the negative space. In essence, the mind 'closes' a form, object, or composition. In the example above , the triangle is formed by the viewer's mind, which wants to close the shape formed by the gaps and spaces of the adjacent circles and lines. The partial triangle, outlined in black also hints at the missing shape.

Proximity

Figure 3.22 Proximity

Proximity is an arrangement of elements that creates an association or relationship between them (see Figure 3.22). If individual elements are similar, they will probably be perceived first as a whole and second as discrete components. If, like the example above, some of the components form to create a large 'whole,' similar elements positioned away from the main shape will also be associated with the large shape. In this case, the viewer interprets them as falling off or away from the main shape. The shapes used do not have to be geometric to create the effect of proximity. Any components have a strong commonality in shape, colour, texture, size, or other visual attribute can achieve proximity. Proximity can also be achieved with dissimilar shapes and textures if cleverly and conceptually composed.

Figure/Ground

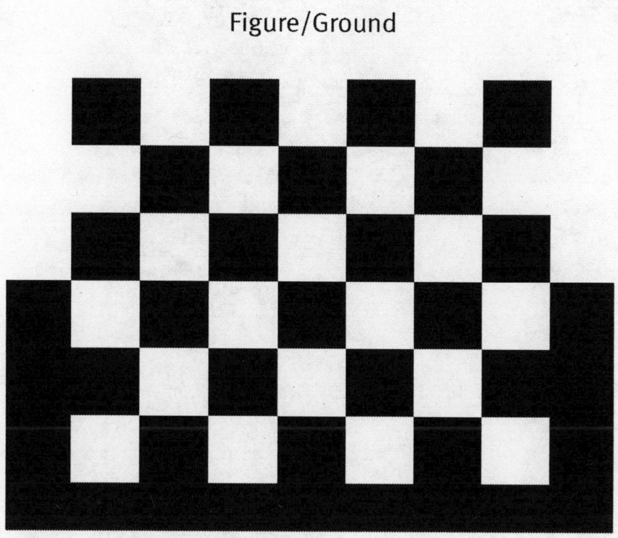

Figure 3.23 Figure/Ground

Figure/ground was discussed earlier, but it is part of Gestalt theory, so we present it here again. This principle describes the mind’s tendency to see as two different planes of focus, information in both positive and negative space (see Figure 3.23). It works if those spaces are suggestive enough in their composition.

Symmetry and Order

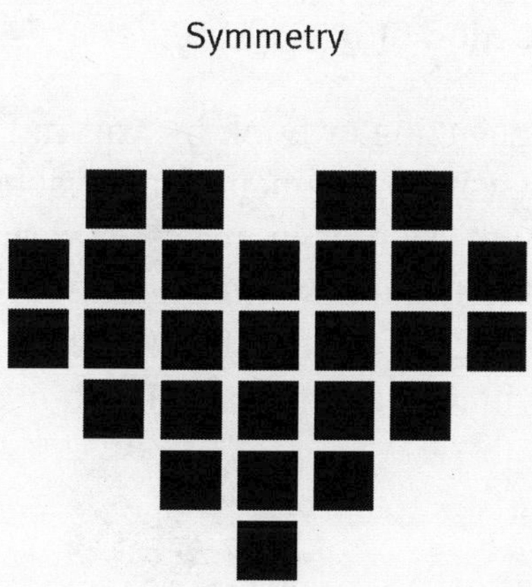

Figure 3.24 Symmetry

Symmetry and order follow the premise that a composition should not create a sense of disorder or imbalance (see Figure 3.24), because the viewer will waste time trying to mentally reorder it rather than focus on the embedded content. The photographic example in Figure 3.25 is composed symmetrically and allows the viewer to concentrate on the figure in the centre. Achieving symmetry in a composition also gives the composition balance and a feeling of harmony.

Figure 3.25 Example of symmetry and order

Rhythm

Rhythm is integral to the pacing of a design composition and is also necessary for creating a pattern, as used in the example in Figure 3.26. The pacing of a repeating motif or element at regular or irregular intervals within a design determines the energetic quality of a composition; it also creates a consistent and unifying backdrop for the introduction of new elements.

Rhythm is the effect produced in a magazine or book by varying the placement of elements within the grid structure. The changes in the density of elements and visual tones of the spreads translate into a rhythmic visual energy as the energy of each page grows or shrinks. Rhythm is the glue that connects one page to the next; it reveals recurrent themes and creates movement, tension, and emotional value in the content. When viewers understand the rhythm of a book, a magazine, or a website, they will also appreciate the variations that break with or punctuate the rhythm and create interest, change, or tension.

Figure 3.26 Example of rhythm

Repetition

Repetition creates visual consistency in page designs or in visual identities, such as using the same style of headline, the same style of initial capitals, and the same set of elements, or repeating the same basic layout from one page to another (see Figure 3.27).

Excessive repetition, however, creates monotony. This usually leads to viewer boredom and dull, uninteresting compositions for the designer. Be sure to create a design system that allows the repetitions within it to be lively and interesting page after page. The example above uses a simple set of rules, but because the rules allow for colour and compositional changes, each discrete component is as interesting on its own as it is within the whole. If you cannot avoid excessive repetitions, try to add some visual breaks and white spaces where the eyes can rest for a while.

Figure 3.27 Example of repetition

Balance

Balance and symmetry are important design qualities because they are deeply embedded in human DNA. Because our bodies are symmetrical, we have a strong association and satisfaction with centred, symmetrical design. Balancing visual elements compositionally calms the tensions and grounds the design (see Figure 3.28). This is important if you wish to convey a sense of stability to the viewer. When we look at a design, we use our innate sense of what constitutes 'right balance' to assess its stability. If that stability is missing, we feel tension, which can counteract the core of the message. Centred design compositions work very well for stable, security-inspiring content, but what about content that demands attention, or tension, or excitement?

When a centred (or stable) composition is not desirable, developing an asymmetrical composition is the best strategy. Asymmetry has been explored in graphic design for the last 150 years, and designers continue to discover new strategies that feel fresh. Asymmetry has no empirical rules but is guided by balancing the distribution of main elements around the space of a composition in an unexpected way. Contrast and counterpoint are the main tools of composition in asymmetry — large shapes balance small ones; intense colours balance neutrals. Creating asymmetrical design is not easy because there are no firm rules to follow, but it is exciting to create and exciting to see for exactly the same reason.

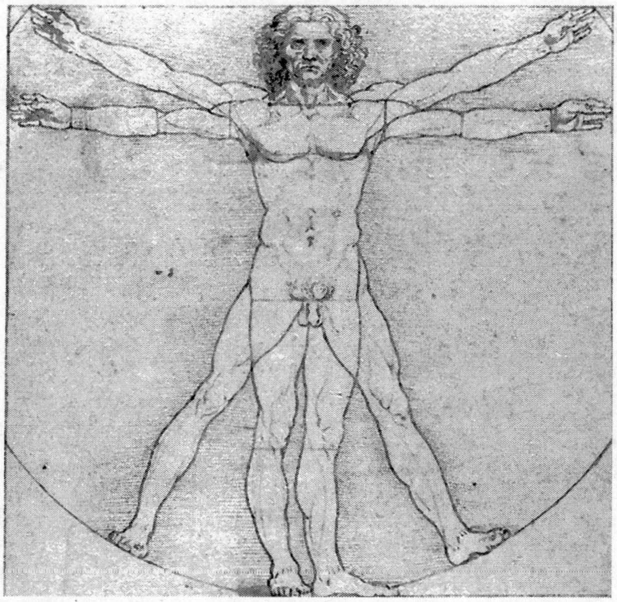

Figure 3.28 Example of balance

Hierarchy: Dominance and Emphasis

Simply put, hierarchy is applying an order of importance to a set of elements. Hierarchical order is apparent in every facet of our lives and is a defining characteristic of our contemporary culture. Hierarchy can be very complex and rigorous — an instruction manual is a good example of this. It can also be uncomplicated and loose. Hierarchy in composition is conveyed visually through variations of all the elements — size, colour, placement, tonal value, and so on (see Figure 3.29).

Figure 3.29 Example of hierarchy

Graphic design does not always embrace hierarchy. There are some messages that are more suited to visual anarchy and chaos (Punk design is a good example). These projects often connect to an audience by experimenting with, and breaking free from universal rules of visual structure. It is important is to match the structure of the composition to the needs of the project.

Typographic hierarchy is very important in design. A body of text is made more comprehensible by imposing order through a system of titles, subtitles, sections, and subsections. Hierarchy is created when the levels of the hierarchy are clear and distinguishable from one another. Subtle signs of difference are not effective. Typography acts as a tonal voice for the viewer, and must create clear variation in tone, pitch, and melody.

Hierarchy is usually created using similarity and contrast. Similar elements have equality in typographic hierarchy. Dominant and subordinate roles are assigned to elements when there is enough contrast between them. The bigger and darker an element is, the more importance it has. Smaller and lighter sizes and tones imply lesser importance.

Every hierarchy has a most important level and a least important level. The elements that fall between the two are ranked according to size and position. However, if you subdivide the text with too many levels, the contrast between different levels will blur their differences in the hierarchical order.

A good strategy to follow with text design is to apply three levels of typographic hierarchy.

Title

The function of a title is to attract the reader to the content of the text block. Often, the title is visually 'flavourful' and possesses a strong visual dynamic and energy.

Subtitle

Second-level typography gives the reader the ability to distinguish between types of information within the text block. This level of type includes subheads, pull quotes, captions, and anything else that can help detail and support understanding of the text-block information.

Text block

The text block is the content. As opposed to the 'display' function of the title and subtitle, the function of the text block is to make the content legible and easy to digest visually. Readers should be able to decide if they want to read this level based on primary (title) and secondary (subtitle) type levels.

Typically, a typographic hierarchy will convey information from general to specific as it progresses from title to text block. The general points presented in the title will be the most important and will be seen by most everyone. Think of how a newspaper is scanned for interesting news items: If readers are interested in the title, they may choose to read more detailed and in-depth information in the associated text block.

Media Attributions

- alignment © Ken Jeffrey
- Blast2_movement © Wyndham Lewis is licensed under a Public Domain license

- gestalt_similarity-01 © Ken Jeffrey
- gestalt_continuity-02 © Ken Jeffrey
- gestalt_closure-03 © Ken Jeffrey
- gestalt_proximity-04 © Ken Jeffrey
- gestalt_figureground-05 © Ken Jeffrey
- gestalt_symmetry-06 © Ken Jeffrey
- Chicago world's fair © Weimer Pursell is licensed under a Public Domain license
- Class of '40 presents LCCN98513436 © Library of Congress is licensed under a Public Domain license
- Flower poster © Alvesgaspar is licensed under a CC BY-SA (Attribution ShareAlike) license
- Da Vinci Vitruve Luc Viatour2 © Leonardo da Vinci is licensed under a Public Domain license

3.4 Organizational Principles

Compositional organization is complex, but even more so when applied to typography. Typography is a complicated medium to work with as it contains two levels of information (display and content), and requires its components to be read in proper sequence with proper emphasis, good legibility, and strong contrast to the substrate. Many elements need to be organized to allow the reader a seamless experience when reading the content. Designing with type requires adept handling of the hierarchy, refining and designing the display elements for focal emphasis and also refining the quiet details of the text block so it sits perfectly and quietly in its space.

Think of these organizational systems as 'large picture' constraints. Constraints (rules) allow a designer to focus on the other aspects of a project. Designers make myriad decisions about concept, style, visuals, form, font, size, spacing, colour, placement, proportion, relationships, and materials. When some factors are determined in advance, the designer is able to spend time with the other parts of the project. A well-defined constraint can free up the thought process by taking some decisions off the table. The following eight organizational systems cover composition for type (but can also be applied to general composition), including the traditional ordering system of the grid.

Grid

A grid is a network of lines that structure the placement of elements and create relationships between them. A grid divides a design space into vertical and horizontal divisions. The grid is a bridge between a design rationale and the beginning of implementation for each project, converting a concept into a structured space. It is an exceptional tool for composing, arranging, and organizing every kind of visual element. The grid usually works invisibly in the background, but it can become an active, visible element as well. Designers use grids in a variety of ways. They can be very disciplined about adhering to their grid structure from the beginning of a project, or use it as a starting point for composition and order.

Grid systems create a formal composition in comparison to more casual compositional approaches like transitional or random structures. Grids are often used in publication and web design because they introduce consistency and guide hierarchy. Consistent margins and columns create an underlying structure that unifies the multiple pages of a document or website, and makes the layout process more efficient.

The plan for the grid comes from the content and concept of the design project. The objective in creating a grid is to set up the relationships between elements in a way that stays true to the concept. For instance, if your publication is a book of poetry, the grid must have generous amounts of negative space and generous leading. If, on the other hand, your publication is a daily newspaper, the spacing relationships cannot be so generous, and have to clearly show which article relates to which image. Hierarchy of information must be very clear as well, and should reveal which news item is most important and which is least important. A well-made grid will naturally allow the designer generous scope for variation in image style, text size, and graphic style. Often, a grid that is complex allows for some freedom where the designer can introduce a new element or effect.

A grid activates the entire surface of a project by making all of it available for active elements. It helps create both stable symmetrical and dynamic asymmetrical compositions. By breaking down space into smaller units, grids encourage designers to leave some areas open rather than fill up the whole page.

Types of Grids

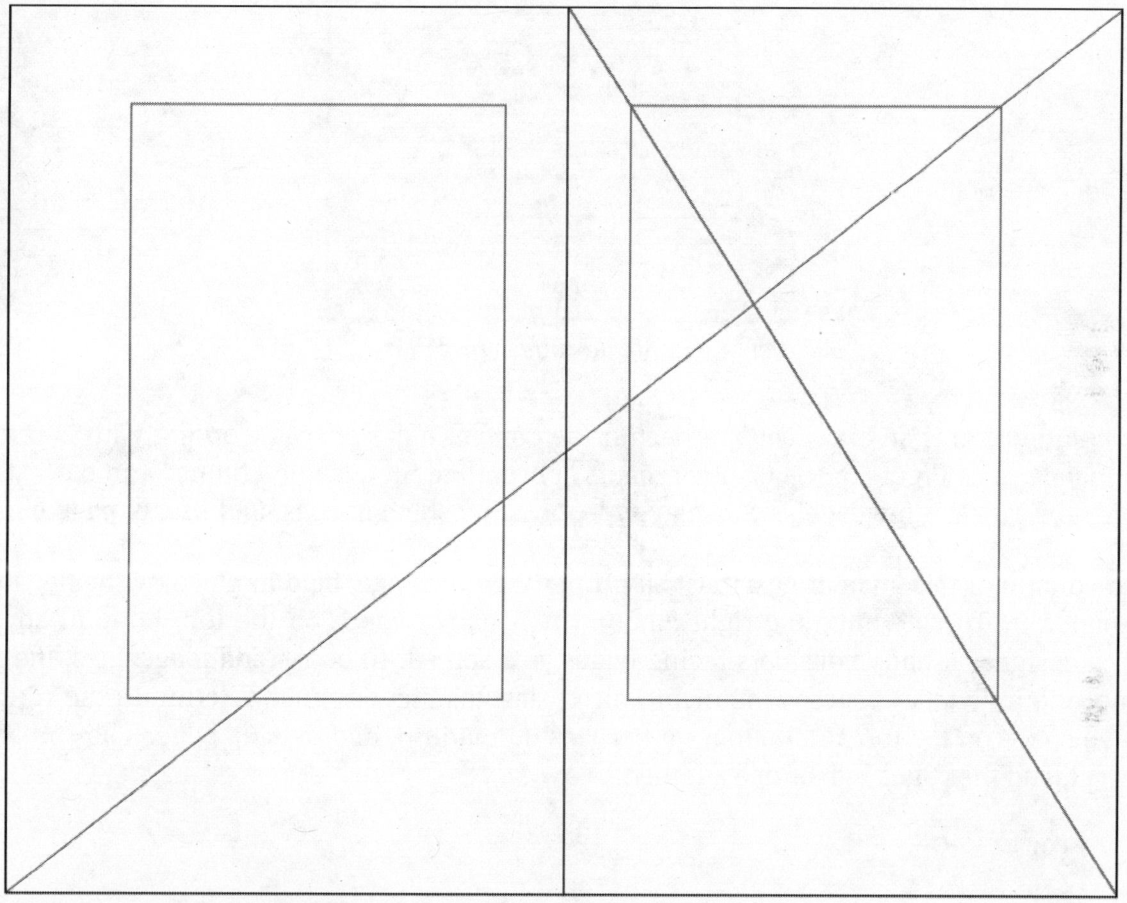

Figure 3.30 The golden section

The golden section is also known as the golden ratio, golden mean, or divine proportion, and it is found in mathematics, geometry, life, and the universe — its applications are limitless (see Figure 3.30)

The golden section is a ratio — a relationship between two numbers — that has been applied as an organizational system in art, design, and architecture for centuries. Expressed numerically, the ratio for the golden section is 1 : 1.618. The formula for the golden section is a : b = b : (a+b). In other words, side a is to side b as side b is to the sum of both sides.

Graphic designers use the golden section to create grids and layouts for websites and books. Photographers use it to compose the focal point of an image and also to compose the elements found in an image.

Single-Column Grid

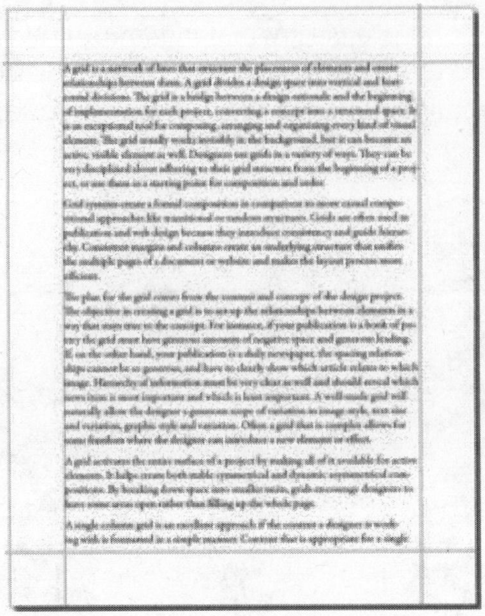

Figure 3.31 Single-column grid

A single-column grid is an excellent approach if the content a designer is working with is formatted in a simple manner (see Figure 3.31). Content that is appropriate for a single-column grid consists of main text for the text block, a few levels of display type, possibly some images, and finally page numbers.

The main column of this style of grid must sit properly on the page, held in place by the negative space that surrounds it. To determine the right amount of negative space on the top, bottom, and sides of the page, a designer usually considers facing pages as a spread. In books and magazines, the two-page spread, not the individual page, is the main unit of design. The designer determines the right amount of negative space on the top and bottom, gutter (inside margin), and outside edge. The spread is often symmetrical, and the pages mirror one another.

Multi-Column Grid

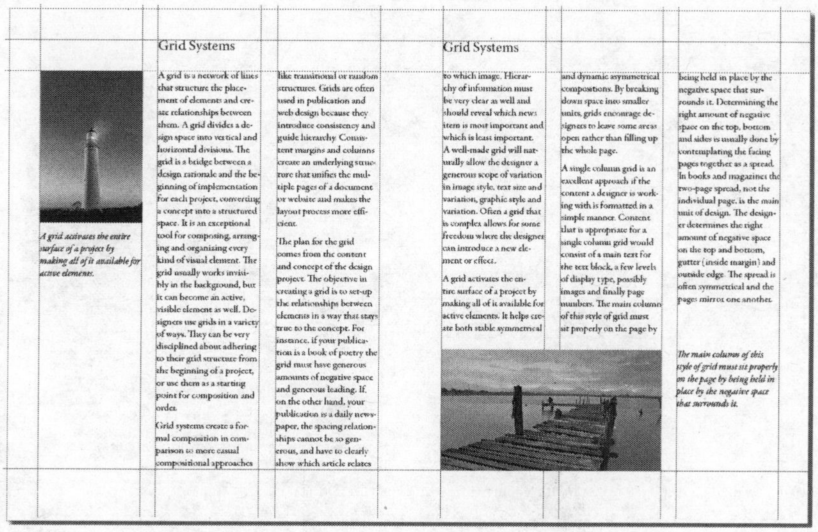

Figure 3.32 Multi-column grid

When a designer creates a grid for a document that is complicated, he or she may use multi-column grids because they allow for a complex hierarchy and provide more options for integrating text and visuals (see Figure 3.32). The more columns you create, the more flexible your grid will be. You can use the grid to articulate the hierarchy of the publication by creating zones for different kinds of content. The columns act as visual units that can be combined or kept separate. A photo can span several columns or be reduced to the width of only one. A text can also occupy a single column or span several.

Hang Lines

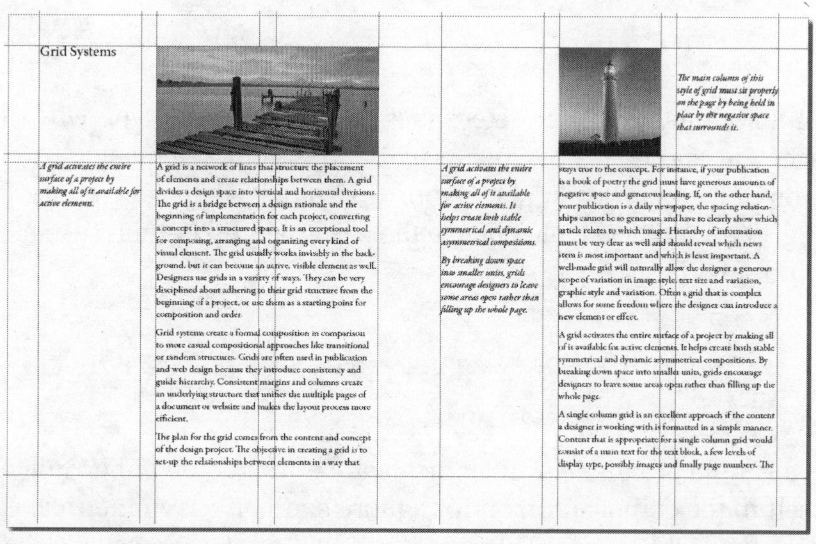

Figure 3.33 Hang lines

In addition to creating vertical columns in a grid, you can also divide the page horizontally. Often, a designer determines the placement of hang lines (see Figure 3.33) by applying the rule of thirds (breaking up the horizontal plane into three equal parts). This compartmentalization allows the designer to reserve certain sections for images and others for the text block.

Modular Grid

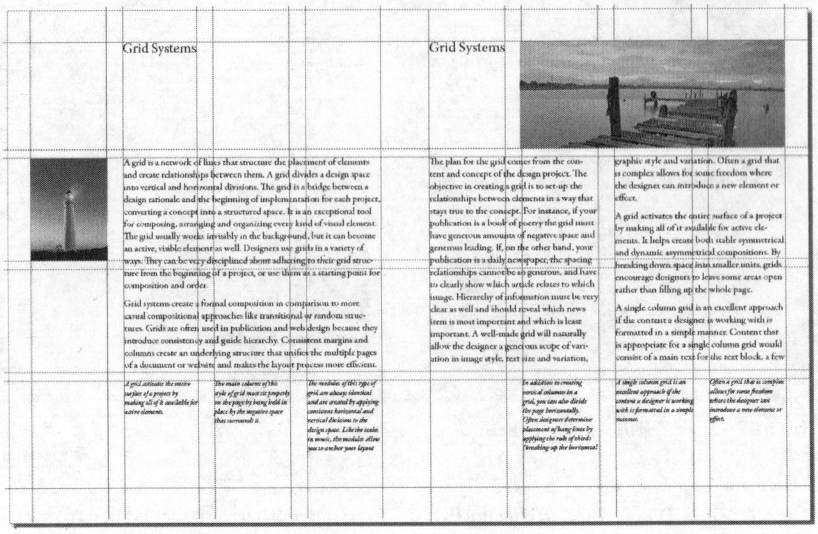

Figure 3.34 Modular grid

The modules of this type of grid are always identical and are created by applying consistent horizontal and vertical divisions to the design space. Like the written notes in a musical score, the modules allow you to anchor your layout elements and typography to a specific rhythm. With a modular grid, the horizontal guidelines are tied to the baseline grid that governs the whole document. Baseline grids serve to anchor most of the elements to a common leading (typographic line spacing). See Figure 3.34.

Baseline Grid

A baseline grid is the horizontal grid that determines where all of the type will sit. You can also use it to determine the placement and edges of your visual and graphic elements. To create a baseline grid, determine the right font, size, and leading for your text block, then go to your baseline grid settings (found with the other grid preferences) and change the baseline grid default (usually 12 pt) to the leading you will be using in your text block.

Axial

The axial system has a simple premise — all elements are arranged on either side of an axis or line. You can centre the axis itself in the composition or, for a more energetic asymmetrical composition, place the axis off centre to either the right or left. This compositional strategy creates a dynamic negative space on the opposite side. To create a more complex composition, designers often employ an axial system combined with another — like the radial or dilatational system (see below). They may also use double-axis compositions with the axes either parallel to each other, or intersecting to create a strong focal point. There are many instances of the axial system in nature — tree trunks, roots, and vines are good examples.

Like these organic examples, an axis does not need to be a straight line — it can be curved, zigzag, or circular.

Modular

Modular organization is a compositional method that utilizes rigour (by constraining the shape) and freedom from structure (modules can be any size and placed anywhere in the space). Modules can also be uniform and contained within a structure (a grid). A module is a fixed element used within a larger system or structure. For example, a pixel is a module that builds a digital image.

Bilateral

The bilateral system is based on mirrored symmetry and is therefore both classic and ubiquitous. Because of its predictability, it is a challenge for designers to work with. Nature exhibits many examples of bilateral composition — the bodies of mammals, the points of a snowflake, and the fractal symmetry of plants are all quickly understood, appreciated, and then dismissed by the viewer. To create a composition based on the bilateral system, a designer must make some part of the composition unusual. The designer can achieve this by moving the axis to a diagonal, off-centre location, which allows the negative space on either side of the bilateral composition to be varied. A second method is to introduce a double axis: the designer uses two columns of bilateral information and varies the size of each.

Radial

The radial system takes its name from the sun — all elements are arranged like rays coming from a central focal point. This is a dynamic compositional strategy as it references dynamic action. Examples of the radial form from the natural world, such as explosions, flowers, spiders, stars, and so on, are all exciting and dynamic. Much like it is difficult to handle the natural objects, reproducing a radial composition is not that easy. There are problems with legibility unless type is very carefully placed and scaled. Every line of type starts and ends in a different place, so continuity is also hard to control. For example, a designer may take a traditional approach so the text reads from top to bottom, or an inverse approach so the text reads from bottom to top. Arranging the text on either side of centre may also be effective. It is important to try placing the type in different positions and in different relationships until it works with the composition and is easy to read.

As in the organizational systems we have discussed, designers can add radial points for a more complex composition or combine a radial system with one that adds stability, such as a grid, axial, or modular system.

Dilatational

Dilatational systems mimic the look of still water when a pebble is dropped into it, creating rings of greater and greater size as they move away from the centre. Like the radial system, this composition has a strong focal point, but unlike the radial system, the composition creates rings, not rays, that expand from the centre. Other examples of this system are the iris of the eye or representations of sound waves.

Random/Spontaneous

Creating a composition that does not follow any compositional principle is not as easy as it sounds. Finding examples of randomness is also one of the most difficult exercises for design students. Random design does not follow any rule, method, direction, or pattern. If a project calls for randomness, it is best to start with materials that are conducive to spontaneity like Jackson Pollock's paint throws. Allow the elements that fall to organize themselves naturally — eventually, a dynamic and fresh composition should emerge. Random compositions exhibit visual qualities that are not patterned, aligned, or horizontal. Instead, they tend toward compositions that exhibit overlapping, cropping, angling, and textures.

Transitional

The transitional typographic system is defined by the layering of lines of text into informal textured planes and shifting tonal bands. The shapes and bands created with this layering approach are not aligned with one another, and create an overall organic atmosphere. This visual approach is often used in Post Modern design where the clear legibility of text is not as important as the visual atmosphere of the design. Text planes in Post Modernist works point the viewer to the main theme of the message rather than articulate the message in clean, concise text arrangements.

Compositions using the transitional approach have a light, airy look that abstractly imply cloud formations or wood grain patterns rather than solid concrete shapes created by using the grid or axial systems. A transitional composition has lively and active negative space, and can create an excellent ground for a vital focal point if it is in sharp contrast to the rest of the composition.

Attributions

Figure 3.32
Image includes: Photo by Stefanus Martanto Setyo Husodo used under a CC0 license and Cape Nelson Lighthouse, Portland, Australia by Joshua Hibbert used under a CC0 license.

Figure 3.33
Image includes: Photo by Stefanus Martanto Setyo Husodo used under a CC0 license and Cape Nelson Lighthouse, Portland, Australia by Joshua Hibbert used under a CC0 license.

Figure 3.34
Image includes: Photo by Stefanus Martanto Setyo Husodo used under a CC0 license and Cape Nelson Lighthouse, Portland, Australia by Joshua Hibbert used under a CC0 license.

Media Attributions

- grid_single column © Ken Jeffrey
- grid_multi column adapted by Ken Jeffrey
- grid_hang lines adapted by Ken Jeffrey
- grid_modular adapted by Ken Jeffrey

3.5 Summary

Exploring the design possibilities that the organizational systems discussed in this chapter possess is an endless undertaking. Once these systems are innately understood individually, a designer can begin to play with layering two systems within one design project. Combining contrasting systems often works well. For instance, an axial system combined with a radial system tempers the axial system's linear focus and anchors and diffuses the rays emanating from the radial shapes. A grid combined with a dilatation system gives the composition both vertical and horizontal structure that is softened by the rounded shapes. Organizational systems give the designer ways to distribute words or images within a structure while allowing negative space into the centre of the design space.

Compositional strategies are design constraints. The definition of a design constraint is to apply or impose limitations on the elements or design of a system. The compositional strategies (systems) discussed above are in fact design constraints, and they should be understood as parameters that assist the designer in the design process rather than as restraints that limit the designer's creativity. Parameters are necessary in every visual system. Applying a visual organizational system also allows the designer to focus on the message and the details of a design project rather than on the structure of the composition that holds the work together. Visual systems create visual unity.

Questions to consider after completing this chapter:

1. Name the design principle that distorts realistic relationships for visual effect and emphasis.
2. Name the three building blocks of design that pertain to form.
3. Describe the eight organizational systems that apply to typography.
4. What are two typographic categories?
5. How many levels of visual hierarchy are needed for hierarchy to exist?

References

Bartel, M. (2012). Principles of design and composition. In *Some ideas about composition and design. Elements, principles, and visual effects*. Retrieved from https://www.goshen.edu/art/ed/Compose.htm#principles

Bradley, S. (2011, January 31). Counterpart and counterpoint in typographic hierarchy. *Vanseo Design*. Retrieved from http://www.vanseodesign.com/web-design/counterpart-and-counterpoint-in-typographic-hierarchy/

Bringhurst, R. (2004). *The elements of typographic style* (3rd ed.). Point Roberts, WA: Hartley and Marks Publishers.

Lupton, E., & Phillips, J. C. (2014). *Graphic design: The new basics* (2nd ed.). New York City, NY: Princeton Architectural Press.

Moholy-Nagy, L. (1947). *The new vision and abstract of an artist.* (1st ed.). New York City, NY: Wittenborn.

Porter, J. (2010, March 12). Visual hierarchy. *52 Weeks of UX*, week 10. Retrieved from http://52weeksofux.com/post/443828775/visual-hierarchy

Suggested Readings

Bradley, S. (2011, January 31). Counterpart and counterpoint in typographic hierarchy. *Vanseo Design*. Retrieved from http://www.vanseodesign.com/web-design/counterpart-and-counterpoint-in-typographic-hierarchy/

Elam, K. (2007). *Typographic systems*. New York City, NY: Princeton Architectural Press.

Designhistory.org (2011). *The Sans Serif* Retrieved from http://www.designhistory.org/Type_milestones_pages/SansSerif.html

Taylor, K. (n.d.). The metaphysics of color. *Philosophy talk*. Retrieved from http://www.philosophytalk.org/community/blog/ken-taylor/2015/04/metaphysics-color

Chapter 4. Colour Management in the Graphic Technologies

4.1 Introduction

Learning Objectives

- Define the relationship between the observer, the illuminant, and the object in colour appearance
- Describe the physics of light and colour
- Recognize how the eye-brain system affects colour perception
- Explain the components of the CIE colorimetric system, specifically the Lab colour space and Delta E measurements
- Differentiate between device specific and device independent colour models
- Describe the role of colour management in achieving consistent appearance between proofing cycles and final printed production
- Define an ICC profile and describe its application in digital imaging
- Use a spectrophotometer to capture colour data from industry standard targets as the first step in profile creation
- Create ICC colour profiles for standard colour transformations
- Calibrate, profile, and colour manage an LCD monitor
- Describe the application of display, input, and output colour profiles in the electronic prepress workflow
- Apply colour profiles in a variety of industry-standard applications to achieve desirable results for graphic reproduction
- Combine source and destination profiles into a single device link profile for device specific colour transformations
- Apply colour management with ICC or device link profiles in the colour control module of Prinergy's Process Plan for proofing output
- Combine surplus spot colours into a single separation for successful printing-plate production

A knowledgeable application of a colour-managed **workflow** is required for the successful and predictable generation of all colour content in print production and related graphic technologies.

This process requires familiarity with the fundamental colour science that drives the practical steps of **colour profile** creation and colour profile use in our industry-standard software applications. From colour science, we can progress to an examination of the tools and detailed steps required for profile creation and successful profile use.

4.2 Colour Science

The Colour Event

The first challenge in dealing with colour in graphic reproduction is to learn to think of colour as an *event* rather than as an attribute or characteristic of a particular object.

Colour is an event because it requires the participation of three components at a particular point in time to take place. In addition to the object, we require a light source and an observer. Only with the interaction of these three things — object, light, and observer — can we have a colour event or experience.

We need some help from three branches of science, physics, physiology and psychology, to understand how the object, light, and observer contribute to the colour event. If you like memory aids, you can use the acronym POLO to remind you of the three science P's and the object, light, and observer.

Object

The object and light fall under the domain of physics, while we need both physiology and psychology to describe the observer's role in the colour event.

The object's role is to interact with light, and the object can either reflect light back from its surface or transmit light through itself. Reflectance and transmission are the two potential interactions. The majority of objects are opaque, so most of the time we are dealing with the reflection of light. If an object is semi-opaque, and transmits a portion of light, we refer to it as translucent.

Light

Visible light is a tiny sliver of the total electromagnetic spectrum. The **electromagnetic spectrum** contains all forms of energy, ranging from kilometre-long radio waves at one end and progressing in shortening wavelengths down through microwaves, infrared waves, ultraviolet waves, X-rays, and finally, gamma waves with wavelengths of a subatomic dimension (see Figure 4.1).

Visible light is nestled in-between the infrared and ultraviolet range (see Figure 4.2). The progression from longest to shortest wavelength is from red (following infrared) to violet (preceding ultraviolet) in the 700 to 380 nanometre (millionths of a metre) wavelength distribution.

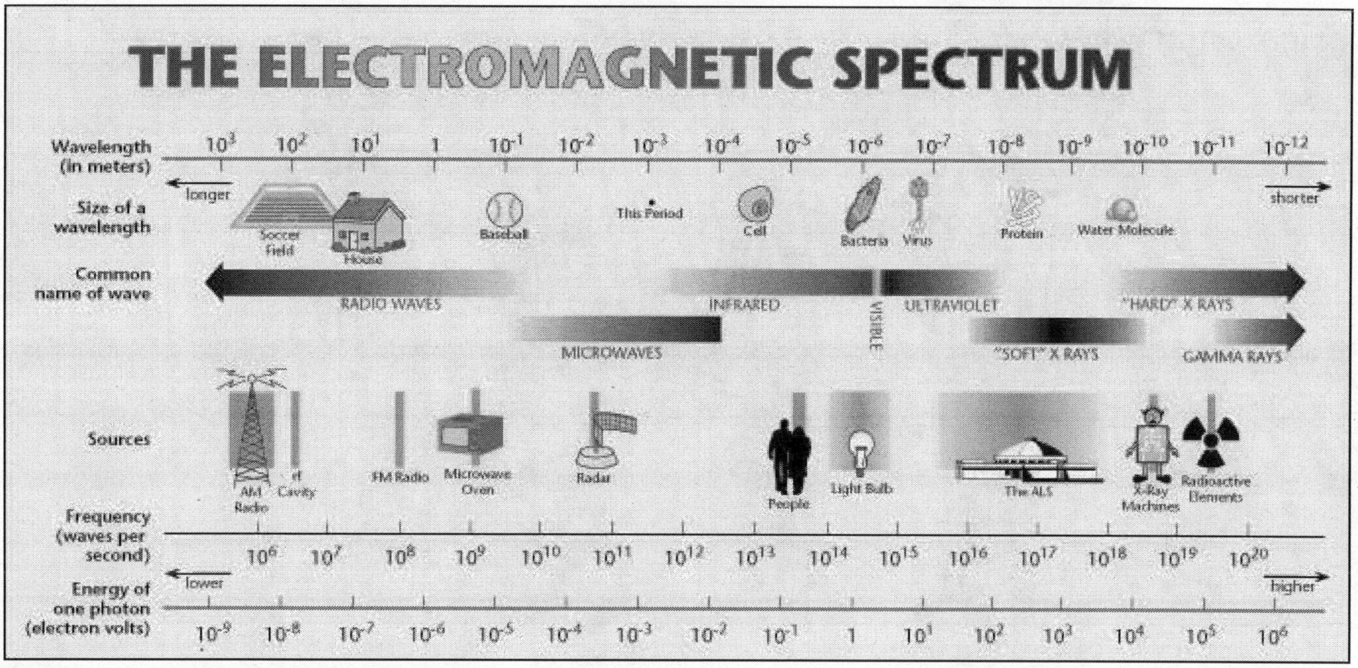

Figure 4.1 The Electromagnetic Spectrum

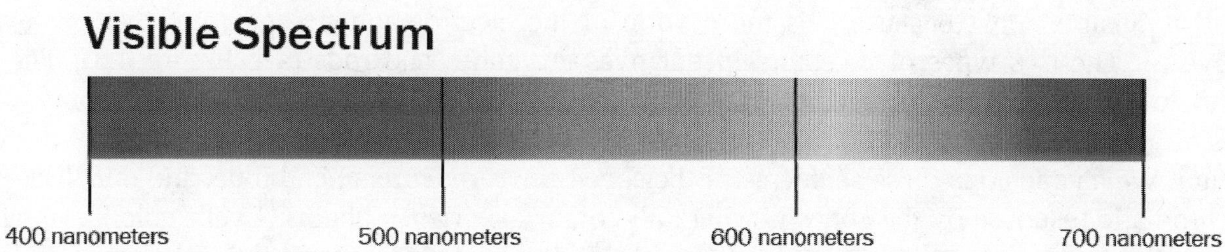

Figure 4.2 Visible Spectrum

We describe the **temperature** (relative warmness to coolness) of light in degrees Kelvin. Typical daylight ranges from 5000 to 6500 degrees Kelvin. We use the labels D50 and D65 to indicate daylight-viewing conditions at these temperature points.

Observer

The greatest complexity of the colour event occurs in the interaction with the observer. The science of physiology, the study of the human body's functions, provides half the story. Psychology, which provides insights about the function of the mind, completes the tale.

We begin with how our eyes, our optic systems, respond to light. Trichromacy and opponency are the key concepts.

Trichromacy

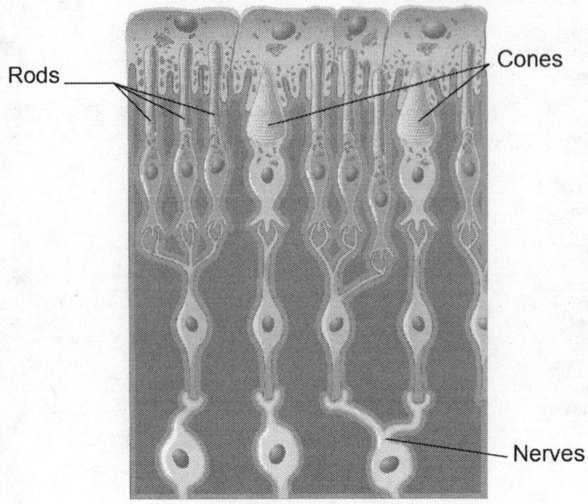

From: http://commons.wikimedia.org/wiki/File%3A1414_Rods_and_Cones_-_ru.svg

Figure 4.3 Rods and cones (adapted by Ken Jeffery)

We call it 'visible' light because it is the portion of the electromagnetic spectrum that our eyes are sensitive to. The two types of receptors in our eyes are cones and rods (see Figure 4.3). The cones respond to colour and the rods come into play in low-light situations when we see only varying shades of grey. There are three types of cones, each sensitive to approximately one-third of the visible spectrum. We characterize those segments of the spectrum as red, green, and blue, and this three-colour or trichromatic response by the cones is where all colour experience begins. Every colour we perceive comes from mixing varying volumes of the red, green, and blue signals from the three types of cones in our eyes.

The Additive Primaries

We refer to the *red, green,* and *blue* colour set (**RGB**) as the **additive primaries**. When we combine or add all three of these, we get the entire spectrum and, thus, white light. This is the primary colour set involved whenever we talk about the transmission of light, such as the display on a computer monitor, a tablet, or from a projector. For this reason, red, green, and blue are also referred to as the **transmissive primaries**.

The Subtractive Primaries

What happens when we project two of the three additive primaries on top of each other? This is the same as removing or subtracting one of the additive primaries from white light. Let's start with red and green. Though not at all intuitive, if you have any experience with mixing paint or inks, the combination of red and green light produces yellow. Remember that we are adding light to light, so the production of a brighter colour is to be expected. Continuing on: combining green and blue gives us a light blue that we call cyan, while the combination of red and blue produces magenta.

Since each of these colours is produced by subtracting one of the additive primaries from the full complement of white light, we refer to this colour set of *cyan, magenta,* and *yellow* (**CMY**) as the **subtractive primaries**. Each of the subtractive primaries acts as a filter for its complementary colour in the additive primary colour set. Cyan absorbs all red light, reflecting only green and blue. Magenta absorbs all green light, returning only red and blue; while yellow absorbs all blue light and reflects back only red and green. What colour would you see if you shone green light on a magenta patch?

Just as we can produce any colour sensation in the transmission of light by mixing the appropriate quantities of red, green, and blue, we can produce the corresponding colour sensation when we put ink on paper by absorbing the necessary portions of the visible spectrum so that only the required amounts of red, green, and blue are reflected back. This is how cyan, magenta, and yellow work as our primary colours in the printing environment, and why we also call them the **reflective primaries**.

Opponency

The second half of the role that our human physiology plays in the observer's part of the colour event is the concept of opponency. Our eyes' tristimulus response (a response to the red, green, and blue portions of incoming light) is the input, but the interpretation occurs when we map that input to a location in a colour space determined by three axes of opposing sensations. We have a built-in colour map where we define our colour perception by identifying the perceived colour based on its degree of greenness to redness, blueness to yellowness, and darkness to lightness.

These three pairs of opposites — green-red, blue-yellow, dark-light — are the fundamental guide posts we use to position any colour we perceive on our internal colour map. These opponent colour pairs are exclusive colour entities, occupying opposing ends of the range of our interpretation. Unlike a yellowish-orange or a reddish-purple, we cannot imagine a colour having the properties of red and green or blue and yellow at the same time.

Lab Colour Space

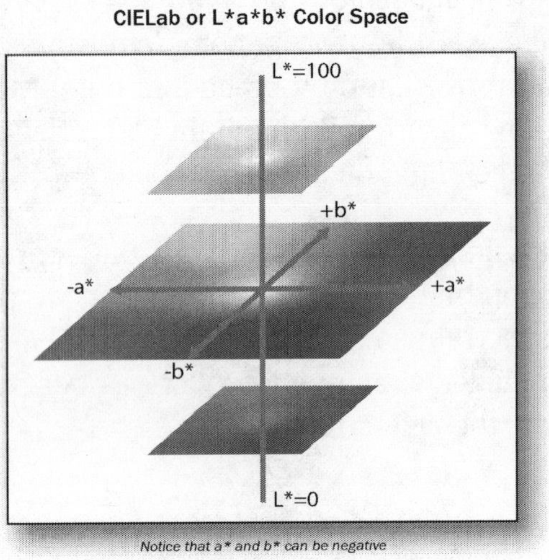

Once the opponent nature of colour interpretation was understood, colour scientists were able to create a model colour space based on the opposing pairs. This is the **Lab colour space** (see Figure 4.4). The Lab variation of interest to us is officially called *CIELAB*, and all references in this textbook to *Lab* will mean *CIELAB*. Additionally, references to *L*, *a*, and *b* in this textbook are equivalent to the *L**, *a**, and *b** units of the CIELAB colour space. Each of the opposing pairs provides one axis of this three-dimensional colour space. L is the axis for darkness to lightness; a is the axis for greenness to redness; and b is the axis for blueness to yellowness. By providing a value for each of the L, a, and b attributes, a colour is accurately and uniquely located in the colour space. The tremendous utility of the Lab colour space is that it allows for the mathematical description of a colour in a non-ambiguous and meaningful way.

Psychology of Colour Perception

We come to the last of our three science P's: psychology. After the trichromatic response is passed to opponent interpretation in the physiology of our optic systems, the final engagement of colour perception occurs in our minds. This interaction complicates and potentially confounds our objective measurements, so it is critical to be aware of the typical issues that the filter of our mind brings to the arena of colour perception.

Colour Constancy

Colour constancy is how our mind adjusts our colour perception to discount or remove the effects of an overall colour cast due to a coloured illuminant. If we see someone wearing a yellow sweater illuminated by a bluish cast of light, we still 'see' a yellow sweater, even though we have no trouble identifying the colour in the sweater as green if it is isolated from the scene. In our mind, we remove the blue constituents of all colours in the scene that we assume are coming from the tint in the light source. This behaviour is also known as **chromatic adaptation**.

The effect of **adjacency** is very similar to colour constancy. A colour placed next to a light colour appears darker than when that same colour is placed next to a dark colour (see examples in Figures 4.5 and 4.6). We make adjustments to our interpretation based on our assessment of the environment.

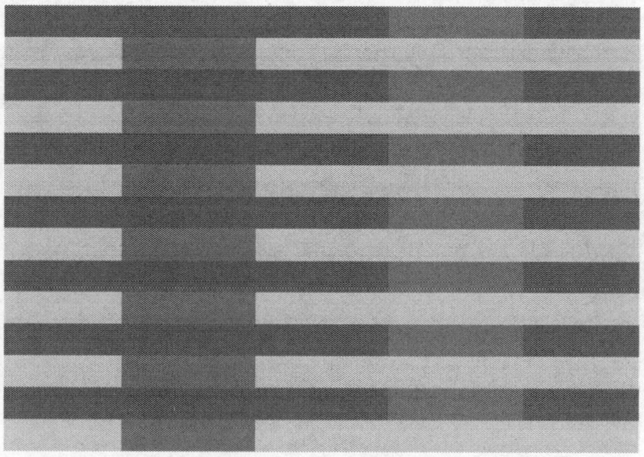

Figure 4.5 Both greens are the same colour

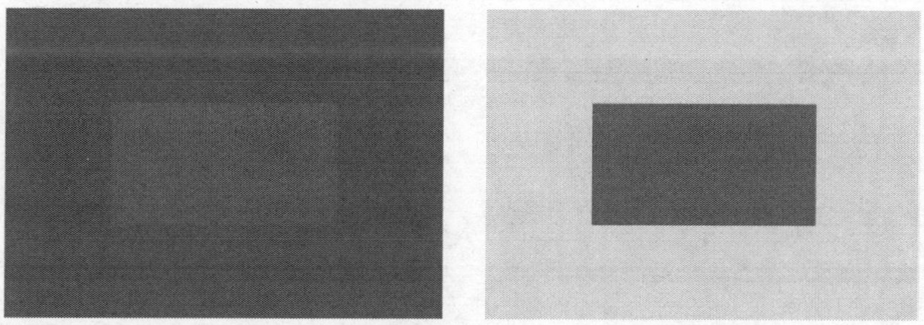

Figure 4.6 Both reds are the same colour

The effect of colour constancy provides a very important lesson in judging our success in colour matching: it is more important to preserve the overall colour relationships in our image than to focus on individual colour accuracy.

Memory Colours

In our mind's eye, not all colours are created equal. Due to their historical importance to our survival, we pay special attention to certain colours. Flesh tones, the blue of the sky, and the greens of grass are known as memory colours due to the additional weight they have in our hierarchy of colour.

We need to give these memory colours a priority when we evaluate our colour management efforts. If these key colours aren't right, then everything will look wrong.

The significant impact of our mind's contribution to colour perception enforces the requirement to take colour matching beyond the raw numbers we can extract from the physics and physiology of light's interaction with an object and our optic systems. The psychological components such as colour constancy and memory colours can only be accommodated by human intervention in a colour management system.

Media Attributions

- 1414 Rods and Cones modified-01-01 © Kaidor, adapted by Ken Jeffrey is licensed under a CC BY-SA (Attribution ShareAlike) license
- Lab colour space © Ken Jeffrey
- green-yellow © Ken Jeffrey
- colours in the middle © Ken Jeffrey

4.3 Measuring Devices

We measure light to provide the data needed to manage colour in a graphic production environment. There are three ways to measure light and three corresponding tools available to take those measurements: densitometer, colorimeter, and spectrophotometer.

Densitometre

To measure only the volume of light, we use a densitometer. The **densitometre** provides a known volume of light and then records what remainder of that light is returned to the device. A transmissive densitometer records how much light gets through a semi-transparent material such as camera film, and a reflective densitometer measures how much light has bounced back. The majority of densitometers in the print environment are reflective.

How does measuring the volume of light help us? Maintaining a consistent thickness of ink in printing is a very good way to control consistency and quality, and measuring the amount of light absorbed by the ink is a very accurate indicator of ink thickness.

Since our eyes have to function over a very wide range of brightness, we have a non-linear response to increasing volumes of light. That means it takes approximately 10 times the amount of light for us to experience one step in our perception of brightness. To match this behaviour of our eyes, the density scale is based on powers of 10, with each larger whole number representing one-tenth the volume of light of the preceding number. A density reading of 1.0 means that 1/10 of the original light has been reflected back. This is a typical reading for a process Yellow patch in offset lithographic printing. A density reading of 2.0 indicates that 1/100 of the original light is returned, while a density reading of 3.0 shows only 1/1000 coming back. Black ink is usually in the 1.7 density range, with cyan and magenta at 1.3 to 1.4.

Scanning or hand-held densitometers are typically found in the viewing station by a press. Densities are recorded when the printed sample matches the desired result and then ongoing adjustments to maintain the target densities keep the printing on target.

Colorimetre

Colorimetres mimic the three-colour response of our eyes by using red, green, and blue filters to measure the amount of light present in each third of the spectrum. They have built-in software to calculate Lab values based on what volume of red, green, and blue is returned from a sample. Colorimeters are particularly useful for calibrating and profiling monitors. Some well-known examples of colorimeters are the X-Rite ColorMunki or i1 Display devices.

Spectrophotometre

Spectrophotometres measure slices of the spectrum to produce a spectral 'map' of the light reflected back from a sample. Spectrophotometers are typically more expensive than densitometers and colorimeters but are employed because they can more accurately do the jobs of both devices. They work by recording the light at specific wavelengths over the wavelength range of visible light, and then by converting this spectral data to colorimetric and densitometric values.

While we are talking about measuring spectral values, it is important to note that we do not depend on identical spectral values to achieve matching colour experiences. Different spectral values can trigger the same volume of colour signals in our optic system and lead to matching colour perception. In fact, we depend on this phenomenon in graphic production in order for proofing devices to simulate the colour output of a printing press or for any two devices to be colour aligned. The ability of the CMYK (cyan, magenta, yellow, black) process colour set to mimic most of the colours in the world is also based on the fact that we can achieve a colorimetric match without having identical spectral values.

4.4 Lab Colour Space and Delta E Measurements

The CIE (Commission Internationale d'Eclairage or International Commission on Light) is a scientific body formed by colour scientists in the 1930s that has provided much of the fundamental colour knowledge we possess today. Three core definitions provided by the CIE are the standard observer, the Lab colour space, and Delta E measurements. The latter two are particularly important for colour management.

The Lab Colour Space Revisited

In section, 4.2, we mentioned the Lab colour space as a natural outgrowth of understanding the function of opponency in human vision. It's comprised of three axes: *L* represents darkness to lightness, with values ranging from 0 to 100; *a* represents greenness to redness with values of -128 to +127; and *b* represents blueness to yellowness also with values from -128 to +127.

Notice that there are no negative values on the L axis as we can't have less than zero light, which describes absolute darkness. The L axis is considered **achromatic** meaning without colour. Here we are dealing with the volume rather than the kind of light. In contrast, the a and b axes are **chromatic,** describing the colour character and the type of light.

The standard two-dimensional depiction is of only the a and b axes, with a as the horizontal axis and b as the vertical axis. This places *red* to the right, green to the left, *blue* at the bottom, and *yellow* at the top. If you found our previous mnemonic aid of POLO helpful, you can use RGBY to remember the colour pairs. For correct placement, remember that *red* is on the *right*, and *blue* is on the *bottom*.

Colours are more neutral and grey toward the centre of the colour space, along the L axis. Imagine that equivalent values of the opposing colours are cancelling each other out, reducing the saturation and intensity of those colours. The most saturated colours are at the extremes of the a and b axes, in both the large positive and negative numbers. For a visual depiction of the Lab colour space, open the ColorSync application found in the Utilities folder of any Macintosh computer and view one of the default profiles such as Adobe RGB.

Now it's time to explore the practical application of this colour map for the comparative analysis of colour samples. We can't make any progress in evaluating our success in colour matching unless we have a frame of reference, some yardstick to determine how much one colour sample is similar or different from another. That yardstick is the Delta E measurement.

Delta E

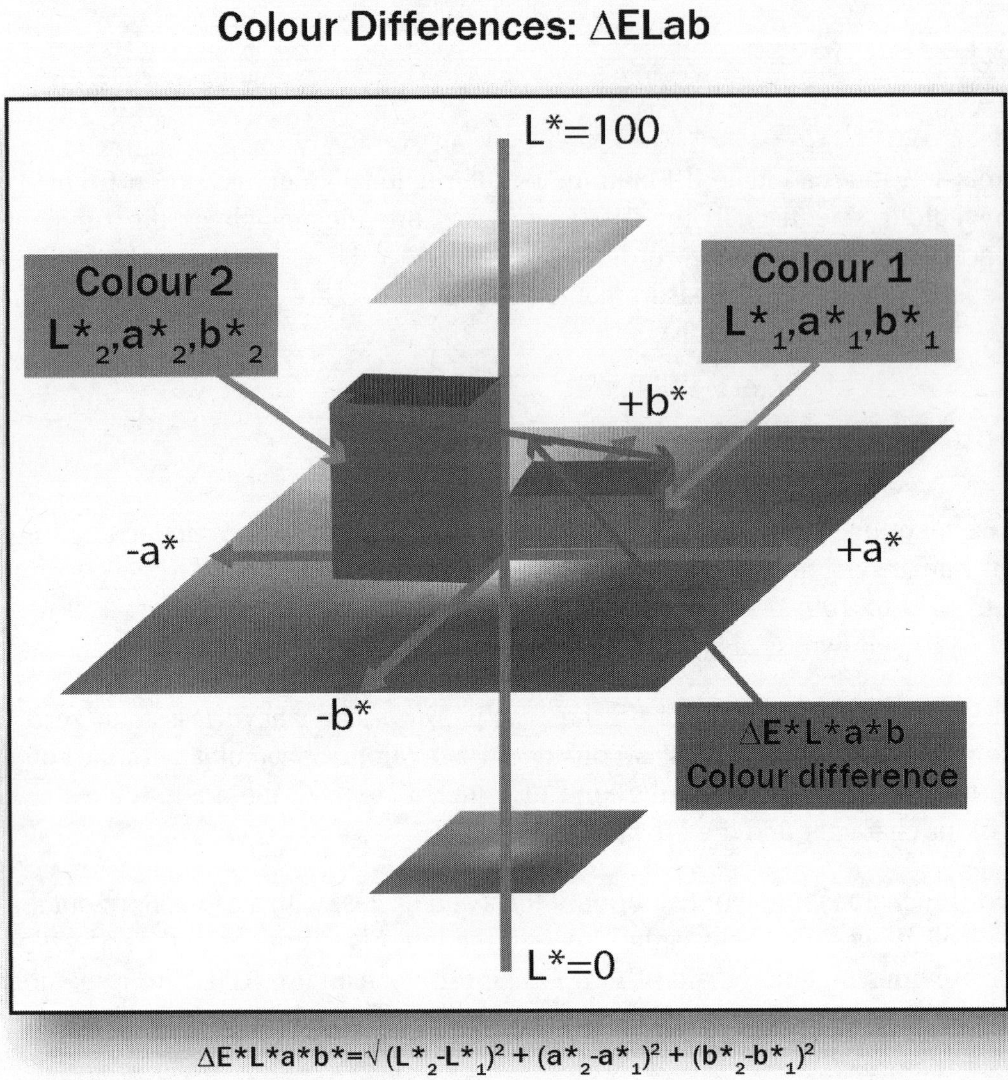

Figure 4.7 Lab Colour Space

Delta, the fourth letter of the Greek alphabet and symbolized as a triangle, is used in science to indicate difference. **Delta E** is the difference between two colours designated as two points in the Lab colour space. With values assigned to each of the L, a, and b attributes of two colours, we can use simple geometry to calculate the distance between their two placements in the Lab colour space (see Figure 4.7).

How do we do that? It looks a lot like the formula used to determine the long side of a right triangle that you may remember from high school geometry. We square the difference between each of the L, a, and b values; add them all together; and take the square root of that sum. Written out as a formula it looks a little more daunting: $\sqrt{(L_1 - L_2)^2 + (a_1 - a_2)^2 + (b_1 - b_2)^2}$.

Let's try a simple example to see what we get. Colour 1 has a Lab value of 51, 2, 2 and Colour 2 is 50, 0, 0 (right at the centre of the colour space):

$L_1 - L_2 = 51 - 50 = 1$, and$1 \times 1 = 1$, so our first value is 1.

$a_1 - a_2 = 2 - 0 = 2$; and $2 \times 2 = 4$, so our second value is 4.

$b_1 - b_2 = 2 = 0 = 2; 2 \times 2 = 4$, so the third value is also 4.

Add them together: $1 + 4 + 4 = 9$; and take the square root: $\sqrt{9} = 3$.

The Delta E (difference) between our two colours is 3. Could we detect that difference if we were viewing those two colours? Probably just barely. The minimum Delta E for seeing a difference is about 2. Smaller differences can normally be detected in neutral colours (such as our samples), while more saturated colours require a slightly larger Delta E. A Delta E of 4 is the upper threshold for acceptable machine repeatability or consistency.

Delta E provides a value indicating the overall difference between two colours. It does not provide any colour-related data such as which colour is lighter/darker, redder/greener, more blue/more yellow. To understand how the colours are different, we have to evaluate the comparative L, a, and b differences independently.

Experimentation over time has come to show that conventional Delta E is about 75% accurate in showing the difference we see between two colours. Delta E numbers exaggerate the differences in yellows and compress our perceptual distance between blues. To improve on the representation of our interpretation of colour difference, scientists have produced a modified formula known as Delta E(94).

Delta E(94)

Delta E(94) is a modified formula that provides about 95% accuracy in correlation to human perception of colour differences. Here it is in all its splendour:

$$\delta E{*}_{94} = \sqrt{(\frac{\delta L^*}{k_L S_L})^2 + (\frac{\delta C^*_{ab}}{k_C S_C})^2 + (\frac{\delta H^*_{ab}}{k_H S_H})^2}$$

where:

$S_L = 1$

$S_C = 1 + 0.045C_{ab}$

$S - H = 1 + 0.015C_{ab}$

$K_L = K_C = K_H = 1$ (for reference conditions)

$C_{ab} = C^*_{ab}(\text{standard})\ \text{OR} \sqrt{C_{ab,1}C_{ab,2}}$

$\delta H^*_{ab} = \sqrt{\delta E^*_{ab}{}^2 - \delta L{*}^2 - \delta C^*_{ab}{}^2}$

You can see that it is still the comparison of three values: L, C, and H, where C and H are produced by applying modifying factors to the original Lab values to compensate for perceptual distortions in the colour space. Each difference is squared and the root taken of the sum of the squares, just as in the original Delta E formula.

There is an additional refinement in Delta E(2000) where further adjustments are applied to blue and neutral colours and compensations for lightness, chroma, and hue. This is a much smaller correction than the change from Delta E to Delta E(94).

The good news is that you don't need to understand or remember any of the details of these equations. Just remember that these are real numbers measuring actual plotted distances between colour samples. Delta E represents the distance between two points in the Lab colour space. Delta E(94) and Delta E(2000) are enhancements, providing improved numbers that more closely match our perception of colour differences.

Media Attributions

- Delta E in Lab Colour Space © Ken Jeffrey

4.5 Working with a Spectrophotometer to Read Standard Colour Charts for Output Profiling

Armed with our fundamental concepts in colour theory, we can apply these principles to the physical process of colour management. The practical application to print production requires a procedure for measurement, colour profile generation, and the correct use of profiles in the manufacturing process. Let's begin with measurement and discuss the working components of a standard graphic arts spectrophotometer and the colour charts we would use it with.

X-Rite i-One (i1) Pro Spectrophotometer

The i1 Pro is one of the most common hand-held spectrophotometers used in the graphic reproduction industry. It can also be mounted in the iO base for automated scanning. As described in section 4.3, the **spectro** works by recording spectral data from incremental slices of the range of wavelengths included in visible light. To do this properly, the spectro must calibrate its white point to establish the baseline for interpretation. It does this by reading the white tile supplied in the baseplate that comes with the spectro. Each baseplate is uniquely matched to a specific spectrophotometer and marked with a serial number that corresponds to its spectro. Make sure you confirm that you have the correct baseplate that matches the serial number on your spectro. When used commercially, the manufacturer recommends that a spectro be returned for factory recalibration every two years. The packaging will include a certificate indicating the expiry date for the current calibration.

The spectro may also be identified (on both the serial number tag and surrounding the light-emitting aperture) as a UV-cut. This indicates it has an ultraviolet filter, which acts to remove the impact of fluorescence from optical paper brighteners. If you have access to more than one spectro device, be sure that any related measurements are done consistently either with or without the filter. Best practice is to use exactly the same instrument for any series of measurements.

The USB cable provides power to the spectro and so should be plugged directly into the computer and not into a peripheral such as a keyboard. Additional typical accessories for the spectro include a weighted strap and screw-in base for hanging the spectro against the screen of a monitor and a proof mount base with sliding rail for the spectro to read printed colour targets.

Colour Charts or Targets

You will typically be dependent on the colour management software application that you have chosen to produce a pdf file of the colour chart that your spectro can read. While in the software, you select a reading device (such as the X-Rite i1 Pro or i1 iO) from the list of devices that the software supports and then provide the dimensions for your output device. The choice of reading device will determine the size of colour patches and page format, and the size of output will define how many pages are ganged to a sheet. When prompted, name the pdf with a clear identifier (output device and date or equivalent) and save it.

Once you have the pdf, use it for any direct output, such as a proofer, or to make a plate for your printing press so that the colour chart can be printed. In all cases, it is critical that no colour management be applied to the output device for the production of the chart so that the natural base state of the device is captured in the colour target produced. It is also essential that the proofer or press be in an optimal operating state so that the output is an accurate reflection of the device's capabilities. This may require a calibration process for a proofer or standard maintenance procedure on the press.

There are several colour chart standards that you should be aware of. The chart produced by your colour management software will likely be one of these or a slight variation thereof. The original standard is the IT8.7/3, composed of 928 colour patches. This was followed by the ECI 2002, which has 1,485 colour samples. There is now an update to the IT8, the IT8.7/4, which has extended the colour sampling to 1,617 patches. The larger number of patches provides a more detailed snapshot of the colour capability of the device that you are profiling. Of course, it takes more time to read the greater number of samples, so the newer sets are more manageable with automated reading devices such as the iO table. If you are reading with a hand-held spectro, choose the IT8.7/3 or smaller patch set if it is offered by your colour management software. The other trade-off between larger and smaller numbers of colour patches lies in the smoothness of colour transitions. Fewer data points mean less interpolation and potentially smoother curves in colour modulation. Be aware that it will require some experimentation on a device-by-device basis to determine the ideal intersection of accuracy and smooth interpretation for your measurement data.

The colour charts come in two standard patterns of organization: random and visual. Random is exactly that, and comprises the vast majority of charts that are produced for measuring. The colour swatches are distributed to provide optimal contrast between adjacent patches to aid the spectrophotometer that is reading them in distinguishing where one patch ends and the next begins. Having the colours scattered over the sheet also generates relatively even distribution of cyan, magenta, yellow, and black ink which leads to better performance from the press. The visual pattern places the colour blocks in a logical and progressive sequence so it's easy to see the chromatic ranges that are covered. Some scanning spectrophotometers can read the visual arrangement.

Measuring Your Colour Chart

Once you have used the pdf to generate the printed sample, you have to measure the sample. For charts from proofers, it is critical to wait a minimum of 30 to 90 minutes after the sample has been produced before measuring in order for the colour to stabilize. To create a measurement file, you need three things: colour management software; a target from that software; and a measuring instrument supported by the software. After connecting your measuring device to the computer (remember to connect directly to a USB port on the computer, not to a peripheral such as a keyboard), enter the measuring step of your colour management software. You will need to point to the correct measurement chart that was used, which can be easily identified if you have named it distinctively, and confirm the right measuring device is indicated. If you are getting errors once you begin measuring and can't proceed, the typical culprit is the selection of an incorrect colour chart or incorrect measuring device.

When you begin the measurement process, there are a few option prompts you may have to respond to. Some software allows for the averaging of multiple press sheets to produce an improved characterization of the device. This software can scan the colour bars placed at the bottom of the sheet and indicate which sheets are the best candidates for measuring. If you have chosen to do multiple sheets, then you will have to record the sheet number on each of the pages that you cut from the full press sheet in order to enter the sheet number correctly as you carry on measuring.

Proofing devices are stable enough that it is not necessary to average multiple sheets. You may still be cutting out single pages from a larger sheet (depending on the size of your proofing device) and should label the individual pages to stay organized. You can skip any of the prompts that deal with choosing multi-sheet options.

Once past the initial options, you will be prompted to calibrate the measuring instrument. Make sure the i1 Pro is correctly seated on its base plate and push the button. After successful calibration, you will be instructed to mount page 1 of your colour chart and begin measuring. For hand-held measuring with the i1 Pro, use the white plastic proof mounting base it came with. Secure your page under the spring clip at the top of the mounting base, positioning it so that the sliding clear plastic guide the spectro rides on can reach the first row of colour patches. The clear plastic guide has a horizontal opening that the head of the spectro nestles into to traverse the horizontal row of colour swatches. There is a cradle for the base of the spectro to rest on that slides horizontally across the guide. The spectro must begin on white paper to the left of the colour patch row, and finish on white paper to the right of the row. If your target has a semi-circle printed to the left of its colour rows, use it to position the chart under the scanning opening of the plastic guide. The left semi-circle on the opening in the guide should align with the printed semi-circle on the chart. If there is no printed semi-circle on the chart, allow ¼ – ½ inch of white space showing in the opening to the left of the first colour patch.

With your chart properly placed in the mounting base, position the spectro all the way to the left on the plastic guide with its base in the sliding cradle and reading aperture in the cut-away channel. Press the button on the left side of the spectro and keep it pressed. Wait one second while the white of the paper is read (there may be a beep to indicate this is done), slide the spectro smoothly and evenly to the right until you reach white paper past the colour patches, and then release the button. You should be rewarded with a prompt to scan row B. Slide the entire plastic guide down one row, move the spectro all the way back to the left, and do it all over again! If you receive an error, clear the prompt and try scanning the same row again. Success at hand-held scanning comes with a little bit of practice and a Zen approach. Your degree of success will be inversely proportional to the amount of anxiety you feel. The techniques that contribute to getting it right are smooth and even passage of the spectro; consistent pressure (make sure you are not pushing down on the head); white paper at either end; and keeping the button pressed from start to finish.

After you receive a couple of errors on the same row, the software may switch to individual patch reading. In this case, the prompt will now say "Scan patch B1" instead of the previous "Scan row B." You must position the read head over each individual patch and press the spectro's button when prompted on screen. After completing one row of individual patches, you will be returned to full row scanning mode. This procedure allows the measurement process to go forward when the software is having trouble detecting colour boundaries in a particular row.

Having completed all rows on all pages (which may take some time), you will be prompted to save the measurement file. Some colour management software will take you directly to the additional settings required to define a profile and then proceed with the profile creation.

4.6 The Measurement File's Role in Colour Profiling

It's important to remember that the measurement file is not a profile! It provides the basic information about the colour behaviour of the device but needs some critical additional instructions and the processing of the colour management software in order to produce a colour profile that can be used for colour transformations. The measurement file is a snapshot in time of device behaviour and depends on the appropriate calibration of the device prior to the chart's creation for its accuracy.

Content of the Measurement File

```
CGATS.5
ORIGINATOR "1.1.6.3.717"
DESCRIPTOR "ColorFlow MeasurementData File"
CREATED    "December 21, 2010 12:24:30 PM PST"
#Filename   measurements547516763086197948.cgt
#Rows 26
#Columns    19
#This chart generated from averaging several files.  This header extracted
from the first file
NUMBER_OF_FIELDS 51
BEGIN_DATA_FORMAT
SAMPLE_ID   CMYK_C        CMYK_M        CMYK_Y        CMYK_K        XYZ_X XYZ_Y XYZ_Z
      LAB_L LAB_A LAB_B D_RED D_GREEN     D_BLUE        D_VIS 380_NM
      390_NM        400_NM        410_NM        420_NM        430_NM        440_NM
      450_NM        460_NM        470_NM        480_NM        490_NM        500_NM
      510_NM        520_NM        530_NM        540_NM        550_NM        560_NM
      570_NM        580_NM        590_NM        600_NM        610_NM        620_NM
      630_NM        640_NM        650_NM        660_NM        670_NM        680_NM
      690_NM        700_NM        710_NM        720_NM        730_NM
END_DATA_FORMAT
NUMBER_OF_SETS    1976
BEGIN_DATA
A01   100   0     0     0     14.9593       24.264        56.2451       56.3512
      -43.1895      -51.288       1.60652       0.381318      0.166744      0.739
      0.7006        0.3927        0.3573        0.4336        0.5074        0.5794
      0.6549        0.7106        0.7356        0.7434        0.7396        0.7272
      0.7008        0.6495        0.5669        0.456         0.3352        0.2187
      0.1228        0.0686        0.0436        0.0327        0.026         0.022
      0.0214        0.0227        0.0256        0.0322        0.0417        0.0476
      0.0458        0.0404        0.0327        0.0274        0.0312        0.0457
```

Figure 4.8 Example of measurement file

We can open the measurement file in a text editor and examine its structure to understand what information it contains (see Figure 4.8). The first section is header info and provides some basic information about the file. This is followed by a key to the colour data that follows. The actual colour information comprises a row and column ID to identify the specific colour patch and then the numerical data that goes with the patch.

The key information is contained in the second section where the data format is laid out. This indicates what colour spaces are captured in the data for each colour patch. The first four values are CMYK; the next three are **XYZ** (a device independent colour space like Lab); the next three are Lab; then RGB; and finally there is a wavelength measurement for each of the 10 nanometer slices of the visible spectrum (380-730 nanometers; violet to red).

The CMYK values for each patch are fixed in the software, coming from either the IT8 or ECI specification. These CMYK values have to remain constant because they are our point of reference for all devices. When we read the patch with the spectro, it uses the spectral information (each of the 10 nanometer slices) to calculate the XYZ and Lab values that describe the colour appearance of the colour swatch. By matching the measured Lab value to the predetermined CMYK value supplied in the original pdf, we have the raw material to build a translation table describing the device's colour behaviour. Once we have this look up table (LUT), we can predict the Lab equivalent for any CMYK value produced on the device. Correspondingly, when we are given the Lab values from another device that we want to match, we can produce the appropriate CMYK values to provide that colour appearance.

Device Dependent Versus Device Independent Colour Spaces

We've defined CMYK, RGB, and Lab colour spaces, and we've seen how the first step in colour profiling is to measure output from a device to define a relationship between the CMYK device dependent and the Lab device independent numbers. Establishing this relationship between device dependent (RGB or CMYK) values and device independent (Lab) values is a fundamental component of the colour management process.

We call the CMYK and RGB colour spaces **device dependent** because the results we get from specific RGB or CMYK values depend entirely on the device producing them. When we tell a device to produce "50% cyan," we are saying, "Give me half of as much cyan as you can produce." Since the capacity and colour appearance of cyan from any two devices will not be the same, it should not be surprising that a specification of "half that much" will also produce colour events that do not match. Similarly, the RGB values on a monitor or projector simply specify some proportion of the full red, green, and blue signals that the device can produce. Since there is no common starting point between two monitors in terms of what a full red, green, or blue signal is, then providing the same RGB values to those two monitors will in no way provide an opportunity to generate the same colour appearance.

For RGB devices, RGB values simply identify the volume of signal for each channel. For printers, proofers, and presses the CMYK percentages dictate what proportion of pigments are deposited. The numbers associated with specific RGB and CMYK colours only have colour meaning when attached to a particular device. There is no inherent consistency between any two devices based on providing the same RGB or CMYK values.

So if the device dependent colour spaces don't give us any consistency or control of colour between devices, where can we turn? Enter the **device independent** colour spaces of Lab and XYZ. We spoke of Lab earlier as the three-dimensional model colour science has produced to map the way we perceive colour. The Lab colour space is device independent because we do not depend on the values associated with the output of a specific device to enumerate the colour. Lab values are calculated from spectral readings in a controlled environment so that they define a consistent colour experience for any circumstance and from any device. Device independent colour is the Rosetta stone of colour management that allows us to translate from the unique dialect of colour behaviour on one device into a universal language and then back to the specific colour dialect of a different device and maintain the colour meaning.

The device independent colour spaces are known as profile connection spaces (PCS) since they provide this gateway service between the device dependent colour spaces of individual devices. Lab and XYZ are the two PCS allowed in the **ICC** specification that defines profile creation. From the examination of the measurement file, we can see how it provides the first step in establishing and tabulating a relationship between the device dependent values of a particular device's output and the corresponding device independent values that characterize the actual colour appearance associated with the output.

We've talked about the measurement file as the gateway to our profile creation, so let's see what steps remain to get us there.

4.7 Profile Creation

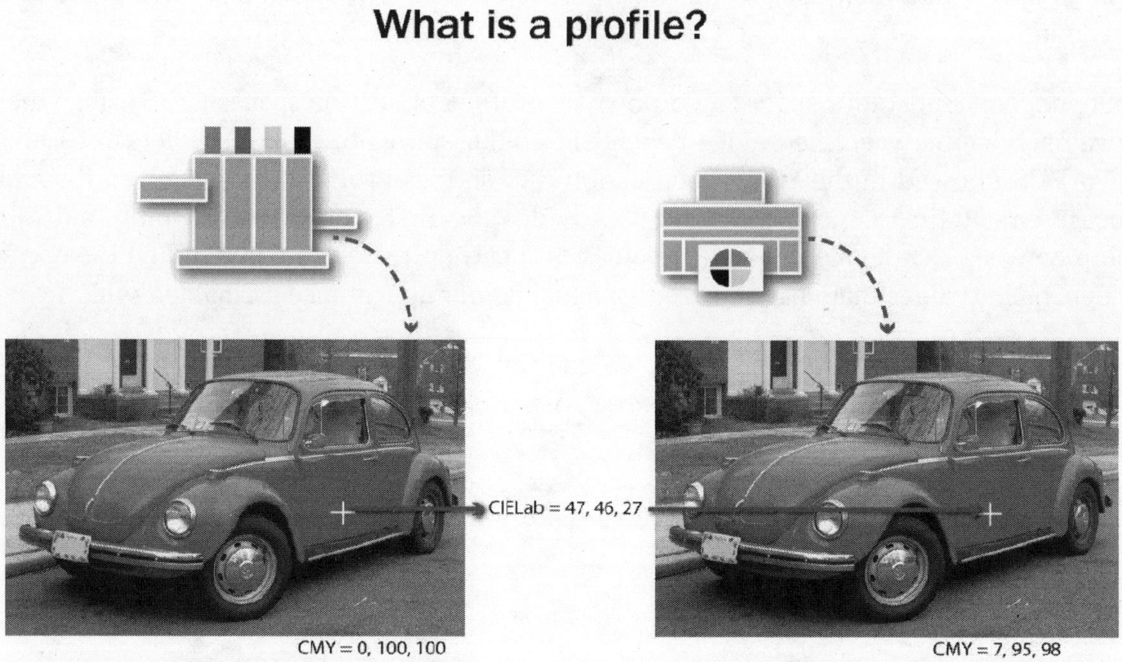

Figure 4.9 what is a profile

The measurement file contains the raw data of the relationship between the device dependent colour space of the device and the device independent colour space of the profile connection spaces (PCS). There are two additional parameters we have to provide along with this data in order for the colour management software to produce an output profile: total ink limit and black generation (see Figure 4.9).

Total Ink Limit

Total ink limit is a percentage, usually between 240% and 400%, that represents the upper threshold that the sum of the four process inks can total. Why would this change? Each device, in combination with its particular substrates (papers) and ink sets, has a different capability in terms of how much ink can be deposited. A coldset web newspaper press might be close to the lower end of 240%, while a high-end inkjet can support 100% from each of cyan, magenta, yellow, and black, and have a 400% rating. This total ink limit setting affects the colour distribution in darker colours. As the total ink limit decreases, dark colours require a higher proportion of black ink relative to CMY to stay within the ink limit percentage. With an ink limit of 360%, when black is at 90%, we still have room left for 90% of cyan, magenta, and yellow (4 x 90 = 360). But if the ink limit is 240%, with black at 90%, we can't exceed 150% for the sum of the other three (150 + 90 = 240). Since cyan leads in a grey balance mix, we might have 60% cyan, 45% magenta, and 45% yellow (60 + 45 + 45 = 150). As the ink limit drops, black has to do more of the work of providing darkness for any heavy colour mix.

Black Generation

We also have to provide instruction on how the black component of the CMYK mix will be created. Remember that our subtractive primaries are CMY and that, theoretically, they provide all the colours in the visible spectrum. Where does K (black) come in? To bridge the gap between theory and real world performance, black ink does some very important things:

- It compensates for the spectral shortcomings of CMY inks: our inks are not perfect representations of what cyan, magenta, and yellow colours should be.
- It eliminates registration problems in black type: if there were no discreet black ink, every time we wanted to print black type we would have to stack cyan, magenta, and yellow on top of one another and make sure they fit perfectly.
- It helps us achieve easier neutrals: we can use black to replace the grey component of colours reducing the amount of CMY required to stay in balance on the press to provide consistent neutral tones.
- It provides cost savings: black ink is cheaper than coloured ink.
- It increases contrast: black's greater density extends the tonal range of CMYK printing and improves the appearance of the final printed piece.

Since black is an add-on to our primary CMY colour set, we must provide instructions for its creation. Typically, we specify the black start point, maximum black, and black strength.

- Black start point: The point at which black enters colour mixes (range of 0% to 50%). If the black start point is 20%, then tones from white to 20% will carry CMY only.
- Maximum black: The upper allowable percentage of black ink used in the K separation (range 70% to 100%).
- Black strength: The relative quantity of black versus cyan, magenta, and yellow in the neutral grey component of colours (range 5 to 75%). As the number increases, colours can contain more black.

Black strength settings are also referred to as grey component replacement (GCR) values in colour separations. These may be set as percentages or simply as light, medium, and heavy, where more equals a larger proportion of black taking the place of CMY in neutral tones. GCR is the successor to UCR (under colour removal), which only moved exactly equivalent amounts of CMY to the black channel. UCR separations exhibit a 'skeletal' black, where there is a small amount of content in the black separation. With GCR, and as the black strength increases, more and more content moves into the black channel.

Final Processing

With the measurement file available, and total ink limit and black generation specified, processing can start in the colour management software and an output profile created. It will take from two to five minutes for all the calculations to complete. You may be prompted to specify whether to save the profile in the system or user location, or both. The system location will make the profile available to all users of the computer, while the user location will restrict it to the current user. Depending on your permissions at the computer, you may not be able to write into the system location. On an Apple OS X machine, the default location for the system is System/Library/ColorSync/Profiles and for the user, Users/(userID)/Library/ColorSync/Profiles.

Viewing Your Profile

The Mac provides a built-in tool for viewing a profile or comparing two profiles. From the Utilities folder, launch ColorSync. Select the second tab from the left and you'll see a selection window on the left and a display pane on the right. The selection window contains a list of all ColorSync aware locations on your computer. Tip open the available folders and browse to find the profile you wish to view. Select a profile and a three-dimensional representation of its **gamut** in the Lab colour space appears on the right. Use your cursor to rotate the profile through all three of its axes. From the drop-down triangle in the display pane, choose Hold for comparison. The current profile is ghosted back, and you can select a second profile to display at full strength on top of it so you can compare the relative gamuts of the two profiles.

Profile Limitations

Remember that your profile represents the behaviour of the device for particular imaging parameters such as a specific substrate, resolution (screen ruling), and ink set. If any of those parameters are significantly altered, it requires a new profile to accurately represent the colour results. For real-world applications, profiles representing related groups of parameters are employed. One profile might represent all uncoated stock at 100 to 133 lines per inch, a second for coated stock at 150 to 175 lines per inch, and a third for a high saturation ink set on glossy stock with high resolution stochastic screening.

Media Attributions

- what is a profile © IFCAR adapted by Ken Jeffrey

4.8 Beyond Output Profiling: Display, Input, and Device Link Profiles

Up to this point, we have focused exclusively on the output profile in our discussion of profiling. This makes sense, since this is the predominant profile we are concerned with in graphic production. Output profiles characterize output devices such as printers, proofers, and presses, but there are other devices that we have to manage in the full spectrum of a colour-managed workflow, and these require two additional classes of **ICC profiles**: display and input.

Display profiles capture the colour characteristics of monitors, projectors, and other display devices. Input profiles characterize devices that capture images such as scanners and digital cameras.

Display Profiling

You may hear this class of profile referred to as *monitor profiling*, but the more accurate designation is *display profiling* to acknowledge the inclusion of components beyond the monitor such as the video card and video drivers. Though less commonly profiled, this class of profile encompasses digital projectors as well.

In preparation for display profiling, the cardinal rule of thumb is to make whatever adjustments we can in the actual monitor. Any software adjustments to the VideoLUT (the look up table stored on the video card) reduce the operating range of the monitor and limit the spectrum of the display. With the predominance of LCD monitors, this means that the brightness or white luminance is the only hardware adjustment available. If you see reference to black level or colour temperature settings, this hearkens back to CRT monitors where these were actual hardware settings. For LCD monitors, these are software controls. For an LCD, all light comes from the backlight, which is a fluorescent array behind a diffuser, so the only monitor control is the brightness of this backlight.

Display profile software typically combines calibration and profiling. A setting called the vcgt (video card gamma type) tag in the display profile can download settings to the VideoLUT on the video card and change monitor behaviour. This is an unusual deviation from the standard protocol in colour management where the profile never alters the behaviour of the device. Calibration is used to optimize device function and characterization or profiling captures a description of device behaviour. Normally, the application of a profile should not have any influence on the device function.

Before calibration, it's essential to warm up an LCD monitor for 30 to 90 minutes. Check the full brightness. If the monitor has aged to the point where it can't achieve adequate brightness, then it should be abandoned as a candidate for profiling. Set the standard refresh rate and resolution that will be used on the monitor. If these are changed after profiling, then the profile cannot be considered accurate. Clean the screen with an appropriate gentle cleaner.

When you begin the profiling software, you will be prompted to identify your instrument. Colorimeters are often provided in display profiling packages, but most software works with standard

spectrophotometers (spectros), such as the i1 Pro.
The recommended settings to enter for the set-up phase are:

- White point: D65 (6500 K)
- Gamma: 2.2

The setting 6500 K is usually close to the native white point of an LCD monitor. You can choose Native White Point if you feel that 6500 is too far from the actual white point of your monitor. Gamma is the tone reproduction curve of the monitor. The setting 2.2 typically provides the smoothest gradients in monitor display.

Next is the choice of a patch set from small, medium, and large options. This determines the number of colour swatches that will be projected on screen for the instrument to read. The trade-off is between calibration time and colour range. Start with the small patch set and see if you are happy with the results.

To start this process, make sure the i1 is on its base plate for the instrument calibration step and then suspend the spectro in the monitor mounting strap on the monitor. The weight at one end of the strap hangs behind the monitor to counterbalance the spectro, and the i1 Pro locks into the mounting plate at the other end of the strap to keep it in place on the monitor screen. The reading aperture of the spectro should be approximately in the centre of the screen. Tip the monitor back very slightly to help the spectro sit flat of the front of the LCD.

When you tell the software to proceed, it begins projecting a series of colour swatches that the colorimeter or spectro records. As you did to produce the measurement file for your output profile, you are building a comparative table of known device values (the RGB swatches projected on the screen), with device independent values (Lab readings from the spectro) that describe their appearance. This may take from three to ten minutes. During this process, make sure that no screen saver becomes active and you keep the mouse out of the scanning area and. If you leave before the process is completed, check that the spectro is properly positioned when you return.

Once the colour patches are done, you will be prompted to name and save the profile. Make a habit of naming your profile with the date so its age can be easily checked. Saving display profiles is similar to saving output profiles, where the user chooses system and user options. With display profiles, there is no value in saving previous versions. All you are interested in is the current state of the monitor.

To see the active profile on a Mac, choose System Preferences/Displays/Color. The active profile will be highlighted at the top of the list. There is a check box toggle limiting the list so only profiles that are known to be associated with the monitor show.

Input Profiles

As mentioned, we need input profiles when we capture images. There are predominantly two types of devices associated with image capture: scanners and digital cameras. The fundamental concept in producing an input profile is that RGB device values scanned or photographed from a target are matched to device independent Lab values either provided by the target vendor or measured from the target itself.

For input profile creation, the targets always consist of two parts: a physical sequence of colour patches and a target description file (TDF) with the profile connection space (PCS) values for the swatches. The TDF accuracy varies from individually measured targets (done by you or a specialty vendor) at the high end to averaged samples from a batch run (an economical alternative).

As with output profiling, there are standard scanner target formats. We have IT8.7/1 for transmissive originals (film transparencies like slides) and the IT8.7/2 for reflective (photo print paper). These targets are available from a variety of vendors and allow you to match the material of the target to the material you will be scanning. If you will be scanning Kodachrome slides, you will want a Kodachrome IT8/7.1 target. Conversely, if your originals are Fuji photo prints, then you will want an IT8/7.2 target on the matching Fuji photo print paper.

The X-Rite ColorChecker targets are commonly used for digital cameras. There is the original ColorChecker with 24 tiles and the later digital ColorChecker SG with 140 colour tiles. The larger target can be used for initial set-up and there is a mini version of the original ColorChecker that will work in most photo shoots for an ongoing reference check.

Though scanners and digital cameras both fall into our domain of input profiling, they have some very different characteristics that we have to take into account when preparing to produce a useful profile. As with output profiling, we need to calibrate the device by stabilizing and optimizing its performance prior to capturing its colour behaviour. In order to stabilize, we need to understand the potential variables that the device presents. Scanners have a controlled light source and stable filters and typically have the option for extensive software intervention. In contrast, cameras have stable filters and moderate software controls but have the potential for hugely variable lighting conditions. The excessive variability of outdoor lighting limits useful profile creation to interior and in-studio camera work. If the lighting conditions can be controlled adequately in the studio, then colour-accurate capture can take place and colour accuracy can be maintained in the production work that follows.

Stabilizing a scanner's performance comes from turning off any automatic adjustments for colour correction:

- White and black point setting
- Removing colour casts
- Sharpening

If you can't turn these off, then the scanner is likely not a good candidate for profiling. Optimize the scanner's behaviour with an output gamma setting of 2.6 to 3.0.

Stabilizing a camera's performance comes from the appropriate lighting and capture settings. Use even lighting and full highlight and shadow exposure for target capture. For colour temperature, use grey balance for camera back devices, and white balance for colour filter arrays (CFA). Optimize the camera's bit depth retention with gamma 1.0 for raw profiling.

With calibration complete, it's time to capture the target. For a scanner:

- Mount straight
- Mask open bed areas

- Scan as high-bit tiff
- Open in Photoshop (beware of any automated conversions or profile assignments) to rotate, crop, and spot

Comparatively, for the digital camera:

- Light evenly
- Capture square
- Open in Photoshop (beware of any automated conversions or profile assignments) to rotate, crop, and spot

With the digital image in hand, we're ready for the input profile creation. Measure the commercial target with the spectro if you are not using a supplied target description file. Launch your colour management software and you will be prompted to identify the target image and the corresponding target description file. The profiling software reads the RGB values from the scanned or captured image, and the software processes the target description file and RGB measurement file to produce the input profile. File-saving options are very similar to what we have previous described for output and display profiles.

Device Link Profiles

Device link profiles are most closely related to the output class of profiles. A device link profile combines two output profiles to provide the specific conversion instructions between two particular devices. It provides the opportunity to maintain black and other separation purity (i.e., what begins as black only in the source colour space emerges as black only in the destination colour space) by removing the need for passing the colour transformation through the PCS. To define a device link, we identify a source and destination profile to our colour management software, specify the rendering intent, and provide details on how constrained the re-separation should be. By avoiding the passage into and back out of the PCS, we can very strictly control the parameters of the colour conversion. The options for conversion are:

- Full re-separation — Complete re-separation. Solid colours in the original file may not remain solid. The black generation parameters that you specify are used, which may result in using less chromatic ink and more black ink.
- CMYK integrity — All colour builds can be adjusted. The relative amount of black versus CMY will be preserved in content processed through the device link.
- Black purity only — Any colours other than the black channel (solid K, K-greys) can be adjusted.
- Colour and black purity — The same as fully constrained, but solid colours can be reduced to a tint.
- Fully constrained — Any colour made with only one or two inks will not have other inks added. Solid (100% tints) primaries and secondaries are not affected and remain solid.
- Ink optimizing — A proprietary term in the ColorFlow colour management software for applying a full re-separation with a heavy grey component replacement (GCR) algorithm.

Colour management software used to be required to preview the results of applying a device link. With the last few versions of Adobe Photoshop, a device link option has been added to the advanced dialog window of the Color Conversion menu, making device link previewing much more accessible. Currently, Photoshop only supports CMYK to CMYK device links. It does not support RGB to CMYK device links. Another alternative for viewing the results of applying a device link is to generate a virtual proof (VPS) in Kodak Prinergy with the device link specified. For details, see section 4.11 in this chapter.

With this extraordinary level of control, why don't we use device links for every colour conversion? The truth is, that with our gain in managing the colour conversion process, we sacrifice an even greater degree of flexibility. The premise of colour management and the use of profiles is that we do not have to generate a unique profile for each pairing of devices. With the power of the PCS gateway to provide the device independent colour description, we only need a single profile for each colour condition of a device and any two profiles can be positioned on either side of the PCS to provide a pathway for the colour conversion.

Where it does make sense to go to the extra trouble of generating a device link profile is a situation where a specific pairing of two devices is used over and over again, such as a proofer for a particular press condition, or to keep two presses in a shop matched for their colour output.
If we process an image from RGB to CMYK at the beginning of our production process, we gain the stability of having the image in our known CMYK space, but we surrender the flexibility of converting to the optimal CMYK space at final output. For final stage or late-binding conversion, we are dependent on the RIP environment for managing the calculations between the profile pair (see Section 5.2). A device link provides additional security in the conversion process by reducing the variability that can come with the processing application input that is part of a profile pair transformation.

4.9 A Review of the Profile Classes

We've now touched on the four types or classes of profiles: display, input, output, and device link. What traits do they have in common? They are:

- Specified by ICC-defined file formats
- Contain colour tables
- Have device colour values associated with device independent colour values (PCS)
- Use a measuring device (spectrophotometer) and targets for creation
- Require a specified rendering intent
- Have standard OS library locations

There are also some unique characteristics for each profile class that help define the role they play in the overall colour management process. The display class of profiles:

- Have no separate, tangible target: the device 'is' the target
- Can affect device behaviour
- Are mostly integrated with device calibration

The input class of profiles:

- Are unidirectional: A to B table only (device values to PCS)
- Are able to exclude any external measuring (with a supplied TDF)
- Ensure that the target's job is tell us how the device 'sees' the target

Output (and device link) class of profiles:

- Use CMYK (versus RGB for display and input)
- Have black handling settings
- Have the largest and most complex colour tables
- Ensure the target's job is to tell us how the device 'makes' the target
- Provides preview capability for upstream editing

We also discussed the functions of a profile in the colour equation. The two functions are source and destination. A source profile is a profile used to convert device dependent RGB or CMYK information to a device independent colour space (Lab). A destination profile is a profile used to convert information from a device independent colour space (Lab) into a device dependent colour space of an output device

(RGB or CMYK). You can think of the source profile as the colour reference or the place from which our desired colour appearance comes. The destination profile describes the location where we are producing colour in the current pairing of devices. If we want a proofer to simulate the colour behaviour of a particular press, the press's profile is the source (the desired colour behaviour) and the profile for the proofer is the destination (our colour output).

Do not confuse a profile's class with its function; they are independent and separate characteristics. A particular output profile can assume the function of source in one colour equation and then turn around and assume the role of destination in a second. Take the example of the press above, where the press profile acted as the source. If we have multiple presses in the printing plant, and we have another press that is our master press for colour behaviour, the press profile that acted as a source for the proofer output will now function as a destination profile to align that press to the colour behaviour of the master press (the master press profile is the source profile in this pairing).
Profiles enable the two key processes of any colour managed workflow: clear communication of colour meaning and the transformation of device values to maintain colour appearance.

4.10 The Components and Purpose of a Colour Management System

Our primary goal in colour management is to provide a consistent perceptual experience. As we move from device to device, within the limits of the individual device's colour gamut, our interpretation of the colour event should be the same.

As we've discussed, but it's worth repeating, we achieve that goal in two fundamental steps:

1. We give colour its meaning through device independent colour values correlated to a specific device's RGB or CMYK numbers.
2. We transform our destination device's specific values to match the perceived colour definitions of our source.

The Components

We have spoken at great length about colour profiles, but there are three additional pieces required to enact a colour-managed workflow: the profile connection space (PCS), a colour management module (CMM), and rendering intents.

The PCS provides the device independent colour definitions to which device values can be matched. The ICC specification allows the XYZ or Lab colour spaces for the PCS.

Profiles provide the look up table for the conversion of device values to PCS and vice versa. Any conversion requires two profiles (or a device link into which two profiles have been merged).

The CMM is the software engine that actually does the conversion. It lives in a product like Adobe Photoshop or Kodak Prinergy, where file processing takes place. The CMM provides two major benefits: it reduces profile size by doing the interpolation in colour calculations and compensates for shortcomings in the Lab colour space. The CMM does the heavy lifting by providing the computation of the conversion. For consistency, it is best to keep to a common CMM as much as possible. The Adobe Color Engine or ACE is the CMM seen referenced in the Color Setup dialog window of the Adobe Creative products.

Rendering intents are the instructions for dealing with out-of-gamut colours (see Figure 4.10). They are user-selectable controls to define colour rendition when you move colour from one device to another. There are four types of rendering intents: perceptual, saturation, relative colorimetric, and absolute colorimetric. Each intent represents a different colour conversion compromise, resulting in a different gamut mapping style.

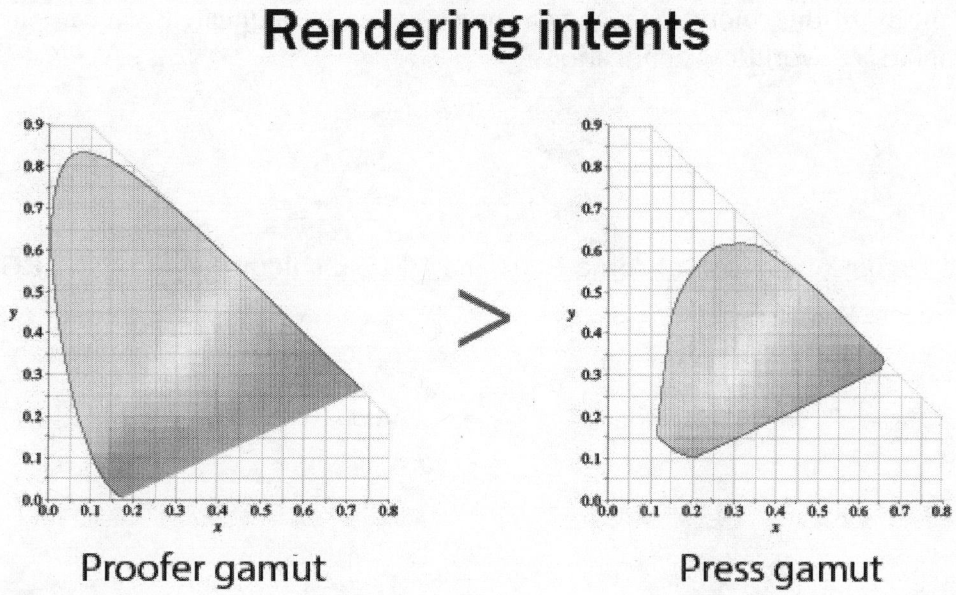

Figure 4.10

Perceptual and saturation intents use gamut compression, where the overall gamut space is adjusted. Relative and absolute colorimetric intents use gamut clipping, where colour matching is maintained throughout the available gamut, and out-of-gamut colours are moved to the available extremes of the destination gamut.

The perceptual intent is used mainly for RGB to CMYK transformations, which are typically image conversions. Since we are moving from a larger gamut (RGB) to a smaller gamut (CMYK), it makes sense to employ a rendering intent that preserves the overall relationship rather than one that emphasizes one-to-one colour matching within the gamut.

The saturation intent is the least relevant for colour-managed workflows. When you use this intent, colour saturation is preserved as much as possible at the expense of hue and luminance. The result is a bad colour match, but the vividness of pure colours is preserved. This intent is usually used for documents such as presentations, charts, and diagrams, but not for graphic arts jobs.

The two colorimetric intents, relative and absolute, are closely related. They are both used for CMYK to CMYK conversions where the gamuts of source and destination are closely matched or the destination is larger (typical of a proofer compared to the press it is matching). They emphasize exact colour matching for in-gamut colours and clip out-of-gamut colours.

The only difference between the two colorimetric rendering intents is in white point handling. The absolute intent pays attention to the colour of white in the source and reproduces that in the destination. Think of newspaper printing where the whitest colour is the paper that has a dull and beige tone. With an absolute rendering intent, a proofer matching the newspaper would add that beige colour to all of the white areas of the proof. This matching of white destination to white source colour is not usually necessary due to the chromatic adaptation or colour constancy that we discussed earlier. We have a built-in mechanism for adjusting to judge the overall colour relationship independent of the appearance of white. For this reason, the relative colorimetric intent is used most of the time and the white of the destination is not adjusted to simulate the white point of the source.

With all of the pieces of the colour management process clearly delineated, we can put them to use in our standard graphic arts workflow applications.

Attribution

Figure 4.10
Image modified from: Comparison of some RGB and CMYK colour gamut by BenRG and cmglee is used under a CC BY SA 3.0 license.

4.11 Applying Colour Management in the Adobe Creative and Kodak Prinergy Software

Colour management comes into play at two primary points in the print production workflow: during file creation with authoring tools like the Adobe Creative applications (Photoshop, InDesign, Illustrator), and then when the file is processed for output with a workflow software program such as Kodak Prinergy. Let's examine the details in these most widely used software tools to provide concrete examples.

Colour Set-up in the Adobe Creative Applications

The primary tool for colour management in the Adobe products is the Color Settings dialog under the Edit menu. Fortunately, these settings can be shared across all of the Adobe applications to coordinate a consistent delivery of colour strategy. Define your settings in Photoshop, as this is the application with the largest number of options, to guarantee that all possible options have been set to your choices.

Launch Photoshop and, from the Edit menu, choose Color Settings. There are three main sections to the dialog window: Working Spaces, Color Management Policies, and Conversion Options. Change the Settings option above the Working Spaces panel to North American Prepress 2. This applies a set of defaults that are optimal for a print production workflow.

Working Spaces is Adobe's name for default profiles. These are the profiles that will be used if no other information is available. If you open a file that is *untagged* (the terminology for a document that has no profile attached to it), the profile listed for the colour space matching the file will be *assumed* and used as long as the file is open. It will not persist with the file once the file is closed. If you create a new file in the application, the profile listed will be *assigned* and the profile reference will move forward with the file.

Let's review and clarify the terminology associated with describing the status of a colour profile relative to a particular document or file. A file that has a profile is referred to as *tagged* while one without profile is *untagged*. A tagged document can have one of two relationships with its colour profile. The colour profile can be *embedded* or *assigned*. An embedded profile is actually written into the file content. This increases the file size, but guarantees that the desired profile will be available. For an assigned profile, only a reference to the profile is contained in the document. File size is reduced, but access to the profile depends on the application and environment processing the object. You can think of an *assumed* profile as a temporary assignment that will only last as long as the file is open.

For Working Spaces options, the RGB default of Adobe RGB (1998) that comes with the North American Prepress 2 setting is a perceptually even RGB space, which makes it better for editing and a good choice. The CMYK field is where you should choose a profile specific to the final output device if it is known. The SWOP profile is a reasonable fallback and is commonly used as the industry standard for generic work. Be aware that choosing SWOP will constrain the gamut to the capability of a web offset print condition.

The list of profiles available for selection comes from the various ColorSync aware folders that we have previously discussed. Priority is given to profiles in the Library/Application Support/Adobe/Color/Profiles/Recommended folder, and these profiles are listed first. If you have a profile that you wish to give prominence to for selection, place it in this folder.

The Color Management Policies subsection controls behaviour when opening or creating documents and when moving objects between documents. There are three options for each of the available colour space settings: Off, Preserve Embedded, or Convert to Working.

The choice of Off is the most misleading, because we can't actually turn colour management off: there is always an assumed profile if no other information is presented. With Off, copy and paste of an object moves tint values: a 50% cyan value from the originating document lands as 50% cyan in the destination document.

Preserve Embedded does what it says and maintains what's in place. New documents use the Working Space profile and become tagged. An untagged file assumes the working space profile but stays untagged. If you copy and paste native RGB objects, they are converted. If you copy and paste native CMYK objects, the tint values are maintained.

Our final choice for colour management policy is potentially the most dangerous. Convert to Working converts tagged documents using the existing profile as a source profile and the Working Space profile as the destination. If you do not have the Alert check boxes ticked, this can happen without your awareness. For an untagged document, it assumes the Working Space profile. Copy and pasting RGB or CMYK objects always converts to preserve appearance (changes the tint values).

After reviewing the choices, the recommendation for Color Management Policies is Preserve Embedded, and make sure all Alert boxes are checked. This allows you to confirm that any action is what you actually want before proceeding.

The last section of the Color Settings dialog window is the Conversion Options. The Engine option refers to the colour management module (CMM) that will be used for calculations in the colour conversions. The default choice of the Adobe Color Engine is good for maintaining consistency. Here we have as well the Rendering Intent entry, which will function as a default unless an alternate intent is specified in any dialog. Relative Colorimetric is a reasonable choice unless you know that almost all of your conversions will be RGB to CMYK for which Perceptual is the appropriate intent option. Always check Use Black Point Compensation. This maps the black point source to the black point destination, avoiding any clipping or flattening of the darkest colours and maintains the full dynamic range.

Now that we have all of our working parameters correctly defined, we can OK the Color Settings dialog and look at the basic mechanism for using colour profiles in the Adobe Creative applications. There are two actions we can invoke from the Edit menu to apply colour profiles: Assign Profile and Convert to Profile.

Assign Profile allows us to select a source profile for the open document. This action will replace the existing profile for a tagged document or provide a new reference for an untagged file. To have the association persist, you must save the file and check the option to embed the current colour profile. Assigning a profile will change the onscreen appearance of the file but not alter any of the file's tint values (colour data). We are simply instructing the computer on how the original CMYK or RGB values would look if they are coming from our new source (described in the look up table of the new colour profile).

Convert to Profile is an immediate and irreversible (once the file is saved) transformation of the document's tint values. The assigned profile is used as a source and the user selects a destination profile and rendering intent. The conversion takes place and the file now has new RGB or CMYK numbers as a result. If you use the advanced dialog to specify a device link profile, then the currently assigned source profile is ignored for the calculations since the device link contains information for both the source and destination conditions.

Both the Assign and Convert dialog windows come with a Preview check box that will allow you to toggle between the before and after state to visually validate your choices and experiment with the effects of choosing different rendering intents.

Assessing the Effect of a Colour Profile

Once the profile is applied, what should we be looking for? Both on screen and when comparing hard-copy (printed) samples, there are specific areas of the image that should be checked. There is also industry-specific language used in describing colour appearance that it is helpful to be familiar with. The areas of the image to pay special attention to are saturated colours, flesh tones, neutrals, and the highlights. Proof and print sample sheets will have four or five images that emphasize these areas along with tone ramps in the process and overprint colours. Focusing on these areas of interest will make it easiest to identify variation when checking for colour matching.

The terminology that is often employed is *colour cast,* to indicate a shift toward a particular colour; *heaviness,* to suggest excessive tone (particularly in the highlights); *dirty,* to specify too much complementary colour resulting in greying; and *flat,* to describe a lack of contrast and/or saturation. Knowing the terminology will help you understand the comments your co-workers may make and will help remind you of the types of analysis you should be doing.

Additional Colour Tools in Adobe Acrobat

In addition to the fundamental profile handling procedures described above, there are several powerful and useful colour tools in Adobe Acrobat that can be used once you have exported your desktop file to a PDF. These are found among the Print Production Tools in the Acrobat Tools menu. Two are of particular note: Convert Colors and Output Preview.

Convert Colors allows you to convert colour spaces, such as changing RGB content to CMYK. It also enables transforming *spot colours* (such as Pantone) to CMYK. In addition, if the file incorrectly contains multiple instances of a spot colour that should all appear together on the same printing plate (i.e., Pantone 283 and s*pecial blue*), they can be linked to behave as a single entry on the colour palette.

Output Preview does not apply any changes to the file, but is an extraordinarily powerful review mechanism. It enables you to confirm that colour elements in the file are as they should be before you commit to the expensive step of actual output. With Output Preview, you can turn individual separations on and off to check overprints and knockouts; check the separation list to confirm which elements are attached to each separation; identify the colour space of each object; and even highlight any area that exceeds your threshold for total ink coverage.

Profile Use in Kodak Prinergy

The final topic in our exploration of colour management in graphic technologies is an example of the application of colour management in a print production workflow. We'll use one of the predominant workflow applications, Kodak Prinergy, as a model.

The processing instructions for file handling in Prinergy are contained in a *process template*. Input files are 'refined' to PDF in the Prinergy workflow and an important portion of the refining process is the instructions relating to colour conversions. In addition, we have process templates for output both to proof and final output. These templates also contain colour control options. For both *refine* and *output* process templates, the colour management information is contained in the Match Colors box of the Color Convert subsection.

Prinergy offers a comprehensive colour management application of its own called ColorFlow. There is a check box in Color Convert to turn on ColorFlow awareness and pass all of the colour management decisions to what has been predefined in ColorFlow. Discussing the structure and functional logic of ColorFlow is beyond the scope of this text. To use Prinergy as a more generic workflow example, we'll uncheck the ColorFlow option and turn off the integration.

The standard location to store profiles for use by Prinergy is \Prinergy\ CreoAraxi\data\ICC-Profiles. Profiles are not immediately available from this location in Prinergy's drop-down menus, but can be browsed to if placed in job-specific subfolders.

Let's look at the Match Colors section of the refine process template. With ColorFlow integration turned off, the entry fields under Assign Input Device Conditions become available. If you check Override Embedded Profiles, then profiles that are checked on in the Assign Input Device Conditions section will replace all existing profiles in the files being processed. Notice that there is a very granular level of control, with independent entries for CMYK images, CMYK graphics, RGB images, and RGB graphics. If you specify a device link profile, it will override any tagged profile whether or not Override Embedded Profiles is checked.

Convert to Destination is where you indicate the destination profile. This will only be used for instances not covered by a device link in the assign section. Remember that any device link contains both source and destination information. Beneath the Convert box is a box for selecting rendering intents. Entries are only available for the options that were checked on under Assign Input Device Conditions. The default entry is Perceptual since most input files will require image conversions from larger colour gamuts.

For output process templates in Prinergy, the options are very similar to what has been described above. We typically use colour management for output to proofs, either single page or imposed. There is a separate ColorFlow section to uncheck to enable the more traditional colour management approach. In the Match Colors box, Match Colors in Page Content must be checked on for any colour profiles to be applied. Also, you must select one of the following radio buttons–As Defined Below, If Not Set in Refining, or Exactly as Defined Below– so you will be able to choose a profile in the Input Device Conditions box. Since all content will now be in the CMYK space from the refine process template, there are no longer independent options for RGB, graphics and images: only one source or device link can be specified. The rendering intent is entered in the Rendering Intent field. The destination profile (usually the proofer profile) goes in the Device Condition box. Once again, this destination profile will be ignored if a device link has been chosen for the source.

By following the steps described, the workflow application user can produce predictable and accurate colour reproduction results through both the file processing and output steps of any print production workflow.

In essence, colour management is a translation process. The tools and precepts of colour science give us the lexicon to populate the dictionaries of each of the devices we use in our graphic technology workflow. Our device's dictionary is the colour profile we generate with the help of a colour target, an instrument to measure the target and colour management software to process the measurements.

Since the device's dictionary (colour profile) defines the specific RGB or CMYK values of that device in a device independent colour language, we have a conduit between any two devices. By aligning the device independent values between the two devices, we can translate from the device dependent values of our source to the new RGB or CMYK values at our destination to provide a common colour experience.

With an understanding of how to configure our standard graphic arts applications to effectively use our device's profiles, we can make successful colour translations happen in our real-world production scenarios. Successful colour translations provide the improved productivity that comes with predictability and confidence in process control.

Questions to consider after completing this chapter:

1. What are the three components of the colour event?
2. How does visible light relate to the electromagnetic spectrum?
3. How does the zone theory of optical systems resolve the apparent incompatibility of trichromacy and opponency?
4. What is the importance of the Lab colour space?
5. Define Delta E.
6. Which of RGB, CMYK, and Lab are device dependent colour spaces, and which are device independent colour spaces?
7. How does a spectrophotometer work?
8. What is the purpose of a colour target?
9. What Mac OS utility can be used to view colour profiles?
10. How does a measurement file relate to an ICC profile?
11. What is the vcgt tag in a display profile?
12. Name the common characteristics of output, display, and input profiles.
13. What characteristics are unique to each of output, display, and input profiles?

14. Working Spaces serve what purpose in Adobe's Color Setup dialog?
15. Which Acrobat tool allows for the merging of spot colours?
16. How do we make a device link profile?
17. Where is a device link profile used in Prinergy's output process template?

References

Fraser, B., Murphy, C., & Bunting, F. (2004). *Real world color management* (2nd ed.). Berkeley, CA: Peachpit Press.

Suggested Readings

Fraser, B., Murphy, C., & Bunting, F. (2004). *Real world color management* (2nd ed.). Berkeley, CA: Peachpit Press.

Sharma, A. (2003). *Understanding color management* (1st ed.). Clifton Park, NY: Course Technology.

Chapter 5. Pre-press

5.1 Introduction

Learning Objectives

- Explain why raster image processing requires so much data for print imaging
- Compare resolutions required for digital media and print media
- Compare and contrast the positive and negative attributes between using process and spot colours
- Discuss why Pantone colours are more accurate on a printed swatch than on screen.
- List a number of different industry standard spot colour systems
- Describe trapping issues that occur when adjacent colours are imaged independently
- Analyze different imaging technologies for trapping requirements
- Interpret how black ink is to be used in overprint and boost situations
- Define transparency within the context of prepress workflow management
- Differentiate between flattening transparency on the desktop, or at raster image processing
- Describe the most common press sheet imposition styles
- Analyze different binding styles to select the correct imposition required
- Identify opportunities for nesting multiple images to save materials
- Explain the importance of preflight within the context of pre-press workflow

North America's fifth-largest manufacturing sector is graphic communications technologies. We can become aware of just how huge this industry is by listing all the manufactured images we see in our day. Your list might include the morning paper or magazine you read, the graphic on the side of the bus you ride to work, and the labels on the grocery shelf where you select your evening meal. Increasingly, more of the graphics that are driving that massive industry are produced with computer graphics software on personal computers. Most of the graphics software used to create the images for reproduction is designed to create images for electronic media — primarily the Internet. Computer graphics designers are not aware of, or concerned with, optimizing their designs for the manufacturing process they are driving. This problem is a root cause of less profitability in most sectors of the graphic communications industry. To tackle this problem, we must become aware of all that happens to a computer graphic from the time it leaves the picture created on the computer screen to the image on the label on the package on the grocery shelf, or the photograph on the side of a bus.

We must first distinguish between traditional pre-press technologies and the pre-imaging processes that are relevant in today's graphic communications industry. Pre-press processes are different from the way we process images for electrophotographic imaging or imaging with an inkjet engine. We must also distinguish between preparing images for a lithographic press and a flexographic press. Electrophotography and inkjet are growing technologies used to produce customized — or individualized — communications materials. Lithography and flexography are used to manufacture mass-produced media products. These four imaging processes are the core imaging technologies that reproduce 90% of the images produced in the graphic communications industry.

Many graphic designers are not aware of what must happen to the computer graphics they produce in order to ready them for manufacturing reproduction. Their experience is limited to hitting 'command P' and their computer graphic magically transforming the illuminated masterpiece on their Apple Cinema Display, to the disappointing rendition that appears on the tray of their inkjet printer. Most of the pre-imaging processes are automated in software functions that are built into the print driver, so people are not aware of how a computer graphic must be prepared for an imaging device. Since more and more of the images produced through inkjet, electrophotography, lithography and flexography start their lives as computer graphics, it is important to understand these pre-imaging processes to properly design computer graphics for the manufacturing process.

This chapter will analyze six pre-imaging processes in detail, and describe how they are altered to prepare computer graphics differently for each of the four imaging technologies. We will refer back to the computer graphic design/creation process to outline how graphics could be altered so they can be more effectively reproduced with each imaging technology. This is the missing link in the graphic communications business in today's marketplace. Designers create computer graphics in software that is increasingly designed for electronic image creation. They do not realize that the same graphic they created for a home page on the Internet should not be used for the cover of a book. They email the image to a lithographic print production facility and the pre-press department of that facility does hand springs trying to alter the image to work on their sheet-fed presses. This adds time and cost to the job that is usually buried. The designer never gets feedback on how the design could be altered to be more effective for lithographic production.

When pre-press was a computer-to-film process, there were two important factors that ensured designers got this critical feedback. The software for computer graphic production was specialized for print creation and content could be photographed or computer-generated and combined on film. Computer graphic designers knew their image was only going to be used for the cover of a book and created it appropriately. They also had to submit their computer graphic to a graphic communications production facility that was separate from the lithographic print facility. If there were extra costs incurred to prepare the computer graphic for a lithographic press, the designer was informed and invoiced for the extra work the image preparation entailed. So the designers were working with computer graphic software that would not let them create imagery that was not appropriate for print production, and if they did dream up an image that did not work well, they were immediately informed of the extra costs they were incurring.

In the 21st-century marketplace, all graphics that drive our four primary imaging technologies are created on the computer. Computer graphics software is designed to create effects for images that will stay in the electronic media: web, broadcast, digital film, and hand-held communication technologies. Pre-imaging processes are either automated or a part of the print manufacturing business and usually considered the painful part of feeding the print machinery that no one wants to talk about. So computer graphic designers drive software that lets them create outrageous images for imaging reproduction manufacture. They are less concerned about the 'print' part of a media campaign, and manufacturers are hesitant to inform them that their designs incurred extra costs to reproduce. We can contribute to a solution to this problem by analyzing all of the pre-imaging processes for each type of reproduction manufacture and link them back to the computer graphic design software.

We will examine six pre-imaging processes:

- Raster image processing (RIP) technologies that are common to all four manufacturing processes
- Colour management for repeatability, as a part of the RIP process
- Trapping to lithographic and flexographic specifications
- Transparency, which is a visual effect that has a great impact on imaging
- Imposition for pre-RIP and post-RIP for media utilization
- Preflight analysis and automation for computer file creation

5.2 Raster Image Processing

The raster image processor (RIP) is the core technology that does the computational work to convert the broad range of data we use to create a computer graphic into the one-bit data that drives a physical imaging device. Let's examine the creation of a single character of the alphabet, or **glyph**. A font file delivers PostScript language to the RIP that describes a series of points and **vector** curves between those points to outline the letter A. The RIP has a matrix grid at the resolution of the output device and computes which spots on the grid get turned on and which are turned off to create the shape of that letter A on the output device. The spots on the grid can only be turned on or off — which is how binary data is encoded — either as 0 or 1. The grid then acts as a switch to turn a mechanical part of the imaging engine on or off.

With computer-to-plate technology for lithographic printing plate production, a laser is used to expose an emulsion on a printing plate. Most plate-setters have a resolution of 2,000 to 3,000 lspi (laser spots per inch). The RIP calculates all the spots that must be turned 'on' to create the graphic that will be imaged on the printing plate. If the image fills a typical sheet-fed press, it is (30 inches x 3,000 lspi) x (40 inches x 3,000 lspi) = 1.08 trillion, which takes 10 gigabytes of computer memory to store and transfer. A printing plate for flexographic print production is created by turning a laser on and off at a slightly lower resolution. An inkjet printer uses the same RIP process to deliver the same one-bit data to each inkjet nozzle for each colour of ink in the printer. Most inkjet engines have a resolution between 600 and 1,200 spots per inch — so the matrix grid is smaller — but if it is an eight-colour printer, the data for all eight nozzles must be synchronized and delivered simultaneously. An electophotographic (Xerox) printer usually has a resolution similar to an inkjet printer and utilizes a similar RIP process to change a grid of electrostatic charges to positive or negative on an electrostatic drum that is the maximum media size the machine can image. Each colour in the printer has a separate **raster image** that charges the drum in the right spot to attract that colour of toner to that exact location. The data for each colour must be synchronized for simultaneous delivery. The data must refresh the charge on the drum after each print in order to pick up new toner. That is a very important fact to remember when we talk about personalizing print with variable data later in this chapter.

This basic understanding of RIP's place in a computer graphic workflow is essential to understanding how to prepare files for, and manage, RIP resources. It is also essential in solving some of the common problems we see in various RIPs. When we compare the two mass production imaging technologies, lithography and flexography, to the personalized imaging technologies, electrophotography and inkjet, we can identify some core similarities. In lithography and flexography, a high-powered laser is used to alter a physical emulsion that is durable and finely grained enough to let the laser image a spot that is one three-thousandth of an inch without affecting the spot of equal size beside it. We can reliably image that spot in a serif of a glyph set in one point type or a hair on a face in a photo that is imaged with a 5 micron frequency modulated (FM) screening pattern. The mass production technology assures us that the first print will be identical to the millionth print.

The raster grid of one-bit data that the RIP produces must be delivered to the imaging drum or the inkjet nozzle for every image that is produced with an inkjet printer or an electrophotographic engine. This is what allows us to make every image different and personalize it for the person we are delivering the image to. It also makes the process slower and less reliable for mass production. The RIP produces a lower resolution raster grid, so the detail in photos and letter shapes is not as precise. We can have a RIP discard data if we have too much detail for the raster grid it is producing. The RIP does not do a good job of interpolating more data to produce additional detail in a photo or graphic shape if that information is missing to begin with.

That brings us to examining the resources that a RIP must have to produce a perfect raster for every graphic shape it renders, and for every colour being reproduced. The resource a RIP consumes is data. In the graphic communications industry, we should all wear T-shirts that say 'Pigs for data!' just to distinguish us from our media colleagues who are producing computer graphics for electronic media. If we think of a RIP as an auto assembly line we are feeding with parts, in the form of files in different data formats, it will help us understand how to make a RIP more efficient. If we feed too many parts into the assembly line, it is easier to throw some parts away than it is to stop and recreate a part that is missing. If we feed the assembly line with five times as many parts needed to make a car, it is still more efficient to throw parts away than it is to stop and recreate a missing part.

If we apply this analogy to image resolution, we can point to examples where designers regularly repurpose images from a web page to use on a book cover or poster print. The web page needs to deliver the photo across a network quickly and only needs to fill a typical computer screen with enough detail to represent the photo. A typical photo resolution to do that properly is 72 pixels per inch. Now remember that the raster grid for a lithographic printing press that will print the book cover is 3,000 lspi. Our RIP needs much more data than the web page image contains! Most of the photos we are reproducing today are captured with electronic devices — digital cameras, phones, scanners, or hand-held devices. Most store the data with some kind of compression to reduce the data the device has to store and transfer. Those efficiencies stop at the RIP though, as this computational engine has to decompress the data before applying it to the graphic page it is rasterizing. It is like breaking a steering wheel down to wires, bolts, and plastic sleeves that efficiently fit into a one-inch-square shipping package, and putting this 'IKEA furniture' steering wheel onto an auto production line for the assembler to deal with in two-point-two minutes!

On the other hand, we can capture a digital photo at 6,000 pixels per inch (ppi) and use it on a page scaled to half the original dimension. That is like packing a finished steering wheel in 10 yards of bubble wrap and setting it on the assembly line in a wooden shipping crate! So it is important for designers to pay attention to the resolution of the final imaging device to determine the resolution that the RIP will produce from the graphic files it is processing.

Halftone Screening

It is important to stop here for a discussion about halftone screening that a RIP applies to photographs and graphics to represent grey levels or tonal values in a graphic element. We described how the RIP makes a grid of one-bit data, but graphics are not just black and white — they have tonal values from 0% (nothing) printing to 100% (solid) printing. If we want to render the tonal values in-between in half percent increments, we need 200 addresses to record the different values. Computer data is recorded in bits, two values (on and off), and bytes, which are eight bits strung together in one switch. The number of values a byte can record is 256 — the number of combinations of on and off that the eight bits in the byte can express. A computer records a byte of data for each primary colour (red, green, and blue — RGB) for each detail in a photo, as a *pixel* (picture element), which controls the phosphors on electronic imaging devices. A RIP must convert the eight-bit RGB values into the four primary printing ink colours (cyan magenta, yellow, and black — CMYK). There are two distinct steps here: (1) conversion from RGB to CMYK continuous tone data (24 bit RGB to 32 bit CMYK); and (2) continuous tone to one-bit screening algorithms. We have to be in the output colour space before we can apply the one-bit conversion. It converts the eight-bit tonal values into one-bit data by dividing the area into cells that can render different sizes and shapes of dots by turning spots on and off in the cell. A cell with a grid that is 10 laser spots wide by 10 laser spots deep can render different 100 dot sizes (10 x 10), from 1% to 99%, by turning on more and more of the laser spots to print. If we think back to the plate-setter for lithographic platemaking, we know it is capable of firing the laser 2,000 to 3,000 times per inch. If the cells making up our printing dots are 10 spots square, we can make dot sizes that have a resolution of 200 to 300 halftone screened dots in one inch. A RIP has screening (dot cell creation) algorithms that convert the data delivered in RGB pixels at 300 pixels per inch into clusters of laser spots (dots) for each printing primary colour (CMYK).

This description of how a RIP processes photographic data from a digital camera can help us understand why it is important to capture and deliver enough resolution to the RIP. It must develop a detailed representation of the photo in a halftone screened dot that utilizes all of the laser spots available. The basic rule is: Required PPI = 2 x lines per inch (LPI) at final size. So if you need to print something at 175 lines per inch, it must have a resolution of 350 pixels per inch at the final scaled size of the reproduction. Use this rule if you are not given explicit direction by your print service provider. You can use a default of 400 ppi for FM screening where lpi is not relevant.

WYSIWYG

It is important to know that each time we view a computer graphic on our computer screen, it is imaging the screen through a RIP process. The RIP can change from one software program to another. This is why some PDF files look different when you open them in the Preview program supplied with an Apple operating system than they do when opened in Adobe Acrobat. The graphics are being processed through two different RIPs. The same thing can happen when the image is processed through two different printers. The challenge is to consistently predict what the printed image will look like by viewing it on the computer screen. We use the acronym **WYSIWYG** (what you see is what you get) to refer to imagery that will reproduce consistently on any output device. Designers have faced three significant challenges in trying to achieve WYSISYG since the advent of desktop publishing in the early 1980s.

The first challenge was imaging typography with PostScript fonts. The second was colour managing computer screens and output devices with ICC profiles. The third and current challenge is in imaging transparent effects predictably from one output device to another. Font problems are still the most common cause of error in processing client documents for all imaging technologies. Let's look at that problem in depth before addressing the other two challenges in achieving WYSIWYG.

Font Management

The development of the PostScript computer language was pioneered by Adobe in creating the first device independent font files. This invention let consumers typeset their own documents on personal computers and image their documents on laser printers at various resolutions. To achieve WYSIWYG on personal computer screens, the font files needed two parts: screen fonts and printer fonts. Screen fonts were bitmaps that imaged the letter shapes (glyphs) on the computer screen. Printer fonts were vector descriptions, written in PostScript code, that had to be processed by a RIP at the resolution of the printer. The glyphs looked significantly different when imaged on a 100 dpi laser printer than they did on a 600 dpi printer, and both were quite different from what graphic artists/typographers saw on their computer screen. That was not surprising since the shapes were imaged by completely different computer files — one raster, one vector — through different RIP processors, on very different devices. Many graphic designers still do not realize that when they use Adobe type font architecture they must provide both the raster screen font and the vector PostScript font to another computer if they want the document that utilizes that font to process through the RIP properly. This was such a common problem with the first users of Adobe fonts that Microsoft made it the first problem they solved when developing TrueType font architecture to compete with Adobe fonts. TrueType fonts still contained bitmap data to draw the glyphs on a computer screen, and PostScript vector data to deliver to a RIP on a print engine. The TrueType font file is a single file, though, that contains both raster and vector data. TrueType fonts became widely distributed with all Microsoft software. Microsoft also shared the specifications for TrueType font architecture so users could create and distribute their own fonts. The problems with the keeping screen font files with printer font files went away when graphics creators used TrueType fonts.

The quality of the fonts took a nose dive as more people developed and distributed their own font files, with no knowledge of what makes a good font, and what can create havoc in a RIP. Today, there are thousands of free TrueType fonts available for downloading from a multitude of websites. So how does a designer identify a good font from a bad font? The easiest way is to set some complicated glyphs in a program like Adobe InDesign or Illustrator and use a 'convert to outlines' function in the program. This will show the nodes and bezier curves that create the glyph. If there are many nodes with small, straight line segments between them, the font may cause problems in a RIP. Remember that PostScript was meant to be a scalable device independent programming language. If the poorly made glyphs are scaled too small, the RIP has to calculate too many points from the node positions and ends up eliminating many points that are finer than the resolution of the raster image. On the other hand, if the glyph is scaled too large, the straight lines between points make the smooth curve shapes square and chopped-looking. These fonts are usually created by hand drawing the letter shapes, scanning the drawings, and auto tracing them in a program like Illustrator. The 'convert to outlines' test reveals the auto tracing right away, and it is a good idea to search out another font for a similar typeface from a more reputable font foundry.

Another good test is to look at the **kerning** values that are programmed into the font file. Kerning pairs are glyph shapes that need the space between them tightened up (decreased) when they appear together. A good font usually has 600 to 800 kerning pair values programmed into its file. The most common pair that needs kerning is an upper case 'T' paired with a lower case 'o' (To). The 'o' glyph must be tucked under the crossbar of the T, which is done by programming a negative letter space in the font file to have less **escapement** when the imaging engine moves from rendering the first shape to when it starts imaging the second shape. If we set the letter pair, and put the curser in the space between them, a negative kerning value should appear in the kerning tool. If no kerning value appears, the font is usually a poor one and will cause spacing problems in the document it is used in.

Another common problem occurred when combining Adobe Type 1 fonts with TrueType fonts in the same document. Adobe was the creator of the PostScript programming language, and although it was easy enough to copy its code and create similar fonts, Adobe has maintained fairly tight control over licensing the PostScript interpreting engines that determine how the PostScript code is rendered through a raster image processor. The RIP stores the glyph shapes in a font file in a matrix that can be speedily accessed when rendering the glyphs. Each glyph is assigned an address in the matrix, and each font matrix has a unique number assigned to it so that the RIP can assign a unique rendering matrix. Adobe could keep track of its own font identification numbers but could not control the font IDs that were assigned to TrueType fonts. If a TrueType font had the same font ID number as the Adobe Type 1 font used in a document, the RIP would establish the glyph matrix from the first font it processed and use the same matrix for the other font. So documents were rendered with one font instead of two, and the glyphs, word spacing, line endings, and page breaks were all affected and rendered incorrectly. For the most part, this problem has been sorted out with the creation of a central registry for font ID numbers; however, there are still older TrueType font files out there in the Internet universe that will generate font ID conflicts in a RIP.

Adobe, Apple, and Microsoft all continued to compete for control of the desktop publishing market by trying to improve font architectures, and, as a result, many confusing systems evolved and were discarded when they caused more problems in the RIPs than they solved. There is a common font error that still causes problems when designers use Adobe Type 1 fonts or TrueType fonts. Most of these fonts only have eight-bit addressing and so can only contain 256 glyphs. A separate font file is needed to set a bold or italic version of the typeface. Some page layout programs will allow the designer to apply bold or italic attributes to the glyphs, and artificially render the bold or italic shapes in the document on the computer screen. When the document is processed in the RIP, if the font that contains the bold or italic glyphs is not present, the RIP either does not apply the attribute, or substitutes a default font (usually Courier) to alert proofreaders that there is a font error in the document. The line endings and page breaks are affected by the error — and the printing plate, signage, or printout generated becomes garbage at great expense to the industry.

To solve this problem, Adobe actually cooperated with Microsoft and Apple in the development of a new font architecture. OpenType fonts have unicode addressing, which allows them to contain thousands of glyphs. Entire typeface families can be linked together to let designers seamlessly apply multiple attributes such as condensed bold italic to the typeface, and have the RIP process the document very closely to what typesetters see on their computer screen. PostScript is also the internal language of most page layout software, so the same OpenType font files are used to rasterize the glyphs to screen as the printer's RIP is using to generate the final output. There can be significant differences in the RIP software, but many font issues are solved by using OpenType fonts for document creation.

One common font error still persists in the graphic communications industry that acutely underlines the difference between creating a document on a single user's computer but processing it through an imaging manufacturer's workstation. Designers usually own a specific set of fonts that they use for all the documents they create. The manufacturer tries to use the exact font file each designer supplies with the document. The problem once again involves the font ID number, as each font file activated in an operating system is cached in RAM memory to make the RIP-to-screen process faster. So the font files the manufacturer receives can be different versions of the same font created at different times, but assigned the same font ID number. For example, one designer uses a 1995 version of Adobe's Helvetica typeface and another uses a 2015 version, but the two typefaces have the same font ID number. The manufacturer's operating system will not overwrite the first font matrix it cached in RAM, so it is the first font file that renders the document on screen and will be sent down to the RIP. Usually, there are few noticeable changes in the glyph shapes. But it is common for font foundries to adjust kerning values between letter pairs from one version to the next. So if a manufacturer has the wrong version of the font file cached in RAM, a document can have line-ending changes and page reflows. This is a hard error to catch. There are programs and routines the imaging manufacturer can implement to clear the RAM cache, but many times, more 'garbage' is generated before the problem is diagnosed. Modern PDF creation usually includes the production of a uniquely tagged font subset package that only contains the glyphs used in the document. The unique font subset ID avoids the potential for font ID conflicts.

Managing fonts on a single user computer has its own challenges, and Apple has included Font Book with its operating systems to help manage fonts in applications on an Apple OS. Adobe offers Typekit with its latest Creative Cloud software to provide greater access to a wide variety of typefaces from a reliable foundry. Third-party font management programs like Suitcase Fusion also help graphic artists manage their fonts for repurposing their documents effectively. It is still the responsibility of individual operators to know how to use the fonts in their documents. They should also make sure that the fonts are licensed and packaged to deliver to other computer systems so that they can drive many different RIPs on a wide variety of output devices.

5.3 Colour

The second challenge with implementing WYSIWYG for electronic documents that are imaged on substrates is managing colour expectations. Chapter 4 discussed the challenges of colour management from the perspective of how we see colour, measure it, and manage output devices with ICC profiles. In this chapter, we will explore colour management from the perspective of how we recognize and manage the ICC profiles that are embedded in client documents. We will also explore the preflight issues in managing spot colours in documents. This will also lead us to a discussion of trapping for lithography and flexography.

To design with colour in computer graphics software, we must understand how the software generates the colour values. Page layout and illustration software usually have several systems for creating colour on a page. The colour settings or colour preferences attached to a file can change from one document to another or in the same document restored from one computer to another. If a designer uses the RGB colour model to specify the colours in a document, the colours on the monitor can change depending on the translations done to the colour settings. This is a major turning point for designers creating documents intended to stay in the electronic media. No one pays much attention to how a particular colour of red is rendered from one web browser to another. Designers pay more attention to how the colours interact relative to one another in web-page documents. It is only when we image a computer graphic on a substrate that we must pay attention to rendering the exact hue of red from one device to another. Coca-Cola has very exact specifications for the red used in its documents that tie into its brand recognition. So designers for documents intended for imaging on substrates must use colour models that are proven to render exactly the same results from one output device to another.

Pantone Colours

This is a lofty ideal that the graphic communications industry aspires to. There are systems in place that are proven to render very accurate results. There are challenges in understanding the systems, and one wrong step in the process and accuracy is destroyed. The process starts with how a designer chooses colours in a document. The most-used system for choosing accurate colours was created by the Pantone company. Pantone has developed a library of ink recipes that are published as swatch books. A designer can buy a printed book of a library of colours that matches an electronic library that can be imported into computer software programs. Designers compare their on-screen rendering of a colour to the printed sample swatch. If a designer is developing a corporate identification package with logos that use Pantone 123 and Pantone 456, the designer can be assured that the documents he or she creates will be imaged with inks that have similar spectral values to the swatch books used to choose the colour. I say similar, because the swatch books fade over time, and the substrates the books are printed on don't usually match all the substrates a corporate logo is imaged on.

It is also important to realize that the Pantone library was created to mix pigments for **spot colour** inks rather than **process colour** inks. Spot colours are mixed independently and must each be applied to the substrate independently. Process inks are only the four primary colours: cyan, magenta, yellow, and black. Process inks are transparent and are intended to be combined by halftone screening different percentages on a substrate to render any colour in the Pantone library. Spot colour inks are more opaque and are intended to be applied to a substrate one at a time, through distinctly separate printing units. Since most colour photography is colour separated to render the photo in only the four primary process inks, most documents are created intending to convert the spot colours to process colours. They can be imaged with the photographs in the document. A designer must know how many colours the output device is capable of when deciding which colours will remain as spot colours and which will be converted to CMYK process colours. Most inkjet and electrophotographic devices are only capable of imaging with the four process colours. Some lithographic presses have extra printing units that can print spot colours, so six- and eight-colour presses commonly print the four process colours and two (or four) extra spot colours in one pass. It is not uncommon to have 10- and 12-colour flexographic presses that image no process colours but use 12 spot colours. This is because, historically, flexo plates cannot consistently reproduce very fine halftone dots reliably. This is changing with the development of high-definition plating technology, so we are seeing more photographic content produced well on flexographic presses. Flexography is primarily used in the packaging industry where spot colours are very closely tied to brand recognition in retail outlets. A designer must be very aware of the imaging technology used to reproduce a document when deciding which colours will remain spot colours.

This is where the next round of challenges begins when preflighting (assessing) documents for imaging to substrates. If design elements stay as spot colours, it is a simple process to maintain the spot colour on the output device and to image with the appropriate ink or toner. Some software will not maintain the spot colour in a document easily in some situations. Usually, the problem comes with applying gradients to spot colours. It is very easy to introduce a median colour value on a spot colour gradient that is simulated with a process colour value. The screen version displays a nice smooth gradient that looks like what the designer intended to create. When imaging on a substrate, the gradient will have to be broken down into individual colours: from the solid spot colour to a value of CMYK and back to spot colour. It is very hard to recognize this by viewing the document, or even a composite PDF file. Viewing separated PDF files, or using a 'separations' tool in Acrobat, will show the problem before it gets to a printing plate.

There are also colour problems associated with nested files generated in different software. For example, if we create a magazine page with a headline colour named "PMS 123," add a logo created in Adobe Illustrator with type in a colour named "Pantone 123," and insert a PDF ad created in Apple's Pages layout with a border specifying "PANTONE 123," then even though they are all the same, colour-separating software will generate three separate spot colour plates for that page. The spot colours have to be named exactly the same and come from the same library. Some modern workflows include aliasing rules that will match numbered PMS colours to try to alleviate the problem. Colour libraries can be a problem as well, especially if our software allows the library to convert the spot colour to a process colour. The same colour library in two different versions of Adobe's Creative Suite software can generate a different process colour recipe for the same Pantone colour. This is not a problem if all the document elements are created within one software package and all spot colours are converted to process colours. The problem arises when a designer places a graphic file from other software on a page with the same colour elements. A logo created in an older version of Adobe Illustrator will use that colour library to look up process colour recipes that can be very different from the recipes in a recent colour library used in Adobe's InDesign software. So all the Pantone orange colours in a document are supposed to look the same, but do not because the spot colour to process colour conversion has not been done with the same library. The problem becomes worse when we combine files from different software vendors, as designers often have to do when building a document. It is common these days to bring together graphics created in Microsoft Office and Apple software and generate a final document with Adobe InDesign. The best way to create consistent documents for reproduction is to specify a common CMYK colour value that will print reliably on the output device.

Pantone also publishes a swatch book that shows the difference between the swatches run as spot colour ink mixes, and the same swatch printed as halftone screen builds of process inks. This is a designer's most valuable tool for specifying process ink recipes. It also illustrates that many Pantone colours cannot be simulated very well using halftone screen values of the four process inks. It is very apparent that very vibrant orange, purple, and green Pantone spot colours are not achievable with process inks. There are systems like Hexachrome for colour separations that use more than just CMYK inks to extend the gamut of the Pantone colours that can be reproduced. There are also more and more inkjet and electrophotographic engines that will use extra spot colours to extend the colour range of the device beyond CMYK. The businesses that employ those devices usually know they are unique in the marketplace and have developed marketing tools to help designers use those capabilities successfully.

Accuracy in Design

If we reflect back to the concept of WYSIWYG for a moment, we can use the Pantone selection process to illustrate the challenge very well. If we ask a designer to choose colours for a document based on computer screen displays, we know that the RGB or HSL values they can select will be far too vibrant for reproduction with any imaging engine. To set proper expectations for WYSIWYG, we ask the designer to calibrate a monitor and select the proper output profiles to tone down the screen view and set more realistic expectations. We also ask that a print designer use printed swatch books to select from a library of specified colours and assign realistic CMYK process colour values to her or his colour palette. If those steps are followed, there is a very reasonable chance that the process will achieve WYSIWYG. However, it can break down in a few places. The spot colour swatch books set expectations about colours that cannot be achieved with process inks. When a mixture of spot colours and process inks are used, it is difficult to display both on the same computer screen with reliable colour. Graphics files can originate in different software with different libraries using different process colour recipes for the same Pantone colours.

There are also many spot colour libraries to choose from, and designers don't know when to use each library. We have described why the Pantone library is a North American standard, and some of its limitations. There are other design communities in the world that use spot colour libraries that are included as choices in graphic creation software tools. There are almost as many spot colours to choose from as there are free fonts files to download from the Internet. Spot colour classification has led to thousands of discrete colours being given unique names or numbers. There are several industry standards in the classification of spot colour systems. These include:

- Pantone, the dominant spot colour printing system used in North America and Europe.
- Toyo, a spot colour system common in Japan.
- DIC colour system guide, another spot colour system common in Japan.
- ANPA, a palette of 300 colours specified by the American Newspaper Publishers Association for spot colour usage in newspapers.

- GCMI, a standard for colour used in package printing developed by the Glass Packaging Institute (formerly known as the Glass Container Manufacturers Institute, hence the abbreviation).
- HKS is a colour system that contains 120 spot colours and 3,250 tones for coated and uncoated paper. HKS is an abbreviation of three German colour manufacturers: Hostmann-Steinberg Druckfarben, Kast + Ehinger Druckfarben, and H. Schmincke & Co.
- RAL is a colour-matching system used in Europe. The RAL Classic system is mainly used for varnish and powder coating.

The guiding principle for using any of these spot colour systems is to check that the manufacturer of the reproduction is using that ink system. The Trumatch library is quickly gaining favour as a tool for colour selection. That library of spot colours has been developed to be exactly replicated with process colour halftone screening. There are no spot colours a designer can choose from that library that cannot be reproduced well with standard process inks. As more computer graphics are being produced on digital imaging devices that only use CMYK, this colour library is becoming the choice for cross-platform or multi-vendor media publications.

5.4 Trapping

Trapping can be a very complex procedure in pre-imaging software for certain imaging technologies. It is an electronic file treatment that must be performed to help solve registration issues on certain kinds of press technologies. Generally, if a substrate has to move from one colour unit to another in the imaging process, the registration of one colour to another will not be perfect. That mis-registration must be compensated for by overlapping abutting colours. As soon as two colours touch in any two graphic elements we must create a third graphic element that contains both colours and overlaps the colours along the abutment line. That third element is called a *trap line* and can be generated many different ways that we will review.

Electrophotography

First let's look at the differences between the four most common imaging technologies and determine where and why we need to generate these trap lines. Electrophotography, or toner-based digital printers, generally use only process colours. Each time an electrostatic drum turns, it receives an electrical charge to attract the toner colour it is receiving. The drum keeps turning until all colours of all toners are on the drum, and then all colours are transferred to the substrate at one time. There is no chance for mis-registration between the cyan, magenta, yellow, and black toners as they are imaged at the resolution of the raster generated by the RIP, and the placement of the electronic charge for each colour can be adjusted until it is perfect, which makes it stable from image to image.

Lithography

Let's compare electrophotography to the lithographic print process. In lithography, a printing plate is generated for each colour and mounted on a plate cylinder. The plates are registered by manually turning wrenches to hold plate clamps, so the plate-mounting procedure can generate registration errors. Each colour printing unit is loaded with a separate ink, a plate that has been imaged to receive that ink, and a blanket that offsets the image from the plate before it transfers it from the blanket to the substrate. This is another mechanical transfer point that can cause registration errors. Most high-end lithographic presses have servo motors and cameras that work together to adjust for mechanical registration errors as the press runs. The substrate must travel from one printing unit to the next, and it is here that most registration errors occur. There are slight differences in the substrate thickness, stability, lead (or gripper) edge, and a different rate of absorbing ink and water that cause slight mis-registration. Also, consider that most sheet-fed litho presses are imaging around 10,000 sheets per hour, and we are only talking about movements of one-thousandth of an inch. On most graphic pages, however, the naked eye can see a mis-registration of one-thousandth of an inch, so the process must be compensated for. The solution is generating trap lines to a standard for lithography of three one-thousandths of an inch. This trap line allowance in abutting colours allows for mis-registrations of two-thousandths of an inch that will not show on the final page.

Inkjet

Inkjet is the next imaging technology we must assess and compare. The print heads on all inkjet machines are mounted on the same unit travelling on the same track. Each ink is transferred one after the other and the substrate does not move after receiving each colour. It is like electrophotography in that mis-registration between print heads can be adjusted electronically, and once in register remain stable for multiple imaging runs on the same substrate. If the substrate is changed between imaging, the operator must recalibrate to bring all colours into registration, and ensure the placement of abutting colours is perfect and no compensation is needed. As a result, no trapping will be needed for most inkjet imaging processes.

Flexography

Flexography is the fourth imaging technology we need to assess. This technology has the most points where mis-registration can occur. The printed image must be raised on the plate to receive ink from an anilox roller that can deliver a metered amount of ink. The computer graphic must be reduced (or flexed) in only one direction around the plate cylinder. A separate printing plate is developed for each colour and mounted on a colour unit that includes an ink bath, anilox roller, doctor blade, and a plate cylinder. The substrate travels from one print unit to the next on a continuous web that is under variable amounts of tension. If a graphic has a lot of white space around it, the substrate can be pushed into the blank space and cause distortion and instability in the shape and pressure of the raised inked image on the substrate. Flexography is used to image the widest range of substrates, from plastic films to heavy corrugated cardboard. This process absolutely needs trap lines generated between abutting colours. Standard traps for some kinds of presses can be up to one point (1/72 of an inch, almost five times our standard litho trap). Graphic technicians need to pay particular attention to the colour, size, and shape of the trap lines as much as to the graphic elements. In most packaging manufacturing plants, there are pre-imaging operators that specialize in creating just the right trapping.

Let's examine some of the ways these traps can be generated. The simplest way is for a graphic designer to recognize that he or she is designing a logo for a package that will be imaged on a flexographic press that needs one-point trap lines generated for all abutting colours. The designer isolates the graphic shapes that touch and creates overprinting strokes on those graphic elements that contain all colours from both elements. That doesn't even sound simple! (And it's not.) It becomes even more complicated when the graphic is scaled to many different sizes on the same package or used on many different packages. So most designers do not pay attention to creating trap lines on the graphics they create and leave it to the manufacturer to create trapping for the specific documents on the specific presses they will be reproduced on.

There is specialized software that analyzes a document, determines where abutting colours are, and generates the tiny graphic lines as a final layer on top of the original graphic. This is done before the document goes to the RIP so it is raster-image processed at the same time as the rest of the document. Most RIPs process PDF files these days, and there are specialized plug-ins for Adobe Acrobat that will analyze a document, generate trap lines, and let an operator examine and edit the thicknesses, shape, and colour of those lines. It takes a skilled operator to examine the extra trap lines and determine if they are appropriate for the press they are going to be printed on. Press operators also need to determine the trap values of their inks. This refers to the ability of one printing ink to stick to another. Inks vary in viscosity depending on the density and types of pigments they are carrying. The trap characteristics and transparency of a printing ink are part of what determines the printing order in which they are applied to the substrate. For example, a process primary yellow ink is very transparent and will not stick (trap) well if printed on top of a heavy silver metallic ink. The metallic silver is thick and very opaque, so it will hide everything that it overprints. A graphics technician must generate trap lines for a graphic that has metallic silver abutting to a process yellow shape. The technician will increase (spread) the shape of the yellow graphic to go under the abutment to the silver. The silver shape will not be altered, and when it overprints, the yellow ink will stick to and hide the yellow trap line shape. The best analogy, we have heard is from a press person — the peanut butter sandwich analogy. We know the jelly sticks to the peanut butter and the peanut butter will not stick to the bread if the jelly is spread first. If a press person does not know the trap values of the inks, he or she can make as big a mess of the press sheet as an upside-down peanut butter and jelly sandwich makes on the front of your shirt! For this reason, trapping should be left to the specialists and is usually applied to a final PDF file before it is sent to a RIP. Ninety percent of trap lines for lithographic and flexographic imaging reproduction are generated automatically by specialized trapping software. Operators are trained to recognize shapes and colour combinations that will cause problems on the press. They will custom trap those documents with the Acrobat plug-ins we talked about earlier.

Special Consideration for Black

There is one trapping combination that should be considered and applied to all four imaging technologies. It is the way that black ink is handled in the document and applied on the imaging device. Most type is set in black ink, and much of it overprints coloured backgrounds. In all four imaging technologies, black is the strongest ink and hides most of what it overprints. It is still a transparent ink and most process black ink is more dark brown than the rich dark black we love to see in our documents. If the size of the black type or graphic is large enough, we will be able to see the black colour shift as it overprints stronger or weaker colours under it. Graphic designers should pay attention to setting whether black type or graphics overprint the background, or knock out the background to print a consistent black colour. A useful rule of thumb is that type above 18 points should be knocked out and boosted. Raise this threshold for very fine faces such as a script where larger point sizes can overprint, and reduce it for excessively heavy fonts like a slab serif. If the graphic is large enough, it should also be 'boosted' with other process colours.

The way we handle black ink or toner deserves special consideration in all four imaging technologies. Black is a supplemental colour to the three primary process colours. It is intended to print only when the other three colours are all present in some kind of balance. In all imaging technologies, we must watch that our **total ink coverage** does not approach 400%, or 100% of each ink overprinting the other inks in the same place. This is usually too much ink or toner for the substrate to absorb. As a result, it will not dry properly and will offset on the back of the next sheet, or bubble and flake off the media in the fuser. Therefore, we must pay attention to how our photographs are colour separated, and how we build black in our vector graphics.

Colour Separations

When colour separating photographs, we can build in an appropriate amount of GCR or UCR to give us the right total ink coverage for the imaging technology we are using for reproduction. UCR stands for under colour removal. It is applied to very dark shadow areas to remove equal amounts of cyan, magenta, and yellow (CMY) where they exceed the total ink limit. For example, in sheet-fed lithography, a typical total ink limit is 360. In areas that print 100% of all four colours, UCR will typically leave the full range black separation, and remove more and more CMY the deeper the shadow colour is. A typical grey balance in shadows may be 95% cyan, 85% magenta, and 85% yellow. Including a 100% black, that area would have a total ink coverage of 365. Other imaging technologies have different total ink limits, and these can vary greatly from one substrate to another within an imaging technology. An uncoated sheet will absorb more ink than a glossy coated sheet of paper and so will have a different total ink limit.

GCR stands for grey component replacement, and it is intended to help improve grey balance stability in a print run and save on ink costs. GCR can affect far more colours than UCR as it can be set to replace equal amounts of CMY with black all the way into the highlight greys. This is particularly useful in technologies like web offset newspaper production. Grey balance is quickly achieved in the **make-ready** process and easily maintained through the print run. Black ink for offset printing is significantly cheaper than the other process colours, so there are cost savings for long runs as well. GCR is used in photos and vector graphics produced for other imaging technologies as well. Any process where grey balance of equal values of the three primary colours could be an issue is a smart place to employ GCR.

You may be wondering how we can check the shadow areas of every photo we use. These GCR and UCR values can be set in ICC profiles by linking the shadow and neutral Lab values to the appropriate CMYK recipes. When the ICC profile is applied for a given output device, the shadows get the proper ink limits, and the grey tones get the prescribed amount of black, replacing CMY values.

Keylines

Black keylines, or outline frames for photos, are common in many documents. This is another place where a document should have trapping software applied for every imaging technology. Outline strokes on graphics can also have a ‘hairline’ setting, which asks the output device to make the thinnest line possible for the resolution of the device. This was intended for in-house studio printers where the resolution is 300 dpi — so the lines are 1/300th of an inch. But the same command sent to a 3,000 lspi plate-setter will generate a line 1/3000th of an inch, which is not visible to the naked eye. These commands must be distinguished in PostScript and replaced with lines at an appropriate resolution — trapping and **preflight** software will do this.

Knock outs

The use of solid black backgrounds is becoming more popular in documents, which can cause problems in reproduction with all imaging technologies. The first problem is with filling in details in the graphic shapes that are knocked out of the solid black background. Fine type serifs, small registered or trademark symbols, or the fine hairlines mentioned above will all fill in and be obliterated when imaged. The problem is multiplied when we boost the black colour by adding screened values of cyan, magenta, or yellow to the colour block. When white type or graphics knock out of these background panels, any slight mis-registration of any colour will leave a halo of that colour in the white type or graphic. This problem can also be solved with trapping software. Essentially, the trapping engine outlines all the white type with a small 'black only' stroke that knocks out the process colour that boosts the black, making the white type fatter in that colour separation. This 'reverse trapping' works well when applied to the four imaging technologies we have been examining: lithography, flexography, electrophotography, and inkjet.

5.5 Transparency

The biggest challenge in reproducing computer graphics on output devices in today's marketplace is dealing with transparency in graphic files. This truly emphasizes the importance of WYSIWYG in proofing for the graphic communications industry. We must first emphasize that page layout graphic software is not developed for producing documents for mechanical reproduction. This software prioritizes the creation of documents for viewing on electronic media; they are created on a computer screen for viewing on a computer screen. We have reviewed some of the issues with rasterizing vector shapes consistently, and reliably representing colour from one device to another. Viewing a graphic with three-dimensional transparent elements is significantly different on an illuminated medium where the light is transmitted compared to an opaque medium where the light is reflected. It is very hard to judge how the transparent effects will translate from one to another. There is room for the same kind of collaborative research in this realm, as there was in developing OpenType font architecture and ICC profiles.

The problems in WYSIWYG production for transparency fall in two categories. The first problem is setting expectations so a designer can make a reasonable prediction of how the document will look when imaged on a given media. The second problem is the sheer proportions of the computational processes we are asking of a RIP. PostScript is a three-dimensional language that allows a creator to stack and prioritize elements on a page. The RIP can literally 'throw away' raster data that is knocked out by graphic elements that completely cover the elements behind. If those elements have to show through the foreground elements by 20%, the RIP must hold much more raster data in physical memory addresses. Many times, data is lost if there are not enough addresses available for the computations, and this can change from one processing of the document to the next.

Designers can employ strategies at each level of document creation to manage these problems. The first strategy is to use layers well in document creation. By isolating different effects on separate layers, it becomes easier to isolate and edit the transparent effects when they don't produce the desired results in the final output. The layers can be included in a PDF file of the document, and this allows the possibility of relatively quick editing in PDF editing software closer to the output stage. This can be a completely different working style for some graphic artists. If we start with the premise that the computer screen representation of the document is NOT good WYSIWYG and will probably need editing, then we can justify working with layers more to isolate effects. We can organize design elements on layers after creation — when we are fine-tuning the effects. Usually, this is a good technique when creating many elements on several page dimensions. Designers can review their documents and decide if there are distinct dimensional levels, as page elements are pushed further into the background to pull other page elements forward. A simple example is a book cover for a retrospective, with pictures from four distinct decades. The photos and type from each decade can be set on distinct layers, and transparent values of 25%, 50%, 75%, and 100% can be set for each layer. The screen will render one version of the document, and the printer will render another. It is easier to fine-tune the four layer levels of transparency than to go back and set new transparency levels for dozens of individual page elements.

Another strategy that must be considered for processing multiple transparent page elements is allowing the page layout software to raster the page elements, so it sends raster data to the RIP. This technique treats the transparent elements, such as a photograph on the page, and allows the creator to choose the resolution of the raster. Care must be taken here to ensure overlapping vector elements will raster at the same resolution in the RIP. Let's say we have a type block that crosses a photo on the page, but it is transparent to let the photo show through the type. If we rasterize the transparent type at 300 ppi — the resolution of the photo — it will be significantly different from the raster of the vector type at the RIP, which might be 3,000 lspi for some plate-setters. The letter shape will be 10 times thicker over the photo, and that will be VERY noticeable if the type crosses the photo in the middle of the glyph. The solution is to make sure to raster the transparent type at 3,000 ppi to match the plate-setter raster. This makes the PDF file very large because it contains lots of raster data. But this solution is also a disadvantage because it does not allow late-stage editing of the transparent values in the PDF file. The advantage is that the transparency elements will have better WYSIWYG, process more consistently in multiple RIPs, and use less RIP resources in processing.

It is very important to be aware of the transparent elements you are creating in a document. It is not always apparent when using effects, plug-ins, or effects filters available in page layout software. Using a bevel or emboss effect, or a simple drop shadow, makes that page element use transparent routines in the RIP. Programs like Adobe InDesign let designers view all the transparent elements on a page. Designers should examine each one to decide if it should be rasterized before RIP-ing or at the RIP. This is a good point at which to decide if transparent elements can be grouped, or organized, on common layers. It is also a good point to decide how the transparent element contributes to the design, and how critical the level of transparency, or WYSIWG value, is in the overall design. In the retrospective book cover design referred to above, WYSIWYG is very important in communicating the message of the book and getting predictable results.

Transparent elements can be rasterized at the page layout stage, the PDF creation stage, and at the RIP stage for the final output device. Adobe Acrobat also has a tool to view transparent elements in a PDF file. It is important for a designer to compare the transparent elements in the PDF to those in the page layout software. The primary concern is that the elements rasterized in the PDF are no longer editable, so it is critical that the levels are right to create the desired overall effect. It is also important for a preflight operator to view the transparent elements in a PDF file to check what the RIP will have to process and to make sure the computational resources are available. If there are processing errors in the final output, they are most likely to occur in rendering the transparent objects. Viewing the transparent elements on a page in Acrobat should provide a mental checklist for the operator when she or he views the final output.

Communication Is Key

The graphic communications industry still has collaborative work to do to make the processing of transparent elements on a page more predictable and repeatable. It is important for designers to understand the problems they can be creating for a RIP, especially for output on an extremely high-resolution device like a plate-setter for waterless lithography. It is also important for operators who are managing documents with lots of transparency to be aware of the checkpoints in a document, and to know when there is not adequate WYSIWYG for the transparent elements on a page. Good questions for all stakeholders to ask when processing a document that relies on many transparent elements are:

- Where are the transparent elements?
- Did they process correctly?
- Is anything missing in the layers that should show through the transparency?
- Are there transparency values that can be adjusted to optimize the overall effect?

Let's review the primary tools for reproducing transparent page elements in a document. We can utilize layers in a document for setting common transparency values. We should view all transparent elements in a document before and after creating a PDF file. There are several stages to rasterizing the transparent elements. The earlier we rasterize them, the less editable the document becomes, and the more consistent the final output will be. We are creating a larger file to process when we rasterize transparent elements early. Much less computational resources are required at the RIP, and the more predictable our final output will be. When managing late-stage processing of transparency, we must be aware that what we are viewing on a computer screen is not necessarily a good representation of the final output. Graphic artists at all levels of production must pay attention to the transparent areas of a document to check for accuracy.

5.6 Imposition

Imposition of individual graphics page files serves two primary purposes. The first, and perhaps most important purpose, is to utilize media and manufacturing equipment with the most economic efficiencies. The second is to add what has historically been referred to as ‘furniture’ to the manufactured sheet to control processes. We will discuss both priorities for each primary imaging technology we are examining in this book. There is also a range of equipment capabilities for each technology that affects how documents are imposed. There are a few ways to impose the files either pre-RIP or post-RIP. We will also look at ways of imposing in graphic creation software and in specialized imposition software.

The first technology we will look at is electrophotography, where imposition is perhaps the most underutilized. Electrophotographic, or Xerox-type copiers are usually used for short-run lengths with demands for instant turnaround. Duplexing is the simplest type of imposition, but there are four choices for how to orient the back of a single page on the front. The duplexing style can be specified in the print driver, in the PDF file, or in the RIP. Most small printers will turn on duplexing, rather than image the fronts, turn the printed paper over the right way, and image the back of the sheet. Fewer will take the time to utilize the machine and media capabilities to step and repeat an image two up on a larger sheet to half the run time. Yet, as a manufacturing process, electrophotography is the slowest technology for image reproduction, and the most in need of saving time. There are simple rules of automation that can be programmed in a RIP to automatically impose if a run length is over 100 copies. For example, letter-size documents are the most often imaged on this type of equipment. If run lengths of more than 100 copies were imposed two up on a tabloid sheet, it would halve the run time and open up more imaging time on the machine. This introduces another process — cutting the sheets in half before final delivery. Management can determine how well the imaging engine run time is utilized and when it is efficient to have the same operator cut printed sheets in half. Making that management decision requires a knowledge of workflow options for efficiency. Those efficiencies are the primary purpose of implementing imposition software.

Using a ‘step and repeat’ or ‘duplexing’ imposition of single-page file is the simplest example of imposing files for electrophotographic workflows. More and more copiers have capabilities to fold and bind the finished product ‘inline’ in one continuous process. This process is driven by imposing the single-page files in the correct order as they are processed in the RIP, so they image in the proper spot on the media to fold, and bind together in the correct order.

Imposing page files for binding styles usually follows two types of machine capabilities: saddle stitching and perfect binding. **Saddle stitching** is a binding process that folds the media after it is imaged on both sides, stacks the printed folded sheets one inside the other, and applies staples to the spine of the book. The other dominant style of book binding built into copiers is **perfect binding**. Media is imaged on both sides and folded, but the folded sheets are stacked on top of each other, glue is applied, and a cover sheet is wrapped around the glued book to encase the spine. The pages have to be imposed in a completely different order on the printed sheets. The first and last sheets of a saddle-stitched book are imaged on the same sheet, whereas a perfect-bound book has the first pages imaged on the same sheet, and last pages on separate sheets of media.

There are many options for folding a sheet of substrate before binding it together. The options increase the larger a sheet is. An imposition must account for the preferences that are best practices for the specific machines involved. If we look at sheet-fed lithography first, we can identify some common best practices that can also apply to toner-based electrophotography and inkjet. We shall leave an examination of imposition for flexography to discuss nested dieline shapes for packaging applications.

Imposition standards are based on workflows for standard-sized pages, primarily letter-sized pages measuring 8½" x 11". We speak of *two up* devices that can generally image substrates up to a maximum size of 12" x 18" or 13" x 19." Two up devices can accommodate two letter-sized pages plus bleeds, grip, marks, and colour bars — sometimes referred to as furniture on an imposed sheet. These four elements all serve a purpose in page reproduction manufacturing that we shall define later. *Four up* devices generally accommodate imaging substrates up to 20" x 29" to image four letter-sized pages. Forty-inch devices are referred to as *eight up* and image on a maximum sheet size of 30" x 40", which can image eight letter-sized pages and the furniture mentioned above.

There are four common styles of imposition for eight up devices: sheet-wise, work and turn, work and tumble, and cut and stack.

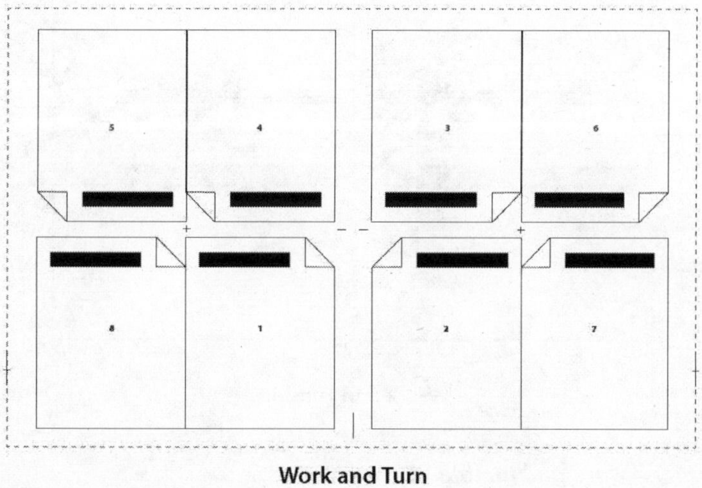

Figure 5.1 work and turn(a)

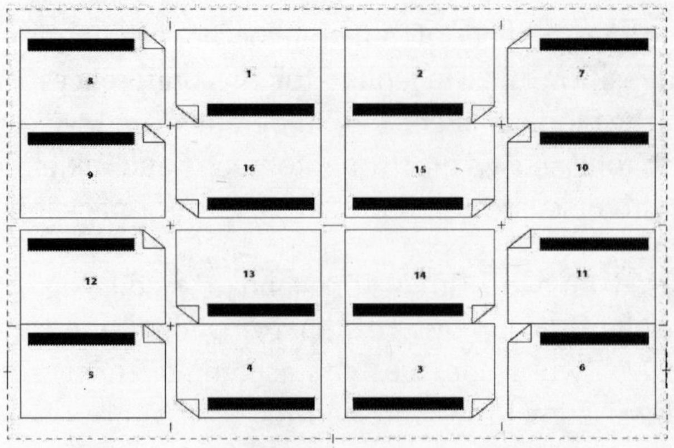

Work and Turn

Figure 5.2 work and turn(b)

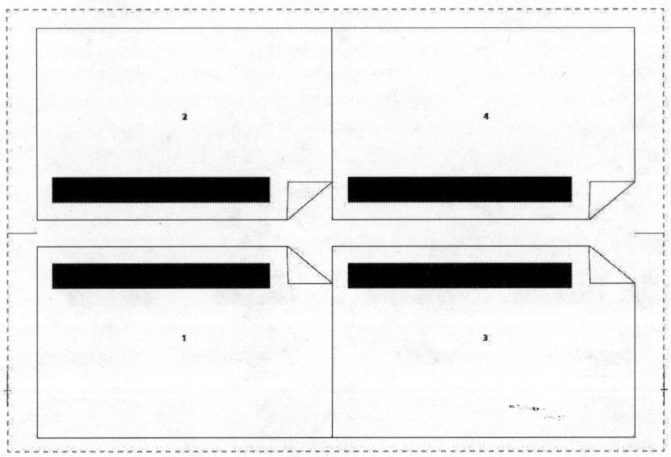

Work and Tumble

Figure 5.3 work and tumble

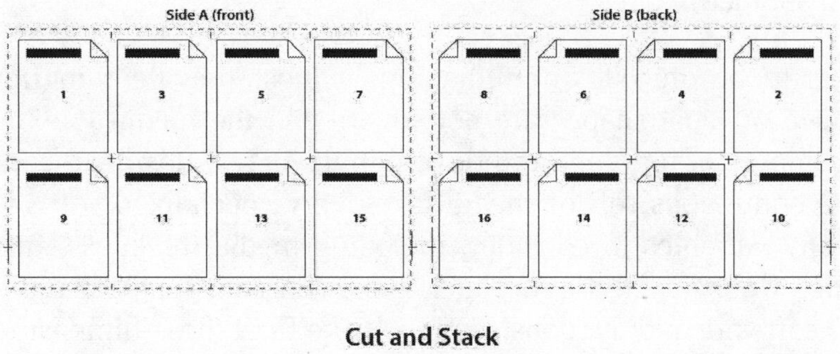

Figure 5.4 cut and stack

Sheet-wise impositions image the fronts of all pages on one side of the sheet and impose all the backs on a separate set of plates for a press run that will back up all the sheets. Work and turn imposes the fronts on one half of the sheet and the backs on the other half, with the axis running perpendicular to the grip of the sheet (see Figures 5.1 and 5.2). Work and tumble imposes all fronts on the bottom half of a sheet and backup images on the top half of the sheet (see Figure 5.3). The sheets are flipped halfway through the press run, with the axis parallel to the grip edge of the sheet. Cut and stack imposes the pages so full press sheets can be collated, and the collated sheets cut and stacked in order on top of each other to make a final book (see Figure 5.4).

Lithographic web offset presses have imposition orders that depend on how wide the web of paper is, and how many web rolls and half rolls will be brought together before folding on a first former, and cutting on a second former. There are many options for configuring a web-fed litho press, depending on the number of pages in a publication. Usually, the entire publication is printed and folded by running the stack of web paper together and folding it in half over a former.

Imposition has to account for creep and bottling when imposing for thicker publications. *Creep* pushes the image on a page closer in to the spine the further the page is toward the spine, by the width of the thickness of the publication at the stapled, spine edge. *Bottling* skews the image on a page to account for the skewing of web rolls of paper that are folded in very thick signatures. The thicker the folded signature of a bound book, the more skewing takes place, which should be accounted for in the 'Bottling' value in an imposition.

Imposition for inkjet mediums is usually done when the image is rasterized. The RIP will store the raster image and nest several raster images together to fill the dimensions of the media being imaged. This is usually set as an automated function in the RIP, and is tied to the size and cost of the media being used. When imaging very low resolution images on very low cost media, the manufacturer is usually more concerned with the speed of the machine than the utilization of the media. If an expensive media is being used, the automatic imposition will be utilized in the RIP to save media. Often inkjet images are not square, and the media will be die cut or cut with a router after imaging. The RIP can be set to impose the images so the shapes nest inside each other. This is usually outside of the automatic features for imposition in a RIP, and requires operator intervention. In that case, the imposition operator must know the die cutting or router processes very well to make sure the imaged media can be cut out even though it is nested with another image.

This nesting of images to be die cut after imaging is most prevalent in flexographic printing for packaging. Most package or label shapes are not square and the media is expensive. The imposition function becomes very important for preparing flexographic plates. Nesting the die cut shapes for several packages together on a continuous roll of media takes very specialized software and a highly skilled operator. There are many variables to consider, including media thickness, ink coverage, die shapes, glue releases, and image floor on the flexo plate. Flexo imaging for packaging generally takes more understanding of CAD software and the construction of the final three-dimensional product. Imposition operators must know the structural requirements as well as the press limitations to nest together several package images on the same press run.

The final consideration for all impositions in all imaging technologies is the computer resource requirements for the RIP. We usually require an imaging engine to raster a single document, and proof it one page at a time through a proofing device. When we impose the same document with many other pages in completely different orientations, sometimes RIP processing errors can occur. Fonts drop out, and more commonly, transparent elements do not process properly. This is another checkpoint to make sure the imposed image matches the proof of the single page. It is essential to discuss preflighting for print at this point to establish where the routine checkpoints in document processing should be.

Media Attributions

- work and turn 01 © Ken Jeffrey
- work and turn 02 © Ken Jeffrey
- work and tumble © Ken Jeffrey
- cut and stack-03 © Ken Jeffrey

5.7 Preflight

We have covered quite a few parameters that must be considered when preparing a computer graphic for manufactured image reproduction. The parameters shift with different substrates and imaging technologies. The task of checking a computer graphic document in preparation for the manufacturing process is called preflight. Most graphics are created by designers who are working separately from the manufacturer. In some cases, preflight preparation is the responsibility of the designer, or graphics creator, and in some cases, it is the responsibility of the manufacturer. Some manufacturers charge extra if they have to correct a graphics file that is not prepared properly for their imaging process. Most do not charge extra for preflighting, trapping, or imposing a file for their imaging process. Problems occur when all parties believe a file is prepared properly, but it causes errors in the RIP process. A poor font, improper colour separations, and transparency settings that drop out layers on a page are problems that occur most often. This is when time, materials, and money are wasted, and critical media campaign deadlines are missed. Preflight tries to catch the problems before they reach the RIP.

Designers or graphics creators can purchase separate preflight software that will generate reports about a PDF or PostScript file before they submit it to a manufacturer. The most popular dedicated preflight software is from Markzware and is called FlightCheck. There are also a few other companies that are popular in the marketplace. Enfocus bundles its preflight software with a suite of PDF editing tools called Pitstop. The Adobe Creative Suite has preflight functions built into its software suite. Adobe InDesign is the page layout software of choice for creating multi-page documents such as brochures, pamphlets , or books. The preflight module in InDesign will generate a report that can be included with the packaged contents a designer should provide to a manufacturer. The report will list important information about the InDesign document, such as that found in the list below. Adobe Illustrator also has a built-in preflight tool, and Adobe Acrobat has preflight tools that designers should use to analyze their PDF files before submitting them to a RIP.

Various industries have set PDF standards. The magazine publishing industry, for example, developed a PDF/X standard to ensure PDF/X files can be written only if they meet a set of specifications that are common for lithographic magazine production. Other manufacturing processes adopted the standards if they were appropriate for their imaging technology and PDF workflows.
Most preflight software checks for the following elements in an electronic document:

- File format
- Colour management
- Fonts
- Spot colour handling
- Page structure
- Thin lines
- Black overprint

- Trapping

5.8 Summary

This chapter has looked at computer graphic creation through the lens of a manufacturer that must reproduce the electronic image on a substrate. The image must be processed through a RIP that drives a laser, or other imaging technology, to transfer pigments to that substrate. There are unique variables that must be considered in preparing the computer graphic for the reproduction process. We have explored routines for processing vector data such as fonts through a RIP, spot colour handling, trapping, and imposition. The next chapter will look at each of the imaging technologies in more depth.

Questions to consider after completing this chapter:

1. Describe six pre-imaging file analysis processes that should be considered when developing a computer graphic for reproduction manufacture.
2. Describe four major imaging technologies that utilize computer graphics to image on different substrates.
3. Describe the difference between raster data and vector data when creating a computer graphic file.
4. Compare the raster resolution of the data for a typical lithographic plate-setter compared to the resolution of a typical inkjet device.
5. How many addressable values can be recorded in an eight-bit byte of computer data?
6. What does the acronym WYSIWYG stand for?
7. How many kerning pairs are present in a 'good' font file?
8. What colour matching library has been developed exclusively for process colour printing inks (CMYK)?
9. What two printing processes must have trapping applied to computer graphics files before making printing plates?
10. What can a page layout artist do to a graphics file if the transparent elements on the page are dropping out or not processing in the RIP?

References

Adobe Systems Incorporated. (1997a). *Adobe postscript*. Retrieved from https://www.adobe.com/products/postscript/pdfs/PostScriptRIPBrochure.pdf

Adobe Systems Incorporated. (1997b). *Adobe postscript printing primer*. Retrieved from https://www.adobe.com/products/postscript/pdfs/psprintprime.pdf

Adobe Systems Incorporated. (2002). *How to trap using Adobe trapping technologies*. Retrieved from https://www.adobe.com/studio/print/pdf/trapping.pdf

Adobe Systems Incorporated. (2004). *A designer's guide to transparency for print output*. Retrieved from http://www.ghpmedia.com/wp-content/uploads/2011/05/Transparency_DesignGuide.pdf

Adobe Systems Incorporated. (2015). *Adobe OpenType*. Retrieved from http://www.adobe.com/products/type/opentype.html

Darlow, A. (2009). Raster Image Processors: RIPs 101. *Professional Photographer*. Retrieved from http://www.ppmag.com/web-exclusives/2009/03/raster-image-processors-rips-1-1.html

Electronics for Imaging. (2011). Fiery servers: The easiest way to get the right color every time. *Electronics for Imaging*. Retrieved from http://www.efi.com/library/efi/documents/476/efi_fiery_spot_on_wp_en_us.pdf

Enfocus BVBA. (2015). *PitStop Pro 13 reference guide*. Retrieved from http://www.enfocus.com/manuals/ReferenceGuide/PP/13/enUS/home.html

Flexographic Technical Association. (n.d.). *First 4.0 supplemental flexographic printing design guide.* Retrieved from http://flexography.org/wp-content/uploads/2013/11/FFTA-FIRST-4.0-Design-Guide.pdf

Gaultney, V., Hosken, M., & Ward, A. (2003). *An introduction to TrueType fonts: A look inside the TTF format*. Retrieved from http://scripts.sil.org/cms/scripts/page.php?site_id=nrsi&id=iws-chapter08

Liquori, E. (2011). *Spot or process color? Essential guidelines*. Retrieved from http://www.instantshift.com/2011/04/29/spot-or-process-color-essential-guidelines/

McCue, C. (2007). *Real world print production*. Berkeley, CA: Peachpit Press.

Muscolino, H., Machado, A., & Corr, C. (2013). Mercury RIP architecture: Adobe's print framework for a one-to-one digital age. *IDC*. Retrieved from http://wwwimages.adobe.com/content/dam/Adobe/en/products/pdfprintengine/pdfs/IDC-WhitePaper-AdobeMercury.pdf

Suggested Readings

Adobe Systems (Ed.). (1990). *Adobe type 1 font format*. Reading, MA: Addison-Wesley Pub. Co.

Adobe Systems Incorporated. (2015). *Adobe PDF Library SDK*. Retrieved from http://www.adobe.com/devnet/pdf/library.html

Adobe Systems Incorporated. (2015). *Font formats*. Retrieved from http://www.adobe.com/products/type/adobe-type-references-tips/font-formats.html

Adobe Systems Incorporated. (2015). *OpenType fonts information.* Retrieved from http://www.adobe.com/content/dotcom/en/products/type/opentype/opentype-fonts-information.html

Adobe Systems Incorporated. (2015). *Transparency flattening*. Retrieved from https://helpx.adobe.com/acrobat/using/transparency-flattening-acrobat-pro.html

Adobe Systems Incorporated. (2015). *Using and creating swatches*. Retrieved from https://helpx.adobe.com/illustrator/using/using-creating-swatches.html

LucidDream Software. (2008). *Trapping tips*. Retrieved from http://www.trapping.org/tips.html

Markzware. (2015). Markzware TV – YouTube Channel. Retrieved from https://www.youtube.com/user/markzwareTV

Montax Imposer. (n.d.). *Imposition types*. Retrieved from http://www.montax-imposer.com/description/imposition-types

Prepressure.com. (n.d.). *Transparency in PDF files*. Retrieved from http://www.prepressure.com/pdf/basics/transparency

TotalFlow MR. (2012). *Imposition for creating a bound book*. Retrieved from http://support.ricoh.com/bb_v1oi/pub_e/oi_view/0001044/0001044134/view/users/int/0085.htm

Chapter 6. Imaging

6.1 Introduction

Learning Objectives

- Describe digital printing methods and their differences
- List the various inks used in inkjet printing and their characteristics
- Identify the key components of electrophotography
- Explain the seven steps of the electrophotographic process
- Describe the differences between toner types and how they affect imaging
- Evaluate the suitability of a paper for a project based on its characteristics
- Convert between paper basis weights and grammage
- Describe the key differences between page description languages
- Acknowledge the historical significance of Postscript in desktop publishing
- Explain the differences between PDF/X versions
- Describe the function of a RIP in a DFE
- Explain why calibration is critical in electrophotography
- Describe the key component in variable data printing
- Identify key benefits of open standard VDP formats

Digital printing can be defined as the reproduction of an image or document onto a substrate, directly from an electronic file, without the use of a fixed image plate. Traditional printing transfers an image permanently onto a fixed image plate, whereas digital printing transfers the image temporarily onto a photoconductive cylinder, called a drum, or directly onto the substrate itself. Printing in this manner provides some unique capabilities that sets it apart from traditional print methods. There is virtually no set-up or make ready, finishing tasks can be accomplished inline, and each sheet can have unique content, which makes this printing method ideal for publication printing, short print runs, or highly dynamic content.

The two most common digital printing methods in use today are electrophotographic (toner based) and inkjet (ink based). Both technologies are used in a wide range of printing devices from small desktop printers to large high-volume, high-speed digital presses. The term *digital press* is often used to describe commercial digital printers. In the past, speed was the determining factor of this designation. Today, we have specific criteria published by Idealliance, a not-for-profit member organization that develops standards and best practices for the digital media supply chain (Idealliance, n.d.). Apart from speed, colour accuracy to meet a specification and consistency over long print runs are key parts of Idealliance's certification process.

For the purposes of this text, we will focus on digital printers and presses used in commercial printing rather than on consumer or office printers.

6.2 Inkjet

Inkjet printing is a type of digital imaging where drops of ink are jetted onto the substrate in a very precise pattern from a nozzle. This nozzle, also called the print head, is required to be very precise and accurate, which is a challenge when you consider that the goal is to get many thousands of tiny drops of ink to land exactly where needed on the printed surface. Over time, inkjet technology has become more advanced, allowing greater resolution, more accurate colour, and overall, finer visual fidelity to the original. The most common method of inkjet printing for commercial purposes is called drop-on-demand (DOD). This type of inkjet print head only fires each individual droplet of ink when needed (on demand) and comes in two types, thermal or piezoelectric (see Figure 6.1). Accuracy in DOD inkjet printing is achieved by keeping the print head close to the surface being printed (substrate) as the velocity of the jetted ink is low.

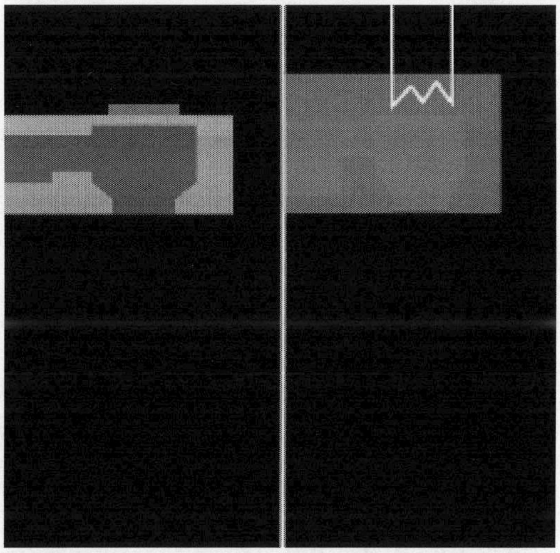

Figure 6.1 Piezoelectric head on the left, thermal on the right

Thermal Inkjet

In a thermal print head, each nozzle contains a special reservoir that is bounded by a heating element. When current is passed through the heating element, it causes the ink to expand rapidly, ejecting out of the nozzle to land on the substrate in a given position. The print head is made up of a matrix of many of these chambers, and each print head is connected to a different colour of ink. As the ejected ink leaves the chamber, fresh ink is drawn into the reservoir by surface tension and the vacuum created by the previous drop of ink leaving.

Thermal inkjet is most common in household and consumer grade inkjet printers. A major benefit to using thermal printhead technology is the relatively inexpensive print head. Since each colour printed requires a separate print head, and some print devices can contain eight or more colours of ink, thermal technology keeps the initial cost of the device low and reduces replacement costs when a print head fails, or is damaged.

Piezoelectric Inkjet

Piezoelectric (piezo) print heads also use a tiny reservoir to hold a droplet of ink. However, unlike thermal printheads, piezo heads contain a small flexible membrane, or diaphragm, that moves up and down to squirt the ink out of the print nozzle. The pressure caused by the flexing of the piezo material is very precise, allowing a drop, or multiple drops, to strike the substrate accurately. Similar to thermal, the print head is made up of a matrix of a number of these individual nozzles. And by using multiple print heads, multiple colours are possible.

Piezoelectric is more common in commercial and large-format printing applications, although there are a few consumer grades of printers that use piezo as well. Piezo is more accurate, and because the ink in the chamber doesn't have to be vaporized to form the droplets of ink, piezo can print with a wider variety of inks such as aqueous, ultraviolet, and latex.

Types of Ink

Inkjet printing has become more advanced not only in the mechanics of how the print heads work, but also in the variety and usage of different types of ink. Below are some common types of ink and a brief explanation of how they might be used.

Aqueous Ink

Aqueous ink, as discussed earlier, is a water-based ink. This type of ink is used in consumer printers using thermal technology, but can also be used in commercial piezo printers as well. Aqueous is well suited to thermal technology because the formulation of the ink allows it to vaporize in the print head for expulsion onto the paper. The water component of the ink, however, also contributes to its greatest drawback: the susceptibility of the finished printed piece to run or smear if it gets wet. Many users of desktop printers in their homes have been disappointed when they take their printed pages outside in the rain. Even a few drops of water can cause the ink to run and bleed into the paper.

In commercial uses, aqueous inkjet is well known for colour fidelity and quality, but the finished piece has to be protected from moisture. These types of print products would most likely only be used indoors, mounted behind glass, or with a laminated plastic layer on top. There are water-resistant coatings that can be sprayed onto a finished product, but even then, you would not want to leave it outside for an extended period of time. Aqueous ink is a common choice for art prints.

Ultraviolet Inkjet

Ultraviolet (UV) ink is a type of **energy-cured ink** that stays wet until it is bombarded with ultraviolet radiation. This UV radiation is commonly projected onto the freshly printed surface by means of a special high-intensity light bulb. Once the UV rays hit the ink, a special molecular process is triggered, causing the chains of molecules in the ink to bond and solidify instantly. UV ink does not dry from exposure to air, nor from heat. Once the UV ink has been cured, however, it is very solid and quite durable.

For commercial use, UV inks tend to be popular for outdoor uses such as banners and signage. Indoor signage is commonly printed using UV as well because of its durability and rub resistance. Since UV inks dry instantly, they can be removed from the printer and handled much sooner. UV inks sit mostly on top of the surface of the substrate, and because of their solid bond are more prone to cracking if bent or folded. UV is not a good choice of ink where flexibility of the substrate is required.

Latex Inkjet

Latex ink is a newer formulation that has exploded onto the inkjet printing scene in the last few years. Latex inks are water based and cure primarily through heat, but more importantly, they are not subject to moisture damage once cured. This is because the pigment is carried by the latex molecules, and once the latex has bonded to the substrate, the pigment stays intact. Latex printed products dry immediately and are ready to use as soon as they come off the print device.

Latex inks are used in many commercial applications, particularly where outdoor durability and flexibility are needed. One of the many common uses of latex inkjet printing is in imaging car wraps. A car wrap is a flexible adhesive material that is printed flat, then stretched or wrapped around the contours of a vehicle, usually for marketing or advertising purposes. Figure I.1 in the introduction of this textbook shows an example of a car wrap. Because of this flexibility, latex printed signage can also be adhered to rougher surfaces such as wood or brick. The popularity of latex can be attributed to a previously popular inkjet formulation that is solvent based.

Solvent Inkjet

Because of the rise in popularity of latex ink over the last few years, there has been a great decline in the use of solvent inkjet inks. Formerly, this was the type of ink needed for flexible, durable printing. Solvent inks are formulated using solvent as a carrier for the pigment, and as the solvent dries, the pigment remains bonded to the substrate. A big concern for the use of solvent-based printing is the release of volatile organic compounds, or VOCs. These VOCs are released into the atmosphere during the printing and drying of solvent prints, and have to be vented outdoors so as not to pollute the workspace. Even newer eco-friendly inks still release VOCs, albeit at a lower level. Some areas have environmental laws that restrict the release of pollutants into the air (United States Environmental Protection Agency, 2000). Customers often complain about the smell of solvent prints, particularly when used indoors. Because of this, solvent inkjet is primarily chosen for outdoor uses such as large-format signage, banners, and car wraps. Solvent can be very economical, and while the quality isn't as sharp as UV or aqueous, it is excellent for very large projects that will be viewed from even a moderate distance. Pressure on the solvent ink market comes because most of these uses can now be achieved with latex inks as well, and the industry has seen a divergence between companies that still use solvent or eco-solvent inks and those that are switching to latex.

Media Attributions

- Micro_Piezo_Comparison © Javachan is licensed under a CC BY-SA (Attribution ShareAlike) license

6.3 Electrophotography

Electrophotography (also known as xerography) is a complex process commonly used in copiers and faxes, as well as in digital printers. It is an imaging technology that takes a digital file and utilizes a photoreceptor, light source, electrostatic principles, and toner to produce the printed output. Before this process was used for digital printing, it was extensively used in analog copiers where a lamp illuminated the page being copied, and then a series of mirrors reflected the page directly onto the surface of a drum. Digital copiers replaced the direct light path with a sensor that converts the analog image into digital information, then a laser or an **LED** array writes the image onto the drum. Many digital printers today are based on the same platform as digital copiers. The technology has seen many improvements over the years, but the electrophotographic process at its core remains relatively unchanged.

Photoreceptor

The photoreceptor is commonly referred to as a drum. It is a cylinder coated with a material that becomes conductive when exposed to light. Areas that are not exposed have a high resistance which allows these areas to hold the electrostatic charge necessary for the process.

Light Source

Light sources used in digital printing include LED arrays or, more commonly, lasers. VCSEL (vertical cavity surface emitting laser) is an advanced type of laser used in the most current digital presses in the market. A VCSEL array can position its beam with high accuracy (addressability) for optimal clarity, resolution, and image positioning. This makes it ideally suited for a digital press.

Electrostatic Principles

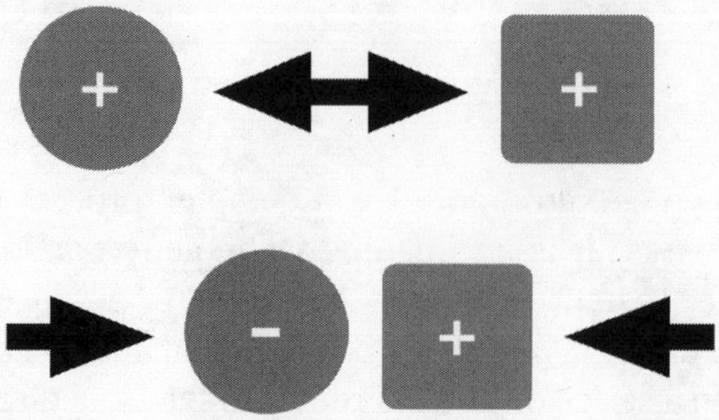

Figure 6.2 Like charges repel each other while opposite charges are attracted

To understand electrophotography, we must first understand some basic electrostatic principles. When certain materials come in contact then separate from each other, these materials can become electrically charged. Rubbing these materials together can increase this effect. This is called the **triboelectric effect.** Static electricity buildup on your clothes in a dryer or from rubbing a balloon on your hair are examples of the triboelectric effect. Charges can have either a positive or negative polarity. Like charges repel each other while opposite charges are attracted, in much the same way as the polarities in magnets (see Figure 6.2).

These properties are at the core of the technology and are utilized in almost every stage of the digital imaging process.

Toner Basics

Toner is a very fine, dry powder medium used in the electrophotographic or xerographic process. It is composed primarily of a resin and includes pigment, wax, and process-enhancing additives. The term *xerography,* in fact, is derived from the Greek words *xeros,* 'dry' and *graphia,* 'writing,' reflecting how toner rather than ink is used in the imaging process. Toner particles become electrically charged when stirred or agitated through a triboelectric effect. The composition of the toner not only contributes to its imaging characteristics but to its ability to maintain and control its charge properties. The shape of the toner also is a factor in its charging capability. This electrical charge is what allows the toner to be precisely manipulated throughout the process.

There are two basic types of toner production, pulverized and chemical (Figure 6.3). Pulverized toner was commonly used in earlier digital printers and is manufactured by successive compound mixing and grinding steps until the desired consistency and size is achieved. The resulting toner particles are irregular in size and shape and typically average around 6.2 to 10.2 microns in size. Pulverized toner produces good results, up to 600 dpi resolution; however, a consistent size and shape along with a smaller particle size is required to produce better clarity and detail at higher resolutions.

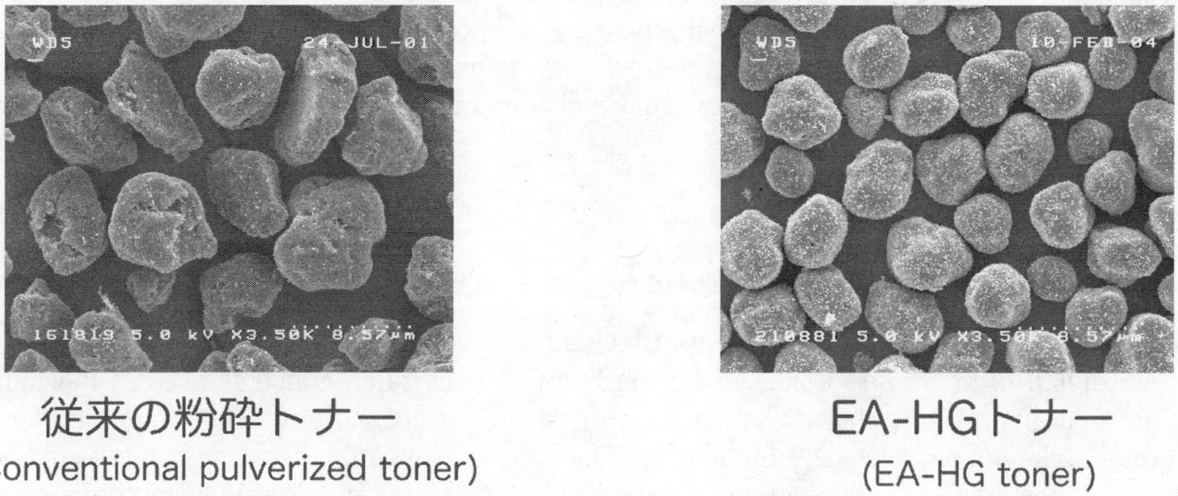

Figure 6.3 Two basic types of toner production

Chemical toners were introduced later to overcome those limitations and are in common use today. Each manufacturer has its own process for creating this type of toner and unique names as well. Xerox's EA toner, Ricoh's PxP toner, and Konica Minolta's Simitri toner are all examples of chemical toners. As the name suggests, chemical toners are created through a process of building or 'growing' the particle chemically. This process allows for the precise control of the shape and size of the toner particle (under 5 microns in some cases), resulting in higher definition and resolution capabilities. Resolutions of 1,200 dpi and 2,400 dpi are possible largely due to the use of this type of toner. Other benefits include much lower energy consumption, both in the manufacturing process and printing process, as well as narrower particle size and charge distributions.

Here is a YouTube video of how chemical toner is made: https://youtu.be/852TWDP61T4

Dry toner comes in two forms: mono component and dual component. Both rely on magnetic iron or iron oxide particles to 'hold' the charged toner on a magnetic roller. Mono component toners incorporate the magnetic material in the composition of the toner particle itself where dual component toners have the magnetic material mixed together with the toner but as separate components. This mixture is called developer.

ElectroInk

ElectroInk is a unique form of toner used in HP Indigo digital presses. The toner comes in the form of a paste and is mixed internally in the press with imaging oil, a lightweight petroleum distillate. This type of toner is considered a liquid toner as the particles are suspended in the liquid imaging oil, but still uses an electrophotographic process for imaging. One of the important advantages of this type of toner is its particle size. ElectroInk toner particles are 1 to 2 microns, significantly smaller than the smallest dry toner particle. At this size, a dry toner would become airborne and would be very difficult to control. The toner and oil suspension achieves higher resolutions, uniform gloss, sharp image edges, and very thin image layers. A thin image layer allows the toner to conform to the surface of the substrate, producing a consistent look between imaged and non-imaged areas. A drawback of this toner, however, is that substrates may need to be pre-treated in order for the toner to adhere properly. There are substrates available for use specifically on HP Indigo digital presses, but typically these are more expensive or may not be compatible with other printing methods. Some Indigo presses are equipped with a pre-treating station that expands substrate compatibility extensively and even surpasses that of other forms of digital printing.

Nanography

Nanography is a very new and exciting print technology currently in development by the creator of the Indigo digital press, Benny Landa. It borrows some of the same concepts used in the Indigo but with a different approach to the implementation of these. The technology centres around NanoInk, a breakthrough ink with pigment sizes in the tens of nanometers. In comparison, pigments found in good-quality offset inks are in the 500 nanometre range. Colorants intensify and ink density increases at this microscopic level, thereby expanding the ink's colour gamut considerably. The ink uses water as a carrier instead of imaging oil making it more cost effective and eco-friendly. Billions of ink droplets are jetted onto a heated blanket, not directly onto the substrate as in inkjet printing. The ink spreads uniformly on the blanket and the water quickly evaporates leaving only an ultra-thin (approximately 500 nanometres), dry polymeric film. This film transfers completely onto the substrate on contact and produces a tough, abrasion-resistant image. This print technology can be used with almost any substrate without pre-treatment and, due to its minuscule film thickness, does not interfere with the finish. Whether high gloss or matte, the ink finish matches that of the substrate. Although the technology is poised to revolutionize the print industry, the first press to use it is currently in beta testing. You can find the latest news and more information on nanography on this webpage: http://www.landanano.com/nanography

Media Attributions

- Electrostatic principles © Roberto Medeiros
- EA-HG_toner © Fuji Xerox Co., Ltd

6.4 Electrophotographic Process

The electrophotographic process consists of seven stages (see Figure 6.4). For the purpose of this text, we will be describing the process using a negatively charged dry toner. The process is the same for a positive toner except the polarity would be reversed in each stage.

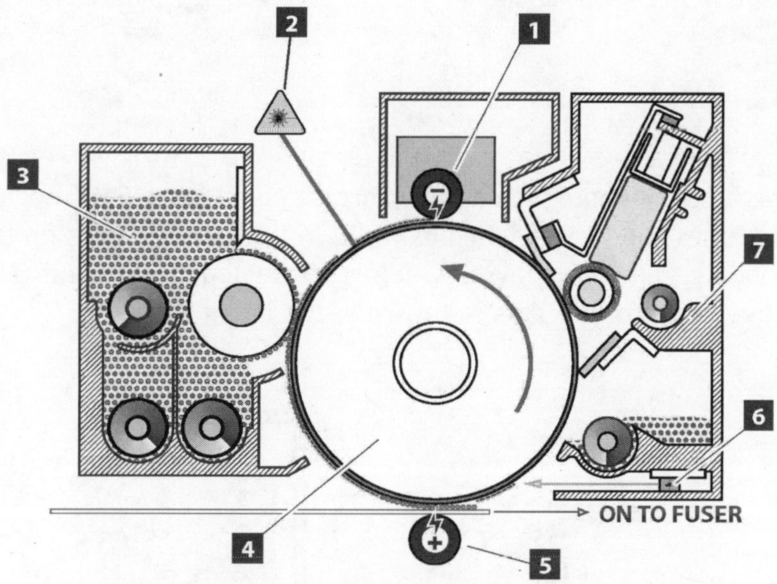

Electrophotographic Imaging System

1	Charging Roller	5	Transfer Roller
2	Exposure Laser	6	Quenching LED Array
3	Developer	7	Cleaning Unit
4	Photoconductor		

Figure 6.4 Electrophotographic Imaging System

Charging

In the first stage, a high negative voltage of approximately -900 volts is provided to a charge roller (see Figure 6.5). The voltage used varies by manufacturer and model. The charge roller applies a uniform layer of negative charge to the surface of the drum. The resistivity of the unexposed photosensitive drum coating allows the charge to remain on the surface.

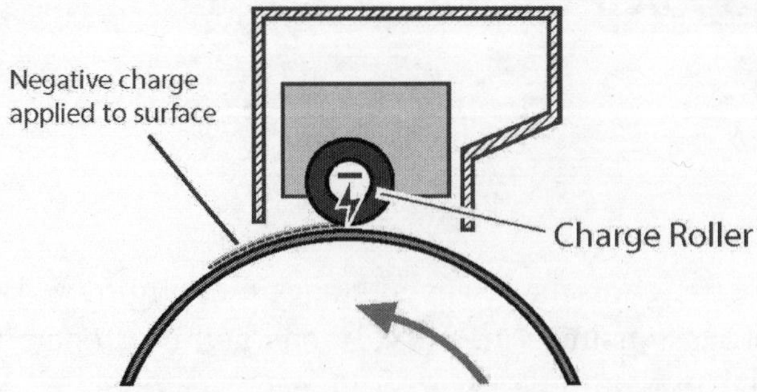

Figure 6.5 Charge roller

Exposure

A laser is used to write the image onto the charged surface (see Figure 6.6). Because the photosensitive coating on the drum becomes conductive when exposed to light, the charges on the surface of the drum exposed to the laser conduct to the base layer, which is connected to a ground. The result is a near zero volt image and a negative background. This is known as the latent image.

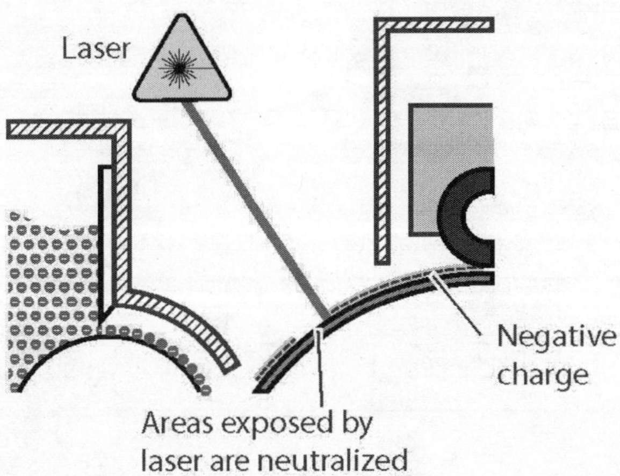

Figure 6.6 Exposure

Development

Many digital printers and presses use a dual component development system (see Figure 6.7). The developer is a mixture of non-magnetic toner and a magnetic carrier. As the developer is stirred and the particles rub up against each other, a triboelectric charge is generated between the them. The toner becomes negatively charged while the carrier becomes positive. The opposite charges cause the toner to be attracted to the carrier. A magnetic development roller holds the mostly iron carrier in alignment with magnetic lines of force forming a magnetic brush. This magnetic brush in turn 'carries' the attracted toner to the surface of the drum. A high negative bias is applied to the development roller repelling the toner onto the drum. The toner is attracted to the areas of the drum exposed by the laser, which, being close to zero volts, is much more positive than the negatively charged toner. In this way, the latent image is developed. As the carrier remains on the development roller, it continues to attract toner from the hopper to maintain the optimal concentration on the magnetic brush.

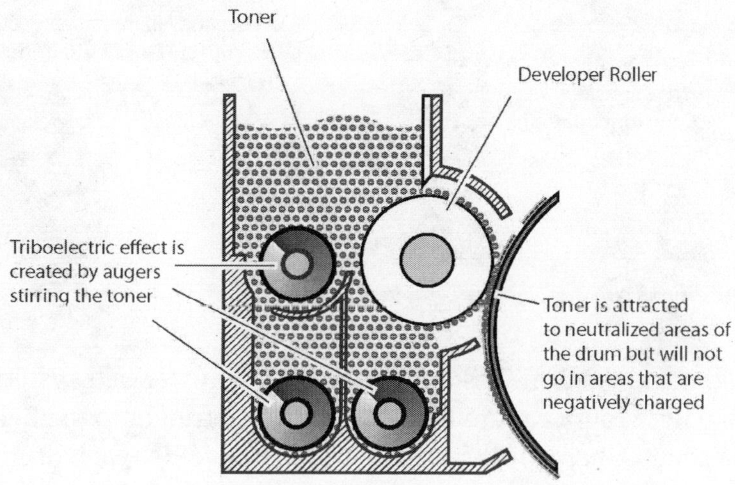

Figure 6.7 Development

Transfer

A sheet of paper or substrate passes between the drum and a transfer charge roller that has a high positive voltage applied to it (see Figure 6.8). The negatively charged toner of the developed latent image on the drum is attracted to the more positive transfer roller and adheres to the sheet in-between. The charge applied to the back of the sheet causes the paper to cling to the drum. A high negative voltage is applied to a discharge plate immediately after the transfer charge roller to aid in the separation of the sheet from the drum. The curvature of the drum along with the weight and rigidity of the sheet also aid in the separation.

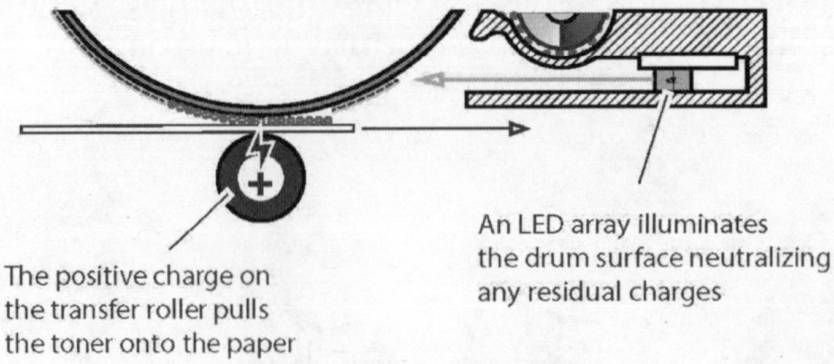

Figure 6.8 Transfer

A more advanced method of transfer utilizes an intermediate transfer belt system. This is most common on colour digital presses where four or more colours are transferred onto the belt before transferring the complete image onto the sheet. Charge rollers beneath the belt, under each drum, pull off the developed **latent images** of each separation directly onto the belt. In the transfer stage, a transfer charge roller beneath the belt applies a negative charge to push the toner onto the sheet. A second roller, directly beneath the first on the other side of the belt, applies pressure keeping the paper in contact with the belt and aiding in transfer for more textured stocks. The lower roller may have a small positive charge applied to it or may be grounded. Some systems can also alternate the charge applied to the transfer charge roller to further aid toner application onto textured substrates.

After this stage, the sheet moves on to fusing where the toner permanently adheres to the substrate. The next two stages described below are post-imaging steps that are necessary to prepare the drum surface for the next print cycle.

Cleaning

After the transfer stage, some toner may be left behind on the surface of the drum. If left there, the background of each successive print would slowly become darker and dirtier. To prevent this, a cleaning blade removes any residual toner from the drum's surface (see Figure 6.9). Some systems will recycle this toner back to the developing unit, but mostly the waste toner is collected in a container for disposal.

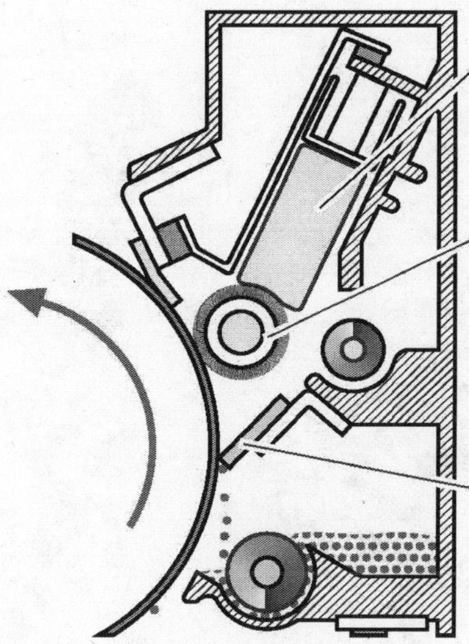

Figure 6.9 Cleaning

Erasing

In this stage, an LED array exposes the length of the drum, bringing this area of the drum to near zero volts. This prepares the drum surface for the charging stage of the next print cycle.

Fusing

This is the final stage in the electophotographic process. The fusing mechanism, or *fuser,* consists of a heat roller, a pressure roller, and cleaning mechanism (see Figure 6.10). Toner is composed mostly of resin. When the toner is heated by the heat roller and pressure applied by the complement pressure roller, it melts and is pressed into the fibres of the sheet. The toner is never absorbed by the paper or substrate but rather is bonded to the surface. A negative charge is applied to the heat roller or belt to prevent the toner from being attracted to it and the cleaning section removes any toner or other contaminates that may have remained on the heat roller. Heat may also be applied to the pressure roller (at a much lower temperature) to prevent the sheet from curling.

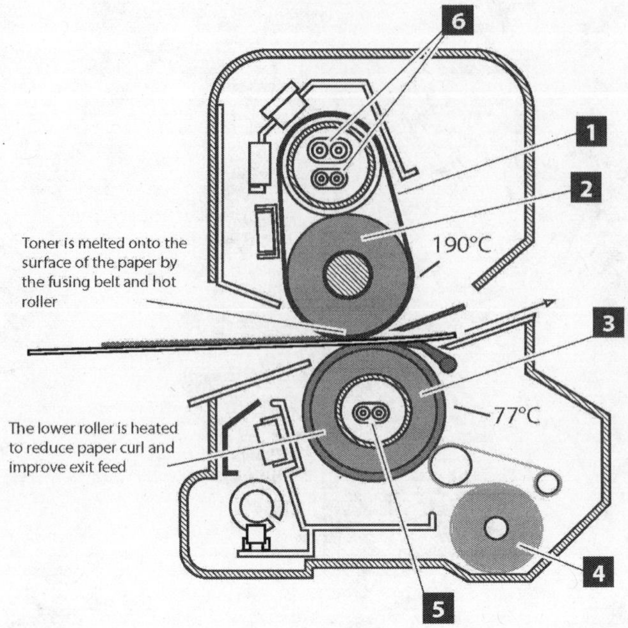

Fuser

1	Fusing Belt	4	Cleaning Belt
2	Hot Roller	5	Lower Heater
3	Pressure Roller	6	Upper Heaters

Figure 6.10 Fusing

Along with the transfer stage, fusing can be greatly affected by the paper or substrate used. The thicker and heavier the sheet, the more heat it absorbs. Because of this, these sheets require higher temperatures so there is sufficient heat remaining to melt the toner. Insufficient heat can cause the toner to scratch off easily or not bond at all. Too much heat can cause moisture in the substrate to evaporate quickly and get trapped beneath the toner causing tiny bubbles that prevent the toner from sticking wherever they occur. This issue is seen more on thinner stocks that do not absorb as much heat. Too much heat can also cause toner residue to stick to the heater roller and deposit it on subsequent sheets.

The heat roller can heat up quite quickly but may take much longer to cool down. This can cause delays in producing work that switches between different paper weights. To combat this, some devices use a thin belt that can be both heated and cooled quickly in place of the heater roller. In some cases, a cooling mechanism is also employed further mitigating the cooling lag.

Media Attributions

- EP Imaging System – Complete © Roberto Medeiros
- EP Imaging System – Charging © Roberto Medeiros)
- EP Imaging System – Development © Roberto Medeiros
- EP Imaging System – Transfer © Roberto Medeiros

- EP Imaging System – Cleaning © Roberto Medeiros
- EP Imaging System – Fusing © Roberto Medeiros

6.5 Paper Basics

When talking about substrates used in printing, paper is usually what comes to mind. Paper is made most commonly from wood fibre. Today, many papers also have some percentage of recycled fibre as well as fillers and other additives. These all contribute to the quality of the paper itself and to the quality of the printed output. It's important to understand some basic attributes of paper as they all have a direct impact on imaging processes and results.

Formation

Formation refers to the distribution of fibres, fillers, and additives in paper and how evenly they come together. When you hold a sheet up to a strong light source and look through it, the mix of dark and light areas are the result of formation. The more uniform the formation, the less mottling is observed in the paper. Papers with uniform formation accept inks and toners more evenly, have reduced print mottling, and enhance clarity.

Opacity

In strict terms, opacity is the degree to which light is prevented from travelling through a paper. In practical terms, it's how well a paper prevents the image on the backside of a sheet showing through to the front. This is measured on a scale from 1 to 100, where 100 is completely opaque. **Opacity** can be increased with fillers, pigments, or even coatings. In general, a thicker paper, coloured paper, or coated paper is more opaque than its counterparts. Opacity values are very important when projects require thinner paper stocks and both sides of the sheet are being printed.

Basis Weight and Grammage

When looking at the label on a ream of paper used in North America, you usually see two weight designations: the **basis weight**, designated in pounds (#) and the equivalent **grammage**, in grams per square metre (g/m^2 or gsm). In most of the world, grammage is primarily used. In North America, the basis weight is more common. Grammage is simply how many grams per square metre paper weighs. No other factors are represented by this designation. So we can deduce that the higher the grammage, the thicker or denser the sheet. Basis weight is the weight of 500 sheets of paper at a specific size, known as the 'parent' sheet size, which varies based on the historical use of the specific paper. To understand this better, let's examine two different basis weights.

Cover basis weight is based on a 20″ x 26″ parent sheet. So 500 sheets of 80# cover (the # symbol is used to indicate pounds) at the parent sheet size weighs 80 pounds. Likewise, 500 sheets of 80# text at the text-weight parent sheet size of 25″ x 38″ also weighs 80 pounds. This can be very confusing as a cut sheet of letter (8.5″ x 11″), 80# text, is much thinner than the same size of 80# cover. Table 6.1 shows common basis weights, parent sheet sizes, and typical uses.

Table 6.1 Paper weights, sizes, and uses

Basis Weight	Parent Sheet Size	Typical Use
Bond	17″ x 22″	Historically used as writing paper and typically uncoated. Standard office paper is 20# bond, while colour prints are more commonly done on 24# or 28# bond due to the need for higher opacity.
Cover	20″ x 26″	Used for paperback book covers, business cards, post cards. Business cards have typically been 100# cover, but have been trending toward higher weights of 110# and 120#.
Text	25″ x 38″	Used for magazines and posters. Relatively thin sheets with higher opacity. Magazines typically use a coated text weight paper for both the cover and the body. Typical weights are 70# to 100#.
Index	25.5″ x 30.5″	Used for index cards and tab stock. Tab stocks are typically uncoated 90# index.

Although basis weight is used as the primary weight on a paper label and description, a digital press will typically use grammage to define the weight property when assigning a paper to a tray. Paper weight is one of the key characteristics that affect many parameters on the digital press, including how much vacuum strength is used for feeding, how much charge is required to transfer toner to paper, and how much heat is required to maintain a consistent fusing temperature to bond toner to the paper, among others. Entering the wrong values for the paper weight can cause paper misfeeds, poor image quality, or toner not adhering to the paper. Using grammage simplifies data entry and avoids errors due to incorrect basis weight selection for the numeric weight value. It may, however, require one to do a conversion calculation if only basis weight is provided. The following conversion factors can be used to do these calculations.

Conversion Factors:

Bond (lbs.) x 3.7606 = gsm
Cover (lbs.) x 2.7048 = gsm
Text (lbs.) x 1.4805 = gsm
Index (lbs.) x 1.8753 = gsm

Grain Direction

In the paper manufacturing process, a slurry of fibre travels over a high-speed mesh conveyor belt that is oscillating side to side. This action and movement causes the fibres to interlace and develop a predominant alignment along the direction of movement. This predominant alignment of the fibres is called **grain direction**. Short grain refers to fibres running parallel to the short dimension of the sheet, and, conversely, long grain refers to fibres running parallel to the long dimension of the sheet.

It is important to keep grain direction in mind when choosing a paper for a project. You need to consider the print process and binding or finishing method you will use, as choosing the wrong grain direction can produce poor results or may be incompatible with the printing method you have chosen. Sheet fed offset lithography papers are often long grain and are most common. Digital presses require the grain to run perpendicular to the feed direction in order to feed properly and make the sharp turns typically found in a digital press. In this case, most sheets are fed into the press with the short edge first therefore requiring short grain paper. When folding is required, folds that run parallel to the grain will be smooth and sharp while folds that run across the grain will be ragged, and the fibres on the top of the sheet may pull apart. Toner used in digital printing bonds to the surface of the paper and does not penetrate. Folding across the grain will cause the toner to break apart where the fibres separate.

The second or underlined dimension of the sheet will indicate the direction of the grain. For example, 18″ x 12″ is a short grain sheet, and 12″ x 18″ is long grain. If the underline method is used, short grain would be <u>12″</u> x 18″ and long grain would be 12″ x <u>18</u>“. If the dimensions are not noted or the sheet is not in its original packaging, grain direction can be determined by folding the sheet along both dimensions. As noted previously, a fold that runs parallel to the grain will be smooth and sharp while a fold that runs across the grain will be ragged. You can also gently bend the paper in either direction. The bend running in the direction offering the least resistance is the grain direction.

Caliper

Caliper, unlike grammage and basis weight, is a measure of thickness. The most common measurement used in North America is thousandths of an inch, designated as points (common for paper) or mils (common for synthetic paper). This terminology can be confusing, however, as points can also refer to 1/72 of an inch when referring to font size, line thickness, and dimensions on a page. Mils can be confused with millimetres as well. A common misconception is that points and mils can be converted to grammage or basis weight. This is not true. The caliper can vary depending on the coatings or finish. In general, a rougher finished stock will have a higher caliper than the same weight of a smooth stock. Coatings can be heavier than paper fibre so coated paper can have a smaller caliper than the same weight of an uncoated counterpart. A process called calendaring, which irons the paper between two highly polished chrome rollers, improves smoothness and printability but also reduces the caliper without changing the weight of the paper.

Brightness and Whiteness

Brightness and **whiteness** define the optical properties of paper and differ mainly in how they are measured. Whiteness measures the reflective properties of the paper across the entire visible spectrum of light (defined by CIE). In other words, it defines how white the paper is. A perfect reflecting, non-fluorescent white material measures 100 whiteness. Brightness also measures the reflective properties of paper, on a scale of 1 to 100, but specifically in the blue area of the spectrum at a principal wavelength of 457 nanometres and 44 nanometres wide (defined by TAPPI and ISO standards). This wavelength coincides with lignin absorption. Lignin is what binds the cellulose fibres in wood and pulp and gives it its initial dark brown colour. The more bleaching done to the pulp, the more lignin is removed, and the higher the blue reflectance and therefore brightness. In most parts of the world, paper whiteness measurement is used; however, in North America, most papers use brightness measurement instead. Some papers have brightness values that exceed 100. This is due to the addition of fluorescent whitening agents (FWAs), which return additional blue light when exposed to UV light. The same is true for whiteness, as papers with higher blue reflectance levels tend to have higher whiteness levels.

Finish

Finish defines the look and feel of the paper's surface and can be achieved during the paper-making process (on-machine) or after (off-machine). On-machine finishes are achieved by the application of a pattern onto the paper by a marking roller while it is still wet. Examples of on-machine finishes are smooth, vellum, laid and felt (see Table 6.2). Off-machine finishes are accomplished with rollers that press the pattern into the paper after it has been made. Off-machine finishes are also known as embossed finishes. Linen, stipple, and canvas are examples of these; Table 6.3 gives a description of each.

Table 6.2 On-machine finishes

On-machine Finishes	Description	Typical Uses
Smooth	Paper is passed through various calendaring rollers, producing a finish that is uniform, flat, and smooth to the touch.	Ideal for general digital printing and copying as toner is applied to the surface and does not penetrate the fibres.
Vellum	A consistent eggshell appearance that is not quite as smooth as smooth finish but has a velvety feel. Not to be confused with the substrate called vellum, which is translucent.	Used most commonly for book paper.
Laid	Consists of a series of wide-spaced lines (chain lines) and more narrowly spaced lines (laid lines), which are at 90 degrees to the chain lines.	Used for letterhead, reports, presentations.
Felt	A felt-covered roller is used to produce this finish. The appearance resembles that of felt.	Used for letterhead, reports, presentations.

Table 6.3 Off-machine finishes

Off-machine Finishes	Description	Typical Uses
Linen	A cross-hatch pattern resembling linen fabric.	Used for personal stationery, letterhead, fine-dining menus, business cards.
Stipple	A fine bump texture that resembles the painted surface of a wall.	Used where a subtle uneven texture is desired.
Canvas	Simulates the surface of canvas.	Used for art prints or where a 'painted' appearance is desired.

Coated papers have calcium carbonate or china clay applied to their surface. The coating fills in the spaces between the fibres on the paper's surface, resulting in a smoother finish. The amount of coating and calendaring produces different finishes and gloss appearance. Examples of coated finishes are matte, dull, satin, silk, and gloss, described in Table 6.4.

Table 6.4 Coated finishes

Coated Finish	**Description**	**Gloss Level**
Matte	Roughest surface of coated paper. Very flat, no lustre, no glare, no calendaring applied.	None
Dull	Smoother surface than matte. No luster, no glare, minimal calendaring.	Very low
Satin	Smooth and soft to the touch. Slight lustre, low glare, light calendaring.	Medium low
Silk	Smooth and silky to the touch. Low lustre, low glare, light calendaring.	Moderate
Gloss	Smooth and slick. Shiny, high calendaring.	High

Cast coated paper has a very high gloss finish on the front side and is uncoated and rough on the back. The high gloss finish is created by applying a heated chrome roller to the coated surface to quickly dry it while moisture is released through the uncoated back of the sheet. Calendaring is not used, allowing the back surface to be rough and ideally suited for labels. Cast coated paper holds ink well, but the toner used in digital printing may not adhere to it.

6.6 Page Description Languages

Many page description languages (PDL) exist today; however, Printer Command Language (PCL) and PostScript are the most common and widely adopted. Each has its strengths, weaknesses, and jobs for which it is best suited. It is important to understand these differences and choose the method best suited to your particular printing requirements.

PCL

PCL is a page description language developed by Hewlett-Packard (HP) and was originally used on HP impact and inkjet printers. PCL 3 was the first version to be used with a laser printer, the HP LaserJet, released in 1984, around the same time PostScript was introduced. The goal of PCL was to have an efficient printer control language that could be implemented consistently across HP's printer line. Simple commands and functionality would not require expensive print controllers, making it very attractive for utility-level printing. Many other printer manufacturers implemented PCL for this reason. Commands are embedded at the beginning of the print job and set the parameters for the printer to use for the job. These commands remain set until a new value is assigned for the command or the printer is reset. If the printer does not support a specific command, it ignores it.

When colour laser printing became available, PCL 5c was developed with similar goals. New commands were added to the existing command set, as was the case with all the predecessors, to add support for colour printing. This ensured backwards compatibility while minimizing development. When it came to colour, HP's goal was to have colour on the printed page look the same as what was displayed on screen. There were many challenges to achieving this, so print quality adjustments were included to give users the ability to fine-tune the output. With the emergence and widespread adoption of the sRGB standard to define and describe colour on a display, the PCL colour command set could be simplified by adopting this standard for colour printing. Thus, HP's goal could be achieved without the complexity and overhead of a full colour management system. Operating systems and applications, for the most part, have standardized how they display colour in sRGB, so this approach is the simplest way to achieve acceptable colour between display and print. PCL is most appropriate for general office use where a simple, low-cost print device that produces good quality colour is expected. It is not suitable, however, for a colour critical or print production environment where precision and full colour management is required.

PostScript

PostScript is a page description and programming language developed by Adobe that describes text, graphics, and images, and their placement on a page, independent of the intended output destination. The code created is in plain text that can be written and examined with a basic text editor. The output itself can either be to a printer, display, or other device possessing a PostScript interpreter, making it a device independent language. The interpreter processes the PostScript instructions to create a raster image the device can render. The interpreter is often referred to as a RIP or raster image processor for this reason. It is possible to write valid PostScript code from scratch, but it is impractical as page composition applications can either generate the PostScript code directly or can utilize a print driver, which can convert the page to the PostScript language.

Since PostScript is a general-purpose programming language, it includes many elements that you wouldn't associate specifically with printing such as data types (numbers, arrays, and strings) and control primitives (conditionals, loops, and procedures). It also has an interesting feature called *dictionary*, which stores information in a table consisting of a collection of key and value pairs. The values can be entered into the dictionary while the keys are used to reference the information needed. These features made possible documents that acted like an application which could generate pages dynamically from data directly on the printer itself. These printer-based applications were stored temporarily in memory or permanently in the printer's hard drive, and triggered by a command in the print stream. These capabilities made variable data printing possible using PostScript and are still being used today for that purpose.

The first printer to use PostScript was the Apple LaserWriter in 1985. The same day that Apple announced the LaserWriter, Aldus Corporation announced PageMaker, a page layout application developed to take advantage of the Apple Macintosh computer's GUI (graphical user interface) and the PostScript PDL. This series of events is considered by many as the genesis of the desktop publishing revolution. In fact, the term *desktop publishing* is attributed to the founder of Aldus Corporation.

PDF

Portable document format (PDF) is one of the most popular file formats for displaying and printing documents. When this format was released by Adobe in 1993, it shared many of the same concepts and components of PostScript. But where PostScript was designed primarily to provide device independent consistency in print output, PDF was focused on maintaining the visual appearance of a document onscreen, independent of the operating system displaying it. Over the years, PDF has expanded to more specific-use specifications for engineering, archiving, health care, universal access, and printing.

PDF/X is a branch of PDF and an ISO standard that deals specifically with print. It was developed by the Committee for Graphic Arts Technologies Standards (CGATS). Table 6.5 shows the evolution of the standard.

Table 6.5 Evolution of PDF
Data source: Adobe Systems Inc, 2008, p. 4

<table>
<tr><th>Preset</th><th>Compatibility</th><th>Settings</th><th>Usage</th></tr>
<tr><td>PDF/X-1a: 2001</td><td>Acrobat 4/PDF 1.3</td><td rowspan="2">• Convert RGB colour to CMYK (spot colors allowed)
• Transparency flattened</td><td rowspan="2">PDF/X-1a ensures that the files are ready for print production—fonts are embedded, colours must be CMYK or spot, layers and transparency are flattened. Note that there is no minimum resolution required for PDF/X.</td></tr>
<tr><td>PDF/X-1a: 2003</td><td>Acrobat 5/PDF 1.4</td></tr>
<tr><td>PDF/X-3: 2002</td><td>Acrobat 4/PDF 1.3</td><td rowspan="2">• Leave RGB and CIELab color unchanged (profiles allowed)
• Transparency flattened</td><td rowspan="2">PDF/X-3 has all the benefits of PDF/X-1a plus it allows colour-managed workflows.</td></tr>
<tr><td>PDF/X-3: 2003</td><td>Acrobat 5/PDF 1.4</td></tr>
<tr><td>PDF/X-4: 2008</td><td>Acrobat 7/PDF 1.6</td><td rowspan="2">• Leave RGB and CIELab colour unchanged (profiles allowed)
• Live (unflattened) transparency
• Layers allowed</td><td>Has all the benefits of PDF/X-3 plus it allows live (unflattened) transparency and layers for versioning. Print workflows based on the Adobe PDF Print Engine will be able to process PDF/X-4 jobs natively, without flattening artwork or converting to PostScript.</td></tr>
<tr><td>PDF/X-4p: 2008</td><td>Acrobat 7/PDF 1.6</td><td>Use PDF/X-4p when a required ICC profile is unambiguously identified and supplied separately.</td></tr>
</table>

Submitting documents for print using one of these standards is highly recommended as it eliminates many of the causes of print issues and is a more reliable method for graphics file exchange.

Digital Front End

Digital front end (DFE) describes the combination of hardware and software that drives and manages a print device. Hardware is often custom built for this specific purpose and may have proprietary video interfaces that connect directly to the print engine. An operating system serves as the base for the software components of the DFE and is often Microsoft Windows based or a Linux or Unix variant. Although the Windows running on a DFE is much the same as its desktop counterpart, Linux- and Unix-based systems are often custom distributions that are compiled specifically for the DFE.

One of the key components of a DFE is the raster image processor (RIP). The RIP refers to the software component that interprets the PDL and performs the function of rendering or rasterizing the complete instructions into an image or raster the print engine will reproduce. The term RIP is often used interchangeably with DFE. This may have been accurate in the past when a DFE really only performed the ripping function and little else. Modern DFEs, however, do much more. In fact, a DFE may contain multiple RIPs, and within those RIPs they can utilize the multi-threading and processing power of modern computer hardware and operating systems to process many pages or channels simultaneously. PostScript has been the defacto PDL in digital printing for many years but with the development of the PDF/X print standards and the subsequent release of the Adobe PDF Print Engine (APPE), a native PDF RIP, many DFEs now include both PostScript and APPE as their available RIP engines.

ICC-based colour management workflow may be part of the RIP process or can be an independent component of the DFE. Different elements within a print file get processed through their respective channels in the colour management system. Common channels include CMYK, RGB, black, and named colours. The idea is to convert all colour elements into the colour gamut of the print engine's colorants/paper combination. The conversion process can be complicated, but the basic concept is device dependent source colour spaces (CMYK, RGB, etc.) are converted to a device independent colour space, referred to the profile conversion space (PSC), then from the PSC to the output gamut defined in the output ICC profile. The idea is to take the source 'recipe' and define the visual appearance of it first. That is why it needs to convert to device independent colour space, which defines the visual appearance of colour. Once the visual appearance is defined, the 'recipe' for the specific output can be calculated.

Systems that support named or spot colour rendering follow a similar process. The named colour is located in a look up table. The name must match perfectly, including punctuation, spaces, and case. Each named colour is defined in a device independent colour space, typically Lab. There is no calculation in this step. The last step is the same; Lab values are then converted via the output profile.

There is one more calculation applied before passing the information through to the printer. Electrophotography is affected by rapid changes in humidity and temperature. The electrophotographic process relies on components that do become less effective over time and use. These factors all affect the colour output. Calibration should be performed on a regular basis to compensate for these variables. Calibration is a process of creating a correction curve to maintain consistent and repeatable print output. This correction curve is applied right after the conversion to output profile, ensuring output is consistent with what was defined in the output profile itself.

In order to maintain all these aspects of the DFE, an intuitive and user-friendly interface is critical. The user interface includes many components. Here is where you would configure the DFE, find the status of the print device and consumables, view and process jobs and job queues, and examine and export job histories and logs. Many WYSIWYG tools are accessed via the user interface, such as those for workflow, imposition, complex job composition, paper libraries, spot colour refinement, the launching of external tools, and even interfaces into other systems such as web2print. DFEs are becoming more powerful and perform more than just the traditional RIP functions. As the digital print industry continues to evolve, DFEs will be called on to perform more duties and functions. User interfaces will need to evolve as well to maintain usability and stay intuitive.

6.7 Variable Data Printing

Variable data printing, or VDP, refers to a special form of digital printing where document content is determined by entries in a record or data set and can be highly personalized. Varied text, graphics, and images are typical content elements, but layout, element positioning, and even document choice are just some of the other variables. Because the content on the printed page is constantly changing, it would not be feasible to produce this type of print product with traditional offset lithography or with any other process that requires a fixed image plate. Electrophotographic and ink jet printing are ideally suited for this type of printing as each page is imaged individually.

VDP can take many forms. Transactional documents like invoices and statements are probably the oldest form of VDP, but these have evolved to include marketing or informational content. This is known as trans-promo or **trans-promotional**. A mail merge is a simple form of VDP where a static document has data elements added directly to it. Each record in the data set produces one document. Another VDP form is when you enter the record manually or upload a simple text-based data table, which then fills the content of a template. This method is typically found in web2print solutions and produces items such as business cards, where the layout, fonts, and required elements can be predetermined and the content based on the data entered. More advanced VDP solutions may include campaign management tools, workflow management, two-dimensional barcode generation, image-based font technology, and integration into external systems such as databases, email, web2print solutions, data cleansing, or postal optimization solutions.

One of the core purposes of VDP is to increase response rate and, ultimately, conversions to the desired outcome. In order to accomplish this, it is critical that the content presented is relevant and has value for the intended audience. Today, there are massive amounts of data available on customers and their behaviour. Analyzing and understanding customer data is essential to maintaining a high degree of relevancy and engagement with the customer.

VDP can be broken down into six key components: data, content, business rules, layout, software, and output method. Each component can vary in complexity and capability and may require advanced software solutions to implement. However, even the most basic tools can produce highly effective communications.

Data

Data used for VDP can be simply thought of as a table or data set. Each row in the table is considered a single record. The columns are the fields used to describe the contents of the record. Some examples of columns or fields would be first name, last name, address, city, and so on. The simplest and most common form of representing this table is by using a delimited plain text format like comma separated value (CSV) or tab delimited. The *delimiter* separates the columns from one another and a new line represents a new row or record in the table. Here is an example of CSV data:

```
"FirstName","LastName","Gender","Age","FavQuotes"

"John","Smith","M","47","Do or do not, there is no try."

"Mary","Jones","F","25","Grey is my favourite colour."
```

The first row contains the row headers or what the fields represent and is not considered a record. You'll notice that each field is separated by a comma but is also enclosed within quotes. The quotes are text qualifiers and are commonly used to prevent issues when the delimiting character may also be in the contents of the field as is the case with the first record above. Many VDP applications support more advanced, relational databases like SQL, but a query must be performed to extract the data to be used, which ultimately results in the same row and column record structure. The data must be attached or assigned to the document in the page layout or VDP application.

Content

Content refers to elements displayed on each page. This would include text, graphics, and images, both static and dynamic. Dynamic content uses placeholders, typically named by the column headers of the data, to mark the position of the element and reference the data in the specific column of the current record. When the document is rendered, the placeholder is replaced by the record data element.

"Dear <<FirstName>>…" becomes "Dear John…" when the document is rendered for the first record and "Dear Mary…" for the second record, and so on. A complete document is rendered per record in the dataset.

Business Rules

Business rules are one of the key elements that make VDP documents highly useful. They can be thought of as a series of criteria that are checked against the data to determine what gets displayed on the page. They can also be used to manipulate the data or filter out relevant content. In almost every case, some level of scripting is required. Advanced VDP solutions have built-in scripting capability, utilizing either common scripting language such as VBScript or JavaScript, or a proprietary scripting language that is only applicable in that specific application. If the page layout tool you are using to create your VDP document does not have scripting capability, you can apply business rules to data beforehand in a spreadsheet application like Microsoft Excel or even Google Sheets.

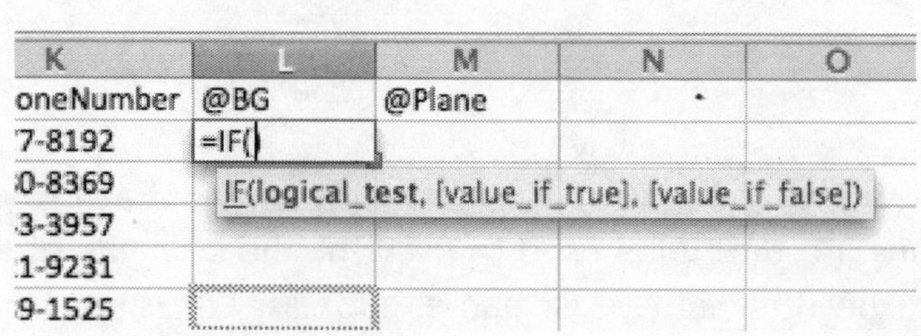

Figure 6.11 Logical test

One of the most common methods for implementing a business rule is using a conditional or IF statement comprising a logical test, an action for a 'true' result, and an action for a 'false' result (see Figure 6.11).

The logical_test means that the answer will be either true or false. In this case, we want to change our graphics based on gender.
In plain English, you may say:

```
"IF gender is male, THEN use plane_blue.tif, or ELSE use plane_orange.tif"
```

In scripting, it would look something like this:

```
IF(Gender="male","plane_blue.tif","plane_red.tif")
```

When doing this in a spreadsheet, you would enter the script in a cell in a new column. The result of the script is displayed in the cell, not the script itself. This new column could now be used to specify the content to be displayed in your layout application. In dedicated VDP applications, the script is attached to the object itself and is processed and displayed in real time.

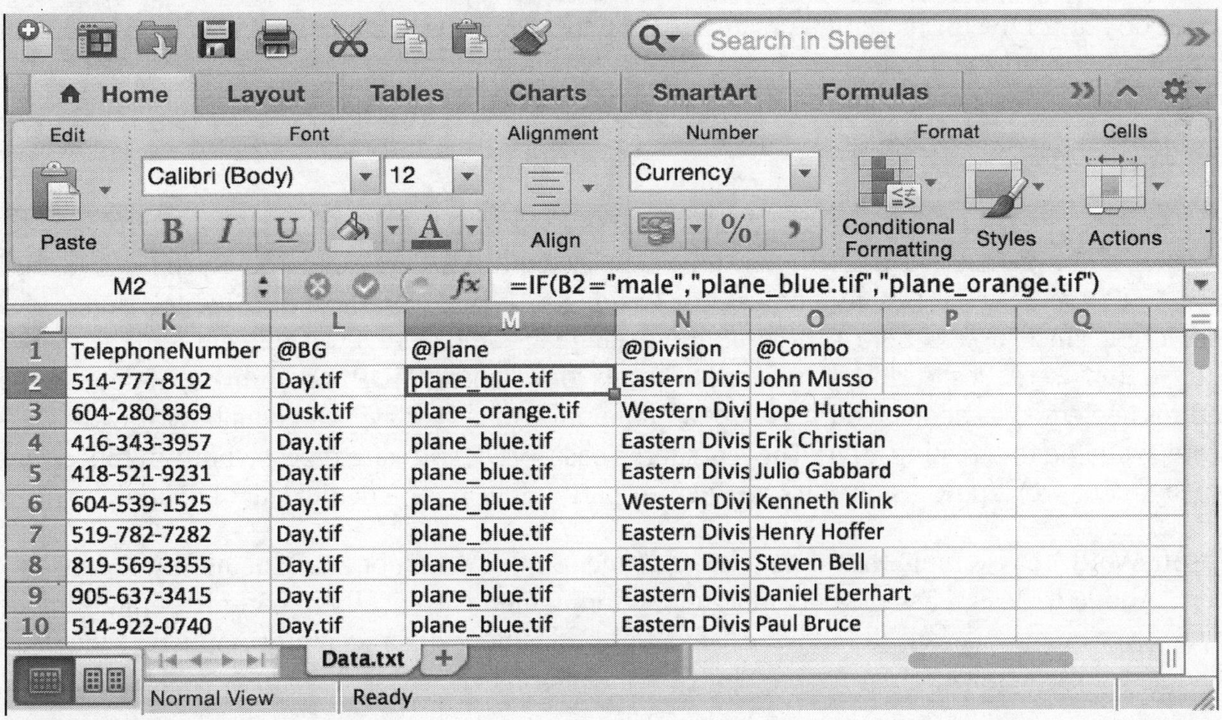

	K	L	M	N	O	P	Q
1	TelephoneNumber	@BG	@Plane	@Division	@Combo		
2	514-777-8192	Day.tif	plane_blue.tif	Eastern Divis	John Musso		
3	604-280-8369	Dusk.tif	plane_orange.tif	Western Divi	Hope Hutchinson		
4	416-343-3957	Day.tif	plane_blue.tif	Eastern Divis	Erik Christian		
5	418-521-9231	Day.tif	plane_blue.tif	Eastern Divis	Julio Gabbard		
6	604-539-1525	Day.tif	plane_blue.tif	Western Divi	Kenneth Klink		
7	519-782-7282	Day.tif	plane_blue.tif	Eastern Divis	Henry Hoffer		
8	819-569-3355	Day.tif	plane_blue.tif	Eastern Divis	Steven Bell		
9	905-637-3415	Day.tif	plane_blue.tif	Eastern Divis	Daniel Eberhart		
10	514-922-0740	Day.tif	plane_blue.tif	Eastern Divis	Paul Bruce		

Figure 6.12 Plane blue

The "@Plane" column was added to dynamically change a graphic based on the contents of the cell in the "Gender" column (B2) (see Figure 6.12).

Business rules can also be applied to the VDP workflow. In this case, the workflow application or component can manipulate the data before applying it to a document, or it can select the document or destination to be used for the record and much, much more.

Layout

When working with variable data documents, there are special layout considerations you should be aware of. Because word lengths will change per record, there needs to be sufficient space to accommodate the largest and smallest record, and prevent **oversetting** while maintaining the desired visual appearance. This challenge is compounded by the prolific use of **proportional fonts**. Character widths differ with each letter so word lengths will vary even when the number of characters is the same. This can also force a paragraph to reflow onto another page and change the number of pages in the document. Additional scripting may be required to handle reflow scenarios. Some applications use special copy-fitting algorithms to dynamically fit text into a defined area. The use of tables for layout purposes can also be helpful. Because we are dealing with dynamically generated documents, we may also want to vary the images. Using images with a consistent size and shape make it easier to work with. Transactional documents, such as statements and invoices, extensively use numbers. Most fonts, including proportional ones, keep numbers mono-spaced. In other words, every number character occupies the same amount of space. This is important because, visually, we want numbers to be right justified and lining up vertically in columns with the decimal points aligned. There are, however, some fonts that do not follow this common practice. These fonts may be suitable for use in a paragraph but are not for displaying financial data.

Software

Software that can generate a data-driven document is required for variable data printing. In the early days of VDP, there weren't many choices for designers. It was common practice to hand code VDP in PostScript, since it was both a programming language and a PDL. Applications like PageMaker and Illustrator were PostScript design applications but lacked VDP capabilities. Applications like PlanetPress emerged as dedicated PostScript VDP applications. Today, designers have a wide variety of software available for creating VDP. There are three basic VDP software types: a built-in function within a page layout or word-processing software, a third-party plug-in, or a dedicated VDP application.

Microsoft Word, for example, has a mail merge function but does not have the ability to vary images, just text. Adobe InDesign has the data merge function, which is basically a mail merge but includes the ability to vary images as well. In both these examples, business rules would be applied to the data prior to using it in these applications.

There are a number of plug-ins available for InDesign that are very sophisticated. These leverage the extensive page layout capability of InDesign while adding scripting and other VDP specific capabilities. XMPie and DesignMerge are examples of these types of plug-ins. FusionPro is another plug-in based VDP product, and while it does have an InDesign plug-in, it only uses this to allocate variable text and image boxes in the layout. Business rules and specific content are applied in its complement plug-in for Adobe Acrobat.

PlanetPress and PrintShop Mail are examples of dedicated applications that combine both page layout and VDP functions. Although they are very strong in VDP functionality, they sometimes lack the sophistication you'd find in InDesign when it comes to page layout. These particular applications have recently moved from PostScript-based VDP to a more modern HTML5 and CSS (cascading style sheets) base, making it easier to produce and distribute data-driven documents for multi-channel communications.

Output Method

The ‘P’ in VDP stands for printing and is the main output method we will discuss here. However, document personalization and data-driven communications have evolved to also include email, fax, web (PURL, personalized landing page), SMS text messaging, and responsive design for various mobile device screen sizes. With the emergence of quick response **(QR) codes**, even printed communications can tap into rich content and add additional value to the piece. In order to take advantage of these additional distribution and communications channels, a workflow component is often employed.

A key element for optimized print output of VDP documents is caching. This is where the printer’s RIP caches or stores repeatable elements in print-ready raster format. This means the RIP processes these repeating elements once, and then reuses these preprocessed elements whenever the document calls for them. This does require a RIP with enough power to process large amounts of data and resources with support for the caching scheme defined in the VDP file but, ultimately, allows the printer to print at its full rated speed without having to wait for raster data from the RIP.

There have been many proprietary VDP file formats that have striven to improve performance of VDP over the years, but the industry is moving rapidly toward more open standards. PODi, a not-for-profit consortium of leading companies in digital printing, is leading the way with two widely adopted open VDP standards. These standards are PPML (Personalized Print Markup Language) and PDF/VT (portable document format/variable transactional).

PPML

PPML, first introduced in 2000, is a device independent **XML**-based printing language. There are two types of PPML: *thin* and *thick*. Thin PPML is a single file, with the .ppml extension, containing all the instructions necessary for producing the VDP document. It does include caching instructions; however, all resources such as fonts or images are stored externally of the file. The path to these resources is defined in the RIP and retrieved during the rendering process of the document. Thin PPML is ideal for in-house VDP development where resources may be shared by multiple projects. These files are extremely small, however, and network speed and bandwidth may affect performance and are more difficult to implement if using an external print provider. Thick PPML is a .zip file containing all the required resources (fonts, images, instructions, etc.). This format makes the file highly portable and easy to implement on the print device, but it has a larger file size when compared to thin PPML. RIPs that support the PPML format can import the .zip file directly. Regardless of the type used, PPML benefits from exceptional performance, an open standard, open job ticketing support (JDF), and overall reduced file size. To generate PPML, an advanced VDP solution is required.

PDF/VT

PDF/VT is a relatively new international standard (ISO 16612-2) that has a lot of potential. It is built off the PDF/X-4 standard, benefiting from its features, such as support for transparency, ICC-based colour management, extensive metadata support, element caching, preflighting, and much more. In short, PDF/VT includes the mechanisms required to handle VDP jobs in the same manner as static PDF printing allows print providers to use a common workflow for all job types, including VDP. Many of the latest releases of advanced VDP solutions already support PDF/VT as well as many DFE manufacturers.

For more information on PPML and PDF/VT, please refer to the PODi website at: http://www.standards.podi.org

Media Attributions

- plane_blue © Roberto Medeiros

6.8 Summary

Digital printing encompasses a number of technologies that each has unique characteristics, strengths, and applications. Digital imaging may even be the only print method able to produce a certain type of work, as is the case with VDP. Paper is also a major factor in the success of a project. Your paper choice can convey a message or set a tone as much as the content printed on it. Having a good understanding of technology and paper fundamentals can go along way when making choices for producing your print project.

Questions to consider after completing this chapter:

1. All xerography can also be called electrophotography, but not all electrophotography can be called xerography. What key element validates this statement?
2. What are the four key components in electrophotography?
3. How does toner acquire its charge?
4. What is the difference between paper brightness and whiteness?
5. Which PDLs support an ICC colour-managed workflow?
6. Which PDF/X standard leaves layers and transparency live?
7. Why are data content and business rules critical in VDP?

References

Adobe Systems Incorporated. (2008). *Adobe PDF in a print production workflow*. Retrieved from http://www.adobe.com/studio/print/pdfs/PDF_wp_A9_updates_july08.pdf

Burton, J. (2008). *A primer on UV-curable inkjet inks*. Retrieved from http://www.signindustry.com/flatbed_UV/articles/2008-11-17-SGIA_Primer_on_UV-Curable_Inkjet_Inks.php3

Idealliance. (n.d.). *Idealliance: About*. Retrieved from http://www.idealliance.org/about

Nanography Lobby – Landa Nanography. (n.d.). Retrieved from http://www.landanano.com/nanography

PPML and PDF/VT. (n.d.). *PODi key standards. Digital print case studies*. Retrieved from http://www.standards.podi.org/

United States Environmental Protection Agency. (2000). *Taking toxics out of the air [Overviews & Factsheets]*. Retrieved from http://www.epa.gov/oaqps001/takingtoxics/index.html

Suggested Readings

Johnson, H. (2004). *Mastering digital printing* (2nd ed.). Boston, MA: Cengage Learning PTR.

Nanography Lobby – Landa Nanography. (n.d.). Retrieved from http://www.landanano.com/nanography

Chapter 7. Web2print

7.1 Introduction

Learning Objectives

- Describe web2print and how it benefits the supplier-customer relationship
- Differentiate between the different business models of web2print implementation
- Explore the economic impact of implementing web2print
- Research target markets that would benefit from online selling processes
- Define business to business (B2B) and business to consumer (B2C) sales models
- Examine variable templates and identify their components
- Discuss how print on demand works and how it affects the sales cycle
- Give examples of print workflows and management information system (MIS) integration
- Discuss how web2print business opportunities might affect return on investment

As modern modes of communication are constantly changing, the print industry has had to become very competitive. Successful print companies have evolved beyond producing only printed products; today, they also provide other services geared to an electronic marketplace. With the ever-growing number of people going online, customers have adapted to having instant information (Poon & Swatman, 1995), which printers can now provide. One such service is web2print. Customers benefit from the ease of ordering print anywhere around the world, with quicker turnaround times than traditional methods. Print companies benefit by building a larger customer base, streamlining workflows, and reducing production costs — all while staying competitive.

Print has traditionally been a service requiring many human touch-points, but with advances in business communication over the Internet, the dynamics of custom manufacturing are changing, particularly with respect to the ordering process (Shim, Pendyala, Sundaram, & Gao, 2000). Putting an effective online service in place involves strategically selecting suitable products and services. Online ordering is not ideal for every print product, but rather for specific products that are unnecessarily labour intensive. Products that were once very labour intensive, such as business cards, can now be ordered online. Customers enter their information directly into a template on screen while they sit in their own offices. A print-ready PDF file enters an automated folder in the print company (called a hot folder) and moves into the print workflow, allowing for a fully automated process called *lights-out prepress*, which saves on labour and allows for greater profits. Web2print provides a client company a value-added feature, while improving workflow process for the print company.

Technology Is the Key

Web2print completely automates the print ordering process by integrating online orders with print production. Using the Internet automates order entry and provides time savings to both the customer and the company.

> Electronic commerce offers the possibility of breakthrough changes: changes that so radically alter customer expectations that they redefine the market or create entirely new markets (Gunasekaran, Marri, McGaughey, & Nebhwani, 2002, p. 195).

This technology allows businesses to interact with customers in a new way in addition to more traditional forms of ordering such as email, file transfer protocol (**FTP**), phone, fax, and face-to-face meetings. While web2print removes the need for more traditional ways of ordering, it does not replace them. Some customers may prefer these ways because they may not know, or be comfortable with, the online options that are increasingly available to them. It is advantageous to a company to inform and educate customers, encouraging them to evolve their buying habits. Traditionally, purchasing involved gaining knowledge about print companies through their sales reps, selecting the appropriate company, and trusting that the sales rep would ensure the product was delivered on time and for the best price. Today, many customers use search engines to obtain information about and decide on which print company to use. Using web2print ensures that the production time frame and the price match what a customer is looking for.

A printing company has to work with and implement many complex and interconnected systems in order to generate a printed product. From the inception of a new item to its delivery to the end-user, there are many opportunities for streamlining. Web2print creates efficiencies at the beginning of the print process, and those benefits trickle all the way through to imaging. The ultimate goal is for the data collected from the customer to proceed directly to the raster image processor (**RIP**) that drives the production process. A print company that takes advantage of this type of automation is positioning itself for smoother and more cost-effective print runs.

7.2 E-commerce for Print Manufacturing

E-commerce is by definition the buying and selling of goods online. Print companies are turning to e-commerce to target the ever-growing number of people who want self-service and a more convenient way to purchase products in their busy lives. Today, many customers are online and the number of users purchasing goods through the Internet is growing substantially (Statistics Canada, 2014). The ability to offer an effective e-commerce service for ordering can put a print company ahead of its competitors. This approach challenges traditional thinking that a printer is only a bricks-and-mortar or face-to-face business. As more and more businesses move online to satisfy their customers' procurement needs, so must print companies (Supply Management, 2014).

A print company should transition with its customers to stay ahead of the competition. E-commerce allows a customer to order any product 24/7 without having to leave the office or pick up the phone. Providing online ordering has other benefits besides increased sales. It can help a company gain more knowledge about its customers and track purchasing trends. As well, online ordering allows print companies to offer customers additional products and services that may not come up in discussions during traditional forms of print procurement.

Not all business can be conducted online, as the more complex a project is the more a company will benefit from offering its services and expertise in traditional face-to-face communications. However, the ability to stay ahead of the competition by using Internet technologies helps solidify a company's relationship with its customers. For example, even if customers are buying products offline, they are likely doing their research online first. Therefore, a company can use the valuable data generated during this research to greatly improve its ability to evaluate and manage its business. When customers place orders, companies can analyze the frequency of those orders, their customers' buying trends, and which products are more successful than others. Data-gathering is the most important advantage online ordering has over traditional offline ordering. Using an e-commerce system allows a print company to learn more about what, when, and how customers are ordering. Online technologies enable a company to broaden the products and services it provides more than ever before.

Templated Variable Data Printing

Templated variable data technology allows a customer to produce a product using a template-driven order-entry system. These templates are used most frequently through an e-commerce store. A variable template allows the user to control the information made available on a product and see the real-time end result. Variable data entry is an ideal solution for direct mailers, promotional flyers, event posters, and stationery. Variable data allows for the custom printing of one-of-a-kind pieces that are unique to the targeted market. The potential for variable data is endless and is only limited by the imagination behind a design.

Variable data is not limited to digital presses, as many lithography presses can incorporate designs with the simple swap of a plate. It is common for companies ordering large quantities of business cards to print blank shells on which they can later imprint a person's information. A print company obtains this information by having the customer use a variable template, which is then uniquely created to ensure all branding standards are consistent. This allows any employee of the client company to order business cards and stay true to the brand. The person fills out his or her name, title, and phone and email contact information, then views the result on a soft-proof. Then the person simply submits the card through a shopping cart system, eliminating the need for multiple communications, and making production efficient by having fewer hands touch the project.

The Benefits to a Print Company

Web2print has multiple benefits for a print company. Software can automate tasks, eliminating the need for staff to touch a project, which makes the service profitable. Allowing the customer to create a print-ready PDF is an asset, not a loss of control, as it allows the customer to assume responsibility for any typos or errors. Web2print also makes the production process much faster and efficient by automating time-consuming steps, and most importantly, helps build solid rapport and customer loyalty.

Once a PDF is ordered, a job ticket (called a *docket*) is automatically generated containing all of the order specifications, including pricing. The PDF then travels to a hot folder where it is accessed by the imposition software, which imposes it onto a press sheet. The press sheet either goes straight to the digital press to be printed or to the plate setter if it is being printed by conventional lithography. The whole process is extremely efficient and takes considerably less time to complete than having staff continually involved as the PDF travels through their departments.

The Benefits to the Customer

Web2print is all about customer satisfaction. That should be the top priority when a print company creates customized online storefronts and variable templates. Customers no longer have to call or physically meet a sales rep, as they now have the ability to order their printed materials at any time of the day and from anywhere. Today, many customers do not sit behind a desk for their entire workday, and establishing an online service allows a company to target those on-the-go customers who need to order print.

Companies can track orders in real time, which helps them predict future buying trends. This is especially beneficial to customers wanting to print blank items, otherwise known as *shells*. Using this information, a company can help a customer determine how many shells to print in the next run.

Business Models: Licensed or Subscribed Software

Web2print services come in two primary types: licensed software and subscribed software. Licensed software allows a print company to own the technology by paying an upfront fee; subscription-based software typically requires a company to pay a monthly or yearly fee to use the software.

Licensed software strategies typically represent a large cash outflow up front. The company can then use the software to create as many portals or implementations as it wishes. While the software is supported through a licence, it is expected that the company will maintain its own web presence, and therefore may require highly trained web developers or programmers. The outlay of expense is gradually recouped over time through increased user implementation.

The subscription model, also referred to as **SaaS** (software as a service) reduces a company's support and maintenance costs up front. Saas allows adding new print products to move forward more quickly because the need to support the same version throughout computers internally is removed. All subscribers operate on the same version at the same time, and are upgraded regularly at the same time. Because the Internet is constantly evolving, the SaaS model is flexible and better aligned to move with it. This business model contributes to a company's return on investment (**ROI**) as well. Since a company typically doesn't pay a large sum of money upfront for the software, it can easily budget for payments based on monthly usage. The company only pays for the services it uses. This business model builds a partnership between the print company and its SaaS vendor, and a positive ROI is beneficial to both parties in the partnership because it keeps both vendor and subscriber focused on mutual success.

7.3 Web2print Strategies and Goals

Evaluating Strategies and Setting Goals

Print companies must have clear strategies and goals to ensure continued success when implementing web2print. The first step is to evaluate the type of sales they make. There are two basic types of sales a print company makes: business to business (**B2B**) and business to consumer (**B2C**). It is very common for a printing company to serve a primarily B2B customer base; however, since B2C requires a vastly different storefront, this decision needs to be made early in the process of implementing web2print.

Once a print company determines the type of storefront its customers need, it should research the three basic types of service: print on demand (**POD**), variable data printing (**VDP**), and static warehoused items. By analyzing its target market, a print company can determine which of these services customers will use most. Once the print company chooses a software vendor that can provide the most suitable storefront, only then can it decide on the specific services to offer each of its customers.
Therefore, to be successful, a print company must:

- Know the target market
- Choose an appropriate vendor and storefront
- Make plans to add new customers to the system by setting goals
- Choose the types of products to offer to each customer based on need

Know the Target Market

Every print company has a different customer base, and thus serves a different market. A print company must analyze the customers it serves to determine exactly what its target market is. The biggest mistake print companies make when committing to the purchase of an online ordering system is not researching the technology in relation to their target market. Print companies should choose the system that best suits their needs and benefits their customers. There are hundreds of vendors and products with thousands of features, so print companies need a strategy to ensure they can maximize their return on investment (ROI) while providing the best possible services to their specific, targeted customer base.

Choosing a Digital Storefront and Variable Software

Since not all vendors of e-commerce systems are the same, print companies need to exercise due diligence in making their choice of vendor. They should analyze their own internal workflow to ensure they find a vendor that best meets their specific needs. As well, print companies should determine what their employees' strengths are and ensure the appropriate staff are hired to accommodate online needs.

Staff involved in the implementation and operation of an e-commerce ordering system need a basic knowledge of many web-based programming languages in order to give them a good grasp of the back-end coding necessary to build and maintain the online system. Every online ordering system uses its own method of coding to create its storefronts and templates, so having previous programming knowledge is a major asset.

Many companies such as IBM, HP, Creo, and EFI are building platforms to provide VDP service to print companies. The software these companies provide creates a web2print workflow. This includes the internal processes needed to print a job, as well as a client-facing website, from which customers can order. It is important to understand the benefits of every digital storefront as they all offer different options. Digital storefronts must provide a simple ordering process for the customer while being very robust and efficient for the print company. Selecting the order quantity and displaying pricing should be simple and not confusing for the end-user. Customizing VDP products or ordering POD or warehoused items should be simple and quick. The ability to split products for multiple-shipping destinations should also be considered.
Selecting a storefront that can be integrated into a management information system **(MIS)** to streamline orders from customization to invoicing is beneficial. The ability to have customers approve or reject orders placed by others is also beneficial, as it allows for an extra review to ensure order information is correct.

To ensure they make appropriate choices, print companies request copies of documentation from a software provider to see what they need to learn if they plan to be a self-service user of the software. They request references and ask how the software provider handles support, system outages, and upgrade development to get a sense of how other users perceive the company. Print companies attend demonstrations of the product and give specifics on what they want to hear beyond the generic sales pitch. Print companies also seek specific information about short- and long-term product upgrades, which gives them a chance to glimpse the software company's strategic vision and how the product might develop in the future.

Other Considerations Before Purchasing

Print companies take other considerations into account before purchasing software.

Usability: If they have current B2B customers, print companies ask them to test the software before committing to a purchase. If these end-users have difficulty using the software, then it is not the right choice. If print companies have B2C customers, they ask someone without any print knowledge or experience to test the product. Testing against online competitors to see how the software compares is another way print companies assess the usability of a product. They also research customer feedback.

Partnership compatibility: The relationship between a print company and a software provider is a partnership, not just a sales interaction. Print companies are in frequent contact with their software provider to solve technical difficulties, arrange training, or add improved services. Therefore, determining if the software provider will make a compatible partner is important. Print companies don't rely solely on what the sales rep tells them; they try to get a sense of the software provider's team by calling the support desk and talking to customer service. This helps print companies determine how well they will be treated and whether the software provider's staff are knowledgeable.

Features: Assessing software features is usually part of the decision-making process. Print companies generally want to know the following before purchasing:

- How easily will customers understand and use the software's features in a self-service situation?
- Was the software built to support the print industry or first created for some other use and applied to the print industry? If the former, are the features transferable?
- Do the features allow set up and administration of the site, creation of B2B storefronts, and product development. Do they enable the print company to add variable elements, create users, and take orders without relying on the software provider?

An important tip when choosing software technology is to not put too much emphasis on the number of features offered. Features tend to constantly change, and more does not necessarily mean better. While software product development tends to centre on adding more features, it is not necessarily adding more value. If a feature is added to a product, but is never used by customers, it is possible that the feature did nothing more than add complexity to the ordering process. Such a feature may result in discouraging customers from using the system, or placing future orders.

Starting with a New Customer

One way to introduce a new customer to web2print is to build a single item for them. This allows the customer to learn the ordering process and the print company to learn and incorporate the customer's products into a production workflow. A workflow should be designed to be as automated as possible, from order entry to production to invoicing. New workflows should include sufficient time to allow a customer to test the variable templates to extremes, entering best- and worst-case scenarios to ensure the template can perform in all situations without errors. Only once the initial workflow has been proven to be efficient should more products be added to the storefront. This ensures that both the customer (external activity) and the print company (internal activity) are confident enough in the workflow to handle more orders.

Setting Goals and Site Testing

Printing companies should allow time to educate their customers in all steps of the process when launching an e-commerce system or when adding a new variable-template-driven item. The easiest way to meet customer expectations is to involve them in the development process, regularly inviting feedback and eliciting suggestions for improvement. Customer satisfaction is important, so a company must ensure that it takes client feedback seriously, incorporating customer input to improve the service process. As the site is being developed, both the programmer and the customer need to rigorously test new products and templates to ensure they are completely satisfied long before allowing product ordering. It is common for a programmer to envision how a template will behave, while the customer intends it to behave in a different way. Often a customer has expectations that the programmer may not have foreseen. Once the entire site, including products and templates, has been developed, it still isn't ready. A testing phase or pilot period is necessary to find any other bugs or shortcomings that may be more easily discovered once real data is being used. Implementing a pilot period before an official launch of the full workflow also allows everyone to learn how the system will impact them, exposes potential workflow issues (which can arise in the many steps between ordering and invoicing), and allows the customer to provide final feedback.

Most important to keep in mind is that the system only works when customers use it. They will often find opportunities during the pilot period to suggest where the process can be improved, as unforeseen problems are discovered only after people start using a new system or variable template. Often these user-experience issues can prevent adoption of the system by the customer. As well, customers may fall back to the more familiar method of traditionally ordering print if they do feel comfortable using the new system. Including the customer in the entire process allows for the greatest chance of success, and is the best way to ensure the success of the site.

Choosing the Right Type of Products

Before setting out to create products, a print company should determine whether it is a variable template, a print-on-demand piece, or a warehoused item. Other key information needed is the name of the product and the communication intent (i.e., Is the piece promotional or educational? What audience is it intended to reach? How knowledgeable is this audience?). Print companies also need to know whether the product will be ordered regularly or be a one-time communication. It is important to choose the right products before the development phase begins. It is common for a product to be almost completely programmed before it is discovered that another similar product would have been more appropriate. Below are explanations of the three most common types of products, followed by a list of more specific options.

Variable Templates

Variable templates contain all the necessary information for a customer to customize and soft-proof a print order. This usually results in the creation of an automated, print-ready PDF, which is generated while the customer is still online.

A PDF of the design is created containing variable fields assigned for every element. Coding is then applied to each field to determine how the template will behave under given circumstances, such as during customization. For example, coding can force a name to be upper case or email to be lower case. Coding can also be used to upload custom images or force phone numbers to use hyphens (e.g., 604-123-4567) instead of dots (e.g., 604.123.1234). Coding is critical for keeping a customer's brand consistent, so regardless of who creates an order, all products will be formatted consistently and have the same look.

Deciding which VDP software or plug-in is more appropriate and how it interacts with the digital storefront is important. VDP software comes in the form of third-party applications such as XMPie or is accessed online through a self-hosted dashboard.

Print on Demand

POD products are the opposite of VDP products. POD allows the customer to order a static product to be printed and shipped. POD products do not require customization and are printed using a completed file uploaded by the customer or stored in the system by the programmer.

Warehousing

Storefronts can act as an inventory management system for any products that can be warehoused. These products can be ordered online using the same process as a POD item. Each product has a real-time inventory count associated with it, which updates after every order. Notifications can be sent about low product inventory levels, reminding a customer that a product needs to be replenished. Inventory counts benefit customers by showing their buying patterns, which helps them to effectively determine future quantities.

Below are other examples of different types of products that can be ordered online:

- *Ad hoc print:* an online print product where the customer provides the content during the ordering process via file upload, such as brochures, flyers, and newsletters.
- *Ad hoc business documents:* an online print product where the customer provides the content during the ordering process via file upload, such as training manuals, presentations, and reports.
- *Ad hoc oversize:* An online print product where the customer provides the content during the ordering process via file upload, such as posters, signs, and banners.
- *Static print product:* An online print product where the content is stored in a catalogue and printed on demand after ordering, such as sales sheets, flyers, and white papers.
- *Inventory product:* An online print product where the content is stored in a catalogue and pulled from existing inventory after ordering.
- *Digital publishing:* An online product where the final product is a downloadable PDF instead of a printed product, such as white papers, personalized sales materials, and presentations.
- *Kit:* An online print product where the customer can buy a basket of goods contained in a single item.
- *Promo product:* A set of products that are branded with a logo for use in marketing or promotional programs, such as mugs, baseball hats, and pens.
- *Integrated campaign:* A product that combines multiple-marketing channels to create an integrated campaign a customer can use to track metrics when launching a new product or sales promotion.
- *Photo product:* An online print product using uploaded photos or photos from online collections, such as photo books, photo cards, and photo calendars.
- *Quote request:* An online print product used to request a quote for a print job.

7.4 Implementation and Workflow Considerations

Implementation and Deployment

By this point, the workflow strategy has been created, the customer has been included in discussions about its goals, and the print company has created some sample products and print items for the customer to test. As well, the print company and customer have completed a pilot period and identified unforeseen workflow issues. What remains is the final step of making the site live.

Making the site live involves 'turning it on' to accept orders from the entire user base. If the above steps have been completed properly, there should be very few issues.

Continuous Assessment

Even after a storefront has been launched, it is not considered complete. There should always be a system of continuous assessment in place to respond to customer feedback and correct any errors as the orders start coming in. Even after the site is live, the programmer should navigate the storefront to ensure its usability, and place a test order to ensure no issues arise for the customer during the ordering process. Also of consideration is a post-order assessment, where the internal processes in the printing company are evaluated for completeness and efficiency, as outlined below.

Workflows and Automation

Orders should enter an automated workflow, creating a seamless transition while bypassing several departments. Once an order has been placed, the appropriate staff are notified to fulfill it. If a VDP product was customized, then a print-ready PDF should automatically be uploaded to a hot folder. At this point, either an automated system or a prepress operator reviews the file for print standards and imposes it on the print template. These files can then be automatically produced on a digital press or be sent to the plate setter to be prepared for litho printing. Throughout every step of the process, email notifications should be sent to appropriate staff so they can fulfill the order, and to the customer so they can be kept informed of anything related to the order such as invoices and product shipping.

MIS Integration

It is beneficial to select a storefront suitable for integration into a management information system (MIS) to streamline orders from customization to invoice. Integration is a connection between two systems that enables the exchange of data. The information is automatically entered into an electronic docket, which is a database that collects and maintains customer information, products ordered, shipping information, and billing information automatically. When integrating two systems, it is important to note which system is the master data holder and which is the subscriber to that data. Only one digital system should 'hold' the data, whereas all the other systems access the same database. In a print environment with a functioning print MIS system, it is the MIS system that should be considered to be the master in every case. The MIS system collects orders from everywhere, not just the orders placed through storefronts online. The web2print system pushes data into the MIS system and subscribes to the master data stored and managed in that system, such as pricing and job specifications. This can be challenging because the web2print software and the print MIS system are often provided by separate vendors, which can prevent a smooth exchange of data.

Web2print is one of many secondary, or subscriber, connections into a printer's business and production workflow. Web2print should serve its main purpose, which is to capture orders in the most efficient manner while maintaining a competitive edge for a print company's sales team. Orders must be transitioned seamlessly and smoothly into the production workflow and MIS system so they can be treated like any other order, whether they were placed online or by traditional means. In this way, web2print is regarded as only one of many business opportunities that bring sales to a print company.

Analyzing the ROI

When making any business decision, investment must be weighed against return. This is known as return on investment, or ROI. Moving a business online to accept orders is a serious business decision. Web2print can be a worthwhile investment and understanding how to measure ROI before investing in a vendor's software is important.

Typically, in a print company, the estimate for the actual printing process is very well defined. The estimating department can provide detailed analysis of all of the costs associated with printing a specific printed product. Where web2print differs, however, is in the costs of capturing the sale and in streamlining the process in the print shop. For example, there are specific increased costs in running a web2print site online. If the system was paid for as a one-time licence, then the total cost must be amortized over the life of the licence, and each print order shares a small part of that overall cost. Some SaaS systems, on the other hand, charge a piece rate or a monthly fee. These are easier to incorporate into the costs of the job. On the savings side, there are processes within the print company that are made more efficient, so an analysis of cost savings can be made there as well. However, print companies should not fall into the trap of thinking that just because a print job can be completed in a shorter time, it is automatically cheaper to produce. In order to assess the total ROI, only real costs that affect the print product's profitability should be assessed.

Timing is important when calculating ROI because a printer must determine when to invest money based on an expected return of that investment. Purchasing or building an online system is not automatically going to generate revenue. It is likely that the print company could invest thousands of dollars very quickly before the system provides any value in return. There is a human aspect to this as well. Sales professionals are still critical for driving new customer sales to the web and finding new online opportunities, both of which will help improve the return on the initial investment.

Systems with monthly payments are sometimes better for new online ventures, as they do not require a huge investment upfront. Up-front payments force a print company to give away all monetary leverage in a single transaction, and while they might be more cost-effective when serving large numbers of customers, they can do serious financial damage in the short term.

7.5 Summary

Web2print is the online connection between a print company and its customers, and the technology should help to solidify this relationship, not hinder it. Print companies offer their services online in response to their customers' needs and buying trends. As web2print becomes more integrated into a print company's day-to-day business, it becomes a main channel for interacting with a customer. A key to the strategy for implementing web services is involving the customer as much as possible, since the customer's use and acceptance of the ordering portal is critical for its success. Print companies should research the types of products and services that will be helpful to customers in the specific target markets they serve, and not add too many products too quickly. Print companies must analyze the types of products their customer needs, and plan how a streamlined workflow will create efficiencies in its operations. Finally, a pilot phase to assess both accuracy of the storefront and user experience is important. To ensure continued customer satisfaction, print companies should be prepared to make ongoing improvements once the site goes live. System integration with print companies' internal processes is also ongoing, as efficiencies and production enhancements are realized. The print industry continues to evolve and a successful implementation of a web2print portal will help print companies keep up with this evolution and stay in front of the competition.

Questions to consider after completing this chapter:

1. How would you describe web2print and the technology involved?
2. How would you describe e-commerce and how web2print utilizes it?
3. What are the benefits of using web2print to a company and it customers?
4. What are the strategic steps in creating a web2print system?
5. What types of products can be offered through a web2print system?
6. In what ways can a web2print system be integrated into a production workflow?

References

Gunasekaran, A., Marri, H. B., McGaughey, R. E., & Nebhwani, M. D. (2002). E-commerce and its impact on operations management. *International Journal of Production Economics*, *75*(1–2), 185–197. http://doi.org/10.1016/S0925-5273(01)00191-8

Poon, S. & Swatman, P. (1995). The Internet for small businesses: An enabling infrastructure for competitiveness. In *Proceedings of the Fifth Internet Society Conference* (pp. 221–231). Hawaii, USA.

Shim, S. S., Pendyala, V. S., Sundaram, M., & Gao, J. Z. (2000). Business-to-business e-commerce frameworks. *Computer*, *33*(10), 40–47.

Statistics Canada. (2014, July 8). Retail at a glance: E-commerce sales, 2012. *The Daily*. Retrieved from http://www.statcan.gc.ca/daily-quotidien/140708/dq140708b-eng.htm

Supply Management. (2014, September 10). *Rise in online purchasing as procurement turns to the internet to research products*. Retrieved from http://www.supplymanagement.com/news/2014/rise-in-online-purchasing-as-procurement-turns-to-the-internet-to-research-products

Suggested Reading

WFTPRINTAM – Web to Print. (n.d.). Retrieved from http://wftprintam.wikispaces.com/Web+to+Print

Index

F

G

H

I

K

L

M

N

O